PATERNOSTER BIBLICAL MONOGRAPHS

The Historical Paul in Acts

Comments on *The Historical Paul in Acts*

'Scholarship have been mesmerized by Vielhauer's short essay pitting the 'real' Paul of his letters against the depiction of Paul's preaching in Acts. Chae's excellent monograph is the most careful scholarly response. He effectively tilts the balance of argument and compels us read the NT in greater historical harmony.'

Prof Dr **Max Turner**

'The question of the unhistorical character of Acts in relation to Paul's epistles is an old problem, but it is tacitly assumed in most of current New Testament scholarship. Dr Chae takes up the challenge of such authors as Ph. Vielhauer and J. Knox and painstakingly shows that their methodology was faulty: they compared apples with oranges and they found them to be different! They did not pay sufficient attention to the different parameters in the writings of these authors: context, audiences, purposes, circumstances. When issues such as these are observed, the affinity between Paul and Luke is found to be astounding. The argument is lucid and the logic undeniable. Dr Chae is to be congratulated.'

Prof. Dr **Chrys C. Caragounis**

'This valuable work does a good job of countering most of the skeptical arguments related to the portrayal of Paul in Acts.'

Prof. Dr **Craig S. Keener**

PATERNOSTER BIBLICAL MONOGRAPHS

The Historical Paul in Acts

Daniel Jong-Sang Chae
(최 종 상)

Copyright © Daniel Jong-Sang Chae 2019

First published 2019 by Paternoster

Paternoster is an imprint of Authentic Media
PO Box 6326, Bletchley, Milton Keynes MK1 9GG

authenticmedia.co.uk

The right of Daniel J.-S. Chae to be identified as the Editor of this Work
has been asserted by him in accordance with the Copyright, Designs
and Patents Act 1988.

All rights reserved. No part of this publication may be reproduced, stored in a retrieval system, or transmitted, in any form or by any means, electronic, mechanical, photocopying, recording or otherwise, without the prior permission of the publisher or a license permitting restricted copying. In the UK such licenses are issued by the Copyright Licensing Agency, Barnards Inn, 86 Fetter Ln, London EC4A 1EN

British Library Cataloguing in Publication Data
A catalogue record for this book is available from the British Library

ISBN 978-1-78893-030-7
978-1-78893-031-4 (e-book)

Unless otherwise noted, Scripture quotations are taken from:
NIV (New International Version) © 1984, Anglicized

Typeset by Daniel Chae
Printed and bound by Lightning Source

In Memory of

Prof. Dr. Martin Hengel

PATERNOSTER BIBLICAL MONOGRAPHS

Series Preface

One of the major objectives of Paternoster is to serve biblical scholarship by providing a channel for the publication of theses and other monographs of high quality at affordable prices. Paternoster stands within the broad evangelical tradition of Christianity. Our authors would describe themselves as Christians who recognize the authority of the Bible, maintain the centrality of the gospel message and assent to the classical creedal statements of Christian belief. There is diversity within the constituency; advances in scholarship are possible only if there is freedom for frank debate on controversial issues and for the publication of new and sometimes provocative proposals. What is offered in this series is the best of writing by committed Christians who are concerned to develop well-founded biblical scholarship in a spirit of loyalty to the historic faith.

Series Editors

I. Howard Marshall	Honorary Research professor of New Testament, University of Aberdeen, Scotland, UK
Richard J. Bauckham	Professor of New Testament Studies and Bishop Wardlaw professor, University of St Andrews, Scotland, UK
Craig Blomberg	Distinguished Professor of New Testament, Denver Seminary, Colorado, USA
Robert P. Gordon	Regius Professor of Hebrew, University of Cambridge, UK
Stanley E. Porter	President and Professor of New Testament, McMaster Divinity College, Hamilton, Ontario, Canada

Contents

Preface -- ix
Abbreviations --- xi

Introduction --- 1
The Nature of Paul's Letters and of Luke's Acts ------------------------ 6
   Paul's letters: follow-up correspondence ---------------------------- 6
   Acts: a record of the gospel message and its progress --------------- 8
Towards an Adequate Comparison --- 9
Luke as the Author of Acts -- 10

1. Vielhauer and 'Paulinism' in Acts -------------------------------- 15
Natural Theology -- 17
The Law --- 22
   Paul's attitude to the law and circumcision ------------------------ 22
   Paul's doctrine of justification by faith -------------------------- 26
Christology --- 29
Eschatology --- 31
   The imminent Parousia: the central Pauline theme? ------------------ 32
   Redemptive history in Paul --- 36
Questioning Vielhauer's Methodology ----------------------------------- 39
Conclusion -- 43

2. Rediscovering Paul's Missionary Preaching --------------------- 45
The Question of Methodology --- 46
The 'Reminder Formula' and Paul's Missionary Preaching ---------------- 50
   The reminders of his preaching to the Corinthians ------------------ 51
   The reminders of his preaching to the Galatians -------------------- 53
   The reminders of his preaching to the Thessalonians ---------------- 54
   The reminders/reports of his preaching to the Romans and the
      Colossians -- 56
   The summary of Paul's missionary preaching ------------------------- 57
*Comparing the Lucan Paul with the Real Paul in Their Missionary
   Preaching* -- 59
   Paul's missionary preaching in Acts -------------------------------- 60
   The corresponding evangelistic topics in Acts and in the letters --- 63
   Paul the preacher of the gospel ------------------------------------ 66
   Comparing Paul's missionary preaching in specific regions ---------- 72
Conclusion -- 77

3. Understanding the Discrepancies --------------------------------- 79
The Silent Topics of Luke and of Paul --------------------------------- 80

The Description of Paul's Jewishness -- 85
The Number of Paul's Visits to Jerusalem ----------------------------------- 89
Paul's Relationship with Jerusalem --- 92
    The description of the Jerusalem Council ---------------------------------- 93
    The relationship during the Antioch incident ----------------------------- 96
    The exchange of co-workers -- 99
    The leadership transition in the Jerusalem church --------------------- 100
Conclusion -- 102

4. The 'We-Passages' and Luke's Portrayal of Paul ------------- 105

The 'we' in Acts 16:10–17 --- 107
The 'we' in Acts 20:5 – 21:18 --- 109
The 'We-Passages' and Paul's Ministry in the Corresponding Regions 113
    Corinth -- 113
    Thessalonica -- 114
    Philippi --- 115
    Ephesus -- 116
Conclusion -- 116

5. Luke's Portrayal of Paul's Life and Ministry ------------------ 119

Paul's Early Life --- 121
    Paul's Jewish background --- 121
    Conversion/call and early Christian years ------------------------------- 122
Paul the Missionary Apostle --- 126
    Paul's missionary journeys --- 126
    Paul the church planter --- 129
    Paul the persecuted missionary --- 131
    Paul's co-workers --- 134
    Paul's characteristics -- 137
Conclusion -- 140

Conclusions -- 142

Summaries --- 144
Contributions --- 147
Implications -- 150

Bibliography --- 152

Index of Authors --- 164

Index of Scriptural References -- 168

Index of Subjects -- 181

Preface

In the last century a consensus was established among the majority of New Testament scholars that the account of the apostle Paul in the book of Acts is unhistorical and thus unreliable. As a result the material about Paul's life and ministry provided in Acts has hardly been used in Pauline studies. However, one must ask whether the consensus had been established on the basis of adequate and objective investigations. This volume is an examination of this subject, and we shall propose that the account of Paul in Acts is much more reliable than is often assumed.

Some of the topics contained in this volume have been presented in academic seminars in draft format. Our critique of Philipp Vielhauer's contention on the unreliability of Luke's account of Paul was first presented in June 1997 to the New Testament Department Seminar of Durham University. Since then Prof. James D.G. Dunn, Prof. I. Howard Marshall, Prof. Chrys C. Caragounis and Dr Conrad Gempf have kindly provided their comments in writing, some of which are implemented in this volume. I am very grateful to them for their generous time and helpful comments. The paper on the reconstruction of Paul's missionary preaching was presented in 1996 at the Paul Seminar of the British New Testament Conference convened at Aberdeen University. I survived and enjoyed the intense debate on that occasion. I am thankful to Prof. Dunn for making many helpful comments in writing on this paper as well.

Since the completion of my doctoral research on the letter to the Romans in 1995,[1] I have been involved in more practical ministries such as church planting and pastoring in north London; carrying out itinerant missionary work around the globe as the managing director of MV Doulos, a missionary community of 350 volunteers from fifty countries; and leading an evangelism and church-planting training college on the outskirts of London. As such, I feel that the alertness of my academic sense is not as sharp as it should be. However, I felt a sense of obligation to revisit this subject on the reliability

---

[1] This research was subsequently published: *Paul as Apostle to the Gentiles: His Apostolic Self-Awareness and its Influence on the Soteriological Argument in Romans* (Carlisle: Paternoster, 1997).

of Luke's account on Paul, and I am grateful to the trustees and staff of Amnos Ministries for granting me part-time study-leave in order to work on this particular volume.

I am most thankful to God for sustaining me so that I could complete this volume. I was conscious that wisdom, insight, knowledge and understanding come from the Lord God:

> God gave Solomon wisdom and very great insight, and a breadth of understanding (1 Kings 4:29).

> To these four young men God gave knowledge and understanding of all kinds of literature and learning (Daniel 1:17).

I am appreciative of Paternoster Press for accepting this work for publication. I would like to thank Prof. Chrys C. Caragounis of Lund University, Sweden, Prof. Craig S. Keener of Asbury Theological Seminary, USA, and Prof Max Turner of London School of Theology, UK for writing most generous words of commendation as well as giving valuable advice to strengthen the case of this study.

It is my honour to dedicate this volume to the late Prof. Dr Martin Hengel of Tübingen University. He showed great interest in my research topic during my research under him there in 1991–2. I am grateful to him for his generosity of time in discussion. His advice to narrow down my doctoral research to Romans alone was most valuable. As one who held the historicity of Acts in high regard, he provided me with much encouragement and sound perspective on Acts as well. I owe a debt of gratitude to him and his writings for their influence on various aspects of the topics in this book.

Abbreviations

AB	Anchor Bible
BAGD	W. Bauer, W.F. Arndt, F.W. Gingrich and F.W. Danker. *Greek-English Lexicon of the New Testament and Other Early Christian Literature*. 2nd edn. Chicago, 1979
BC	*The Beginnings of Christianity*, vol. 5 (ed. F.J. Foakes-Jackson and K. Lake; London: Macmillan, 1933)
BJRL	*Bulletin of the John Rylands University Library of Manchester*
BNTC	Black's New Testament Commentaries
BRev	*Bible Review*
CJ	*Classical Journal*
DPL	*Dictionary of Paul and His Letters* (ed. G.F. Hawthorne, R.P. Martin and D.G. Reid; Downers Grove, IL / Leicester: IVP, 1993)
EvQ	*Evangelical Quarterly*
EvT	*Evangelische Theologie*
ExpTim	*Expository Times*
FRLANT	Forschungen zur Religion und Literatur des Alten und Neuen Testaments
ICC	International Critical Commentary
IVPNTC	IVP New Testament Commentary
JB	Jerusalem Bible
JBL	*Journal of Biblical Literature*
JGRChJ	*Journal of Greco-Roman Christianity and Judaism*
JNT	*Jewish New Testament* (trans. D.H. Stern; Jerusalem: Jewish New Testament Publications, 1991)
JR	*Journal of Religion*
JSNTSup	Journal for the Study of the New Testament: Supplement Series
KERF	Korean Evangelical Research Fellowship
KJV	King James Version
LNTS	Library of New Testament Studies
NAB	New American Bible
NASB	New American Standard Bible
NEB	New English Bible

NICNT	New International Commentary on the New Testament
NIV	New International Version
NJB	New Jerusalem Bible
NovT	*Novum Testamentum*
NovTSup	Supplements to Novum Testamentum
NRSV	New Revised Standard Version
NT	New Testament
NTS	*New Testament Studies*
OT	Old Testament
PBTM	Paternoster Biblical and Theological Monographs
PHILLIPS	*The New Testament in Modern English*, J.B. Phillips
RB	*Revue biblique*
REB	Revised English Bible
RSV	Revised Standard Version
RV	Revised Version
SBG	Studies in Biblical Greek
SBL	Society of Biblical Literature
SBLStBl	Society of Biblical Literature Studies in Biblical Literature
SBT	Studies in Biblical Theology
SLA	*Studies in Luke-Acts: Essays Presented in Honor of Paul Schubert* (ed. L.E. Keck and J.L. Martyn; London: SPCK, 1968 [1966])
SNTSMS	Society for New Testament Studies Monograph Series
SP	Sacra pagina
SwJT	*Southwestern Journal of Theology*
TEV	Today's English Version (= Good News Bible)
TNTC	Tyndale New Testament Commentaries
TynBul	*Tyndale Bulletin*
UBS	United Bible Societies
WBC	Word Biblical Commentary
WUNT	Wissenschaftliche Untersuchungen zum Neuen Testament
ZNW	*Zeitschrift für die neutestamentliche Wissenschaft und die Kunde der älteren Kirche*

Introduction

Paul is one of the most prominent figures in the New Testament and indeed of all times.[1] No fewer than thirteen books of the New Testament bear his name as the author. How we perceive his life and mission substantially influences our approach to his theology and to New Testament studies. We can know about Paul and his theology from his letters. Another important source of information about Paul is the Acts of the Apostles. Acts is an extremely valuable source for studies of Paul and of earliest Christianity.[2]

However, many scholars have hesitated, or even refused, to use the material in Acts for a more adequate study of Paul and his theology. What I.H. Marshall asserted nearly fifty years ago still reflects the scholarly climate today:

> Today it is widely held that the picture of Paul presented by Luke is thoroughly inaccurate – so much so indeed that it is hardly credible that Acts embodies the memoirs of a companion of Paul. Acts, it is held, cannot be used as a primary source in the reconstruction of Paul's career. In other words, the historical capability of Luke is seriously called into question.[3]

Writing in 2009, T.E. Phillips reaffirmed Marshall's assessment: 'The current state of critical scholarship is much the same: those who wish to defend the congruity between the Paul of Acts and the Paul of the letters are in the minority and on the defensive.'[4] So even those who regard Acts as largely historical in its portrayal of the Paul of the letters, acknowledge that the current sceptical stance regarding Acts reflects 'the consensus of modern scholarship'.[5]

Such scepticism rose to prominence through the work of F.C. Baur and his followers in the Tübingen School. In 1845 Baur insisted on this principle:

---

[1] Furnish, 'His apostleship transcends the particularities of time and place and encompasses the world', as quoted in Pervo, *Making of Paul*, 12.
[2] See e.g., Weiss, *Earliest Christianity*, 1:147–8.
[3] Marshall, *Luke: Historian and Theologian*, 74–5.
[4] Phillips, *Paul, His Letters, and Acts*, 193.
[5] Porter, *Paul in Acts*, 189; cf. Pervo, *Mystery*, 151.

'where the accounts in the Acts do not altogether agree with the statements of the Apostle the latter would have such a decided claim to authentic truth that the contradiction in the Acts would scarcely be worth attention'. Baur's rationale is that 'historical truth can only belong to one of them', and, more importantly, Acts contains 'no purely objective statement, but only one which is arranged on subjective grounds'.[6] Baur repeats and affirms his conclusion that Luke portrays a different Paul from the historical Paul:

> It can scarcely be denied that possibly, if not probably, he [Luke] has in many cases altered the true history, not only negatively, by ignoring actions and circumstances which bear essentially on his subject matter, but also positively. The most weighty reason for this opinion is that the Paul of the Acts is manifestly quite a different person from the Paul of the Epistles.[7]

Baur has effectively and profoundly influenced subsequent scholarship on the historicity of Acts[8] for over one and a half centuries, and by the turn of the twentieth century it was widely believed that Luke's material about Paul in Acts[9] was not based on tradition but on his inventive redaction. Adolf Harnack complained of such a tendency in his day:

> Among other things, the thesis that the tradition (that Luke, who presents himself as a companion of Paul in the first-person-plural reports in Acts, is the author of the Acts of the Apostles) is untenable is thought to have been so clearly demonstrated that *people nowadays hardly take trouble any longer to prove it*, and simply note the arguments of those who oppose it. They no longer seem to want even to acknowledge that there are such arguments.[10]

Despite this protest and some counter-attacks on scepticism,[11] the next generation of scholarship went even further in denying the reliability of Luke's account rather than seeking to prove it.[12]

In this regard, it is worth mentioning the two most influential works, which appeared independently of each other in 1950. Both followed on Baur

---

[6] Baur, *Paul*, 1:4, 5.

[7] Baur, *Paul*, 1:11.

[8] Baur's effect is still evident in the twenty-first century. See Phillips, *Paul, His Letters, and Acts*, 33–5 nn. 18–23, for an exhaustive bibliography on the comparative studies on the Paul of Acts and the Paul of the letters since F.C. Baur.

[9] Following the widely accepted tradition, we take Luke, travelling companion of Paul, to be the author of Acts: see below pp. 10–14, 109-13, for our explanation.

[10] Harnack, as cited in Hengel and Schwemer, *Paul Between Damascus and Antioch*, viii–ix: the emphasis is mine. Hengel and Schwemer's assessment is that this perception is still prevalent today.

[11] Notably, Ramsay, *St. Paul the Traveller*; idem, *Pauline and Other Studies*; idem, *Bearing of Recent Research*.

[12] For a helpful survey of critical studies on Acts, see Gasque, *History*.

and strengthened his thesis by introducing new critical methodologies. These new critical methodologies highlighted the fundamental nature of the differences between the Paul of Acts and the Paul of the letters. The first is a short article by Philipp Vielhauer: 'Zum "Paulinismus" der Apostelgeschichte',[13] in which he undertook an investigation of the differences by paying special attention to Luke's portrayal of the four Pauline theological themes, namely, natural theology, the law, Christology and eschatology. His conclusion is straightforward: in these major areas, Luke presents no specifically Pauline theology, but rather that of early catholicism around the turn of the first century. Is he right? This contention deserves our scrutiny in the light of what C.J. Hemer says: 'The problem [of the reliability of Luke's portrait of Paul] cannot be adequately treated today without at least some preliminary consideration of Philipp Vielhauer's essay on the "Paulinism" of Acts'.[14]

The second work is *Chapters in a Life of Paul* by John Knox. Following on his earlier articles,[15] Knox began his investigation in reaction to the scholarship of his day that accepted Luke's account of Paul at face value without any serious examination of its reliability. While Vielhauer focused on comparing Paul's ideas (i.e. *theology*) as portrayed in Acts and in the letters, Knox investigated Paul's life and ministry (i.e. *chronology*) as shown by Luke and by the apostle himself. He then arrived at the same conclusion as Vielhauer: 'Actually the Paul of Acts is in important respects a quite different kind of man and has quite different ideas from the Paul of the letters.'[16] He warned scholars not to use the material in Acts in constructing Paul's life because Luke had 'arranged his materials in the order that best suited the purpose of his book'.[17] Knox's research reinforced the earlier critical contention of his day about the credibility of Acts as a whole,[18] and represents one current extreme position. Baur, Vielhauer and Knox are 'the origins [and architects] of Paul's split personality within contemporary scholarship'.[19]

R.I. Pervo is a more recent notable sceptic of the historicity of Acts. He has written extensively, and he continues somewhat the tradition of Haenchen. He strongly and repeatedly asserts that 'the book [of Acts] is very difficult to use as a firm historical resource because of its many gaps and improbabilities... Acts is not a reliable history of Christian origins... Luke murdered the history of the early church.'[20] 'The greatest enigma is that Paul

---

[13] *EvT* 10 (1950–51): 1–15.
[14] Hemer, *Book of Acts*, 246.
[15] Knox, '"Fourteen Years Later"', 341–9; 'Pauline Chronology', 15–29.
[16] Knox, *Chapters*, 18.
[17] Knox, *Chapters*, 11.
[18] McNeile, *St Paul*, x; Dibelius, 'Acts of the Apostles', 102–8.
[19] Phillips, *Paul, His Letters, and Acts*, 42; see also *ibid.*, pp. 30–42, for brief yet helpful summaries of Baur, Vielhauer and Knox.
[20] Pervo, *Mystery*, 139, 151.

is Luke's hero, but is portrayed so differently from the Paul known from his correspondence.'[21] He contends that Luke wrote Acts 'as a creative author [rather] than as an historian ... Acts is good story but not, all in all, good history.'[22]

However, Martin Hengel stands out in maintaining a high regard for Luke's account of Paul in Acts.[23] A recent trend moves toward greater appreciation for Acts' historical reliability.[24] Many scholars accept it as valuable source, though less valuable than the letters. Nevertheless, the majority of scholars today still refuse to accept Luke's material about Paul as a largely correct source for Pauline studies due to their suspicion (or conviction) that it was coloured by Luke's own theological and ecclesiological agenda.[25] As a result, the extensive information in the book of Acts on Paul's life, ministry and theology has been scarcely used in seeking a better understanding of the apostle.

The liveliness of scholarly study of the Acts of the Apostles has greatly increased in the twenty-first century. Many fresh and stimulating studies have been published in this new millennium. In 2004 two major works appeared, by B. Chilton, and J.D. Crossan and J. Reed.[26] Among others, Craig S. Keener stands out: he has published an exhaustive commentary on Acts in four volumes which runs to over 4,500 pages, excluding the most comprehensive bibliography and the indexes! He argues, contrary to the traditional preference for Paul's writings over Luke's Acts, that one should not always prefer Paul's writings to Luke's without proper grounds.[27] Further, we must accept, Keener insists, that our knowledge of Paul, gained from his letters, is substantially incomplete,[28] because the letters provide limited information about his missionary work during the church-planting stage in various cities. This information belongs to the scope of the book of Acts, and so Luke's portrait of the apostle is able to shed crucial light in our search for the historical Paul. However, a solid, careful and fair appraisal is required to determine the level of the reliability of Luke's portrayal of Paul in Acts.

---

[21] Pervo, *Mystery*, 36–7.

[22] Pervo, *Mystery*, 152, 153; see also his fuller treatment on Luke as an author in Pervo, *Profit with Delight*. See Porter, *Paul in Acts*, 14–21, for a critique of Pervo.

[23] Hengel and Schwemer, *Paul Between Damascus and Antioch*; idem, *Between Jesus and Paul*, 97–128; idem, *Acts and the History*.

[24] Notably, Hemer, Thornton and Riesner. So also Munck, *Paul*, 120; Bruce, *Paul: Apostle*, 245; Holmberg, *Sociology*, 65; Witherington, *Acts*, 430–38.

[25] For example, Segal, *Paul*, 4; Senior and Stuhlmueller, *Foundations*, 162; Jewett, *Dating Paul's Life*, 23; Lake, 'Apostolic Council of Jerusalem', 198–9; Knox, *Chapters*, 18.

[26] Chilton, *Rabbi Paul*; Crossan and Reed, *In Search of Paul*.

[27] Keener, *Acts*, 1:231–3.

[28] Keener, *Acts*, 1:228.

Introduction

In this volume we attempt to investigate these issues as we engage with Vielhauer, in Chapter 1, on the four theological themes he has chosen. We will expose the critical weakness in Vielhauer's contention, which comes from comparing Paul's *missionary* preaching to convert his audience in Acts with his theological and pastoral teaching for the converted in the churches shown in the letters. In Chapter 2, therefore, we attempt to reconstruct Paul's missionary preaching from his letters. We will then be in a better position to compare the content of Paul's *missionary* preaching rediscovered from his letters with the Lucan Paul's *missionary* message as reported in Acts. In Chapter 3, we examine the discrepancies between the letters and Acts to assess the level of Luke's reliability. In Chapter 4, we study the 'we-passages' of Acts to determine the level of the author's personal involvement with Paul in his travels and ministries. In Chapter 5, we engage with J. Knox, though not directly, and examine more general themes on Paul's life and ministry to assess the level of compatibility between Luke's portrait of the apostle and Paul's own description of himself and his theology.

In 1989 C.J. Hemer observed, 'Although there has been no lack of debate about the book of Acts, the question of its historicity has been strangely neglected'.[29] The scope of this volume is not the historicity of Acts in general, but is largely confined to Luke's portrayal of Paul in Acts. One of the ways to test the historical reliability of Acts is to compare the materials related to Paul in Acts with those contained in his letters. The main purpose of this volume is to examine the level of reliability of Luke's portrait of Paul. So, we shall revisit the old questions such as, 'Is Luke's account about Paul reliable?', and 'To what extent can a student of Paul use the material provided by the author of Acts in Pauline studies?' Our main methodology will be to compare the internal materials in Acts with those in Paul's letters. We will use the letters that bear Paul's name, including the Pastorals.[30]

For a comparative study such as ours, however, it is crucial to establish two fundamentals immediately. First, a proper understanding of the nature of Paul's letters and Luke's Acts is required, for this will provide us with the basis for the methodology to be employed. Second, an adequate method of comparing their writings must be adopted. We shall thus examine, briefly in this introductory section, both the nature of these writings and the methodologies which Vielhauer and Knox have employed. We shall attempt to show to what extent we can 'prove', as Harnack urged, that Luke's account of Paul is more reliable than the modern sceptical scholarship allows.

---

[29] Hemer, *Book of Acts*, 1.
[30] The discussion on the authorship of the Pauline corpus is beyond the scope of this work. See Keener, *Acts*, 1:224–5 nn. 17–20, for the list of scholars who are in favour of the Pauline authorship of the Pastorals, and of those who contend their pseudonymity.

The Nature of Paul's Letters and of Luke's Acts

Paul's letters: follow-up correspondence

In most cases Paul's letters are 'follow-up' correspondence written in response to specific situations in, or questions from, the first Christian churches.[31] This is indicated by such statements as: 'So then, brothers, stand firm and hold to the teachings we passed on to you, whether *by word of mouth* or *by letter*' (2 Thess 2:15). Whether one accepts the Pauline authorship of 2 Thessalonians or not, it is absolutely clear that Paul's teachings were given by two means: by word of mouth and/or by letter. The letters are aimed to reinforce or clarify his earlier teachings given during his missionary work. Paul often assumes that his recipients know of his earlier instructions: 'I praise you for remembering me in everything and for holding to the teachings, just as I passed them on to you' (1 Cor 11:2; also 2 Cor 13:2; 1 Thess 4:6, 12; 2 Thess 3:7–10, etc.). Paul's converts would read and understand his letter(s) on the basis of their knowledge of his previous teaching in person.

It is important to note that Paul's letters do not contain his complete thought,[32] but rather supplement his previous teachings. His teaching given verbally during his missionary work, which comprises the earliest and probably larger part, is largely missing from the letters. For example, Paul reminds the Galatians of 'the gospel [he] preached' (Gal 1:11), but he does not write the content of that gospel message he preached to them. What Paul preached 'as of first importance' during his ministry in Corinth for a year and a half is summed up in only a few verses (1 Cor 15:1–8). We have hardly any information about what Paul taught in Ephesus for three years. Therefore, it is not credible to assume that what is not discussed in his letters had no place in his theology, or that his complete theology can be formulated solely from his letters.

Furthermore, as Paul unfolds his theological teaching on certain topics, or explains the implications of his earlier teachings, he sometimes indicates how his theology has unfolded or developed. He says that sometimes he deliberately withheld some teachings due to the spiritual immaturity of the converts: 'I gave you milk, not solid food, for you were not yet ready for it' (1 Cor 3:2). At the same time, certain teachings were not given orally because they were not raised as important issues during his missionary work. These topics include the instructions, for example, about marriage (1 Cor 7), food sacrificed to idols (1 Cor 8), spiritual gifts (1 Cor 12 – 14), the resurrection of the dead (1 Cor 15; 1 Thess 4:13–18) and the collection for the poor (1 Cor 16).

---

[31] Caird, *Apostolic Age*, 37.
[32] So rightly, Ladd, *Theology*, 377.

Introduction

The fact that Paul expounds the resurrection of the dead (i.e. of believers who have died) in great detail in 1 Corinthians 15 implies that he did not explain it fully while he was in Corinth. Paul's question, 'But if it is preached that Christ has been raised from the dead, how can some of you say that there is no resurrection of the dead?' (1 Cor 15:12), indicates that he preached the resurrection of Christ, but most probably did not explain its specific implication with regard to the resurrection of believers. He seems to have expected his converts to understand that they too would be raised from the dead *because* Christ has been raised from the dead. But some of the believers in Corinth could not grasp this implication, and so asserted that there was no resurrection of the dead. When this news reached Paul, he explained the implications at length. The extent of Paul's teaching on this issue in the letter suggests that he did not teach or elaborate on the resurrection of the dead during his missionary days in Corinth. This line of thought can be supported further by his discussion of the same topic in his letter to the Thessalonians (1 Thess 4:13–18). It is clear that Paul had not previously explained what would happen to 'those who fall asleep'. These passages suggest that the resurrection of the believers was not an important topic of preaching during Paul's missionary work. It was the resurrection of Christ (and his exaltation and return as its implication) that was preached as of foremost importance (1 Cor 15:1–8; 1 Thess 5:1–2; 2 Thess 2:1–5).

We can detect something similar in the case of Galatians. During his time in Galatia Paul clearly portrayed Christ as crucified, and the Galatians believed what they heard (Gal 3:1–5). In other words he preached justification by believing in the death and resurrection of Christ. But the fact that the Galatians were so quickly persuaded by the Judaizers indicates that Paul had not taught them as clearly as he now writes about the implications of justification by faith with regard to the law. Although Paul preached the doctrine of justification by faith all along, in the letter he shifts his emphasis from 'justification by *believing in the death and resurrection of Christ*' to 'justification by faith *apart from the law*' in order to win the Galatians back from the Judaizers.

Likewise Paul's writings are often 'highly retrospective'[33] and rhetorical. They are often written polemically to achieve specific aims in critical situations. We can see a glimpse of this tendency in the Lucan Paul as well: 'I have done nothing wrong against the law of the Jews or against the temple or against Caesar' (Acts 25:8; similarly 24:12; 26:22–23; 28:17). In the course of his writings Paul may have added to his teaching or argument some taint of personal bias and self-interest. As H.D. Betz says, 'Paul's own account in Galatians 2 is that of a first-hand witness and it must have priority in case of doubt. But the circumstance and function of the defence in his letter to the

---

[33] Gager, 'Some Notes', 699.

Galatians have coloured his account'.[34]

So also H. Räisänen asserts that 'naïve trust in a man's testimony about himself is a curious fundamentalistic survival within critical scholarship.'[35] It is not only the credibility of Acts but also that of Paul's letters that is at stake. However, the fact that Paul's letters are often retrospective and rhetorical does not necessarily mean that they do not serve as a correct description of his life and ministry.[36] In addition, Acts can supplement the letters with some valuable material. One must admit that on certain points Luke's record could be more objectively presented, as C.J. Hemer suggests, for sometimes the testimony of a witness carries more weight than that of the person concerned.[37] The key is the adequate understanding of the correlation between Paul's letters and Luke's Acts. Although they are different in nature, scope and primary aim, they may still be able to complement each other.

Acts: a record of the gospel message and its progress

One must take into account that Luke's primary concern in Acts is different from Paul's in the letters. Luke records the evangelistic progress of the earliest church from Jerusalem to Rome. As far as his portrait of Paul is concerned, his first interest is in describing Paul as a missionary apostle. The scope of his writing is often limited to Paul's *pioneering* missionary work. For example, he writes about what happened when Paul first preached in Corinth and planted a church there, but he does not record at all what Paul taught and did during his work there for a year and a half, except simply commenting that he taught the word of God (Acts 18:11). Luke also does not record anything of what Paul taught for two years in the lecture hall of Tyrannus in Ephesus (Acts 19:9–10). He simply sums up how Paul taught the word of God during this period. Paul's role as a pastor (or a theologian) does not belong to Luke's main scope in Acts. Hence he often jumps to other events without giving us sufficient chronological or biographical details.[38]

Furthermore, as an author Luke does not repeat what he has already written. For example, after recounting at some length Paul's sermon preached in the synagogue in Pisidian Antioch, Luke does not record the details of Paul's sermon delivered in the synagogues in Iconium, Thessalonica, Berea, Corinth and Ephesus, except for simply mentioning that Paul reasoned to persuade both Jews and Greeks.

---

[34] Betz, *Galatians*, 81.
[35] Räisänen, *Paul and the Law*, 232; similarly, Riesner and Lüdemann in Walton, *Leadership*, 48.
[36] *Pace* Watson, *Paul*, 53–6; Taylor, *Paul*, 62.
[37] Hemer, *Book of Acts*, 244.
[38] Conzelmann, *Acts*, xli.

Introduction

Towards an Adequate Comparison

Paul's letters and Luke's Acts were written with two different primary purposes and scopes. In the letters Paul is a pastor and theologian, while in Acts he is presented as an evangelist and church planter. So Luke's Paul is a missionary preacher. It is methodologically perilous, therefore, to compare Luke's record of Paul's *missionary* preaching with Paul's own *theological and pastoral* teaching expressed in his letters (often in reaction to the disturbance of the Judaizers), even though we would not expect them to contradict each other.

A more plausible methodology is to reconstruct Paul's *missionary* preaching and teaching as far as possible from his letters, and then to compare it with the evangelistic sermons attributed to Paul in Acts. As we noted above, Paul's letters contain few references to his missionary message. Nevertheless, we shall demonstrate that it is possible to reconstruct it by paying attention to Paul's use of a 'reminder formula' scattered throughout the letters. Paul often reminds his converts of his earlier preaching and teaching: 'I want to remind you of the gospel I preached to you' (1 Cor 15:1), or 'Don't you remember that when I was with you I used to tell you these things?' (2 Thess 2:5; so also 2 Cor 13:2; 1 Thess 3:4; 4:6b, 11; 5:1–2; 2 Thess 2:15; 3:6, 10).[39] These brief reminders can provide us with crucial clues in recovering the core of Paul's missionary preaching.

Thus, we propose comparing the Lucan Paul's *missionary* preaching with Paul's *missionary* preaching rediscovered from the letters, not with his 'developed' teaching expressed in the more rhetorical letters.[40] So, for example, since Paul's letters are sent to the *believers* for pastoral purposes, the Lucan Paul's farewell sermon to the Ephesian elders is one that can be compared with Paul's pastoral teachings in the letters. When we compare the materials that are mutually compatible, we see that Luke's Paul 'speaks to Christians as a pastor [Acts 20:18–35], [and] sounds like Paul writing as a pastor'.[41] Furthermore, since Paul's letters are sent to churches where *Gentiles* are predominant, the Lucan Paul's sermons to *Gentiles* in Acts 14 and 17, rather than to Jews in Acts 13 and 22 – 26, should be compared with his missionary preaching to Gentiles which can be recovered from his letters. We need to note that we do not have any letter from Paul's hand to a church which is

---

[39] See Chae, *Paul*, 305–6, and see Chapter 2 below for the methodology used in this book to recover Paul's missionary preaching and teaching from the Pauline letters.

[40] Keener, *Acts*, 1:228, acknowledges the difference in the scope of Acts and of Paul's letters. However, he seems to suggest that these two scopes cannot therefore be truly comparable.

[41] Walton, *Leadership*, 212–13.

predominantly Jewish. In this respect, Romans is arguably an example. The fact that Paul establishes his argument in that letter by quoting numerous quotations from the Old Testament may indicate that some of his arguments were directed more to Jewish believers in Rome.[42]

We will therefore attempt to compare many related details and accounts in Acts and in Paul's letters, especially relating to Paul's life and ministry.[43] By carefully collecting and comparing information about Paul from the letters and Acts, we may be able to acquire a more adequate picture of the historical Paul. John Knox himself has admitted the difficulties of reconstructing Paul's life and ministry independently of Acts.[44] Ben Witherington rightly says:

> Since Paul himself provides few autobiographical remarks in the undisputed letters, we can hardly do without some help from Acts in any case. Because the Pauline letters are not by and large autobiographical in *subject matter*, it is a mistake to consider them an overwhelmingly more primary source for reconstructing a picture of the historical Paul than Acts. As with Acts, the letters must be critically probed if we are to get at the historical Paul, and we need to take their epistolary and rhetorical character and function fully into account when assessing these matters.[45]

We shall then be able to evaluate not only the reliability of Luke's account of Paul in Acts in the light of what Paul writes in his letters, but also the credibility of Paul's accounts of his life and theology in the light of what Luke writes in Acts.[46] But the first step is to determine the reliability of Acts, and we shall attempt to do this as we interact with Vielhauer and Knox in Chapters 1 and 5 respectively.

Luke as the Author of Acts

So far we have used Luke as a convenient name for the author of Acts. However, the authorship of Acts deserves further treatment[47] as it is closely related to the reliability of the author's portrayal of Paul in Acts. To be sure,

---

[42] See Chae, *Paul*, 150–52, 285–8.

[43] Keener, *Acts*, 1:237–50, has provided sets of extremely comprehensive lists of comparison between Acts and Paul's letters, including the earlier works of A. Harnack, T.H. Campbell, M.D. Goulder and B. Witherington.

[44] Knox, *Chapters*, rev. edn, 346–7.

[45] Witherington, *Paul Quest*, 10.

[46] The value of Luke's contribution in understanding Paul is advocated in Hengel and Schwemer, *Paul Between Damascus and Antioch*, 6–11.

[47] For detailed studies on the topic, see Hemer, *Book of Acts*, 308–64, where he devotes a chapter to 'The Authorship and Sources of Acts'; and Barrett, *Acts*, ICC, 1:30–48.

Introduction

the book of Acts itself does not give us an answer as to who the author is. However, the contention that Luke is the author of Acts has been supported for at least three factors. First, church tradition testifies to it. The Anti-Marcionite Prologue to the Gospel of Luke (*c.* AD 150–80) contains a statement: 'Moreover, the same Luke afterwards wrote the Acts of the Apostles'. The Muratorian Canon (*c.* AD 180–200) also testifies that 'Luke compiled [Acts] for "most excellent Theophilus"'. Irenaeus, Clement of Alexandria, Eusebius and Jerome also identified Luke the physician and Paul's companion as the author of Acts.[48]

Second, there are some internal pieces of evidence that point to Luke as the author of Acts. The author of Acts makes it clear that this is his second volume dedicated to the same recipient, 'most excellent Theophilus', and the only book that was also addressed to Theophilus is the Gospel of Luke (Luke 1:3; Acts 1:1). Thus it is clear that the same author wrote both the Gospel of Luke and the Acts of the Apostles. Although the traditional title of the Gospel, *Kata Loukan* ('According to Luke'), is not an authentic part of the Gospel, Luke's authorship of the third Gospel is universally accepted. For these reasons, his authorship of Acts can be accepted as well. Furthermore, the style and vocabulary are very similar in the two volumes,[49] especially the author's use of medical vocabulary which appears to affirm the authorship of Luke the doctor (see Col 4:14). A. Harnack found many medical references unique to Luke and concluded that 'the evidence is of overwhelming force; so that it seems to me that no doubt can exist that the third gospel and the Acts of the Apostles were composed by a physician'.[50]

Another important piece of internal evidence is the 'we-passages' in Acts.[51] In these sections the author shows himself as a travelling companion of Paul, and the apostle mentions Luke as his companion in his letters. This indicates that Luke is most likely the author as he must have been able to see and experience what Paul had gone through. The author presents himself as an eyewitness, and asserts the authenticity of his reports on Paul's life and ministry. That Luke's name is not mentioned in Acts at all is also suggestive of his authorship. Both the letters and Acts contain many overlapping names of Paul's co-workers who were travelling with him during his missionary journeys. However, Luke and Titus are not mentioned in Acts. This seems to suggest the possibility that Luke was the author of Acts, and deliberately hid his own name out of modesty, just as the apostle John did not mention his

---

[48] Irenaeus, *Against Heresies* 3.14.1; Clement of Alexandria, *Stromata* 5.12; Eusebius, *Ecclesiastical History* 3.4.1.

[49] Carter and Earle, *Acts*, xi; Dunn, *Beginning from Jerusalem*, 64–5.

[50] Affirmatively quoted in Carter and Earle, *Acts*, xi–xii. However, this position was thoroughly refuted by Cadbury, but reopened on a different lever by A. Weisserieder, *Image*: See discussion in Witherington, *Acts*, 51-60; Keener, *Acts* 1:402-22.

[51] See Chapter 4 of this book for a detailed discussion.

own name explicitly in his Gospel (cf. John 13:23; 19:26; 20:2; 21:7, 20).

Third, the apostle Paul testifies that Luke was his travelling companion. Luke accompanied Paul as a doctor, and he did not leave Paul when the other companions left him for various reasons (Col 4:14; Phlm 24; 2 Tim 4:11). In Colossians 4:10–15 he is mentioned in the Gentile group of Paul's companions. Here Paul describes him as 'our dear friend Luke, the doctor' (*Loukas ho iatros ho agapētos*). Just as *ho iatros* is Luke's identity as a doctor, so is *ho agapētos* – Luke's other identity, 'Luke the beloved'. K.S. Wuest is of the opinion that 'Luke was the personal physician of Paul. The words, "the beloved one," breathe with Paul's gratitude for his service.'[52] Luke seems to be a very special companion to Paul, because the apostle had a physical weakness.

Paul writes to the Galatians that 'it was because of an illness [*di astheneian tēs sarkos*: 'weakness in the flesh'] that I first preached the gospel to you. Even though my illness was a trial to you, you did not treat me with contempt or scorn' (Gal 4:13–14). Paul had a health issue which would be a stumbling block for his missionary work. He may have strongly felt the need of a doctor who would look after him, and hopefully travel with him, so that he would be able to focus on preaching the gospel in good health. According to tradition, based on the anti-Marcionite prologue and Eusebius, Luke was a native of Antioch.[53] Since Paul was unwell and was severely stoned during the first missionary journey in the region of Galatia (Gal 4:13–14; Acts 14:19–20),[54] it is possible that he visited Luke for treatment after his return to Antioch. Luke may have been a Christian and a member of the church in Antioch. We see that the author of Acts is with Paul during his second journey (Acts 16:10). Thus it is likely that when Paul set out on the second missionary journey, Luke volunteered to join him, and stayed with him ever after. The medical care Luke provided to Paul must have made it possible for the apostle to carry his heavy load of preaching and pastoral ministries.

As we have seen above, the evidence for Luke's authorship of Acts is very strong. The ascription of Luke as the author of Acts was universally accepted until the critical studies of the Tübingen School in the nineteenth century.[55] However, critics have not suggested any alternative author for Acts,[56] and many scholars agree that the author of Acts knew Paul well. For

---

[52] Wuest, *Word Studies*, 238.
[53] Eusebius, *Ecclesiastical History* 3.4.6.
[54] Here we presuppose a South Galatian view. The most notable early contender for this opinion is W. Ramsay; see, for example, his *Church in the Roman Empire*; *St Paul the Traveller*; *Galatians*. More recently Keener, *Acts* 1:582–96, has strongly affirmed this view. For the summary of the debate over North Galatian and South Galatian positions, see Longenecker, *Galatians*, lxiii–lxx; Bruce, *Galatians*, 5–10.
[55] See Hemer, *Book of Acts*, 308–9.
[56] Foakes-Jackson, *Acts*, x.

example, S.E. Porter has cautiously suggested that 'the author of the book of Acts had some form of close contact with Paul and his beliefs'.[57] So contended J. Jervell: 'I do not for a moment doubt that the author of Acts knew Paul well, if not personally'.[58] However, we see no reason why we should not accept R.B. Rackham's conclusion: 'We can then without hesitation conclude that both the Gospel and the Acts were written by S. Luke, the companion of S. Paul.'[59]

That the author of Acts is Luke, a companion of Paul, has huge implications. The reliability of this source becomes much greater. The Gospel of Luke is proven to be an accurate account when it is compared with the other Synoptic Gospels.[60] Here we need to note that Luke produced an accurate and reliable account of Jesus from his research and the collection of his material, most probably carried out during his visits to Jerusalem and Caesarea. If he could produce such a reliable account of Jesus whom he never met, we should note how much more reliance can be placed on a report written by him of Paul, given that he spent years together in missionary ministry with the apostle himself!

If Luke already had in mind to write something about the expansion of the gospel from Jerusalem to Rome, he must have been keen to collect material for his second volume. Much information on Paul's apostolic ministry must have been collected from his own experience as an eyewitness to many of Paul's messages and to the miracles and events of Paul's ministry. Furthermore, he no doubt had opportunity to ask Paul questions about his life and ministry for information and clarification.

We can also infer that Paul shared stories with Luke while the two were together (2 Tim 4:11).[61] Luke was able to visit Paul during his imprisonment in Caesarea (Acts 24:23; 24:27 – 26:32),[62] and Luke must have heard from Paul such accounts as his hearing before King Agrippa. Paul himself was the main source of Luke's material on Paul and the stories connected to him, such as his pre-Christian persecution of the church, Stephen's speech and martyrdom, his Damascus experience, his time in Arabia, Tarsus and Antioch, his experience during the first missionary journey with Barnabas, his second and third missionary journeys, his trials in Caesarea, and so on. Paul

---

[57] Porter, *Paul in Acts*, 206.

[58] Jervell, 'Paul in the Acts of the Apostles', 302; Jervell argues, by disputing the more traditional view, that Luke was more likely a *Jewish* Christian.

[59] Rackham, *Acts of the Apostles*, xvii. Those who maintain the same position include Foakes-Jackson, *Acts*, x; Hengel, *Between Jesus and Paul*, 128; Hengel and Schwemer, *Paul Between Damascus and Antioch*, 7, 9, 18; Wuest, *Word Studies*, 238.

[60] Dunn, *Beginning*, 65, 77.

[61] Even if 2 Timothy was written by someone other than Paul, the author testifies that Luke stays close to Paul till almost the end of his life.

[62] See below, pp. 108-12.

must have shared or shown his passion for Christ and for lost souls, and his struggle with his fellow Jews and Jewish believers.

If Luke was in Antioch, he might have heard the missionary report from Paul and Barnabas (Acts 14:27). He also would have known the occasion that triggered the church to send Paul and Barnabas to Jerusalem to resolve the issue described in Acts 15:1–2. He could have also heard their report on the discussion and decisions of the Jerusalem Council. Even if Luke did not spend extensive time with Paul in Antioch, his experience for a few years with the apostle as a travelling companion is certainly enough for him to have learned about Paul's ministry in other places. It is also likely that Luke collected various pieces of information from personal conversations with Paul or from his sermons while travelling with him.

It is also probable that Luke collected some of his sources from Paul on the earliest church community in Jerusalem. This is assuming that Peter told Paul (during the fifteen days they spent together) about the stories of Jesus' life, teaching, ministry, death, resurrection, ascension, the outpouring of the Holy Spirit, Peter's experience of seeing thousands of people converting to Christ, his trials before the Sanhedrin and imprisonments, and information about the Jerusalem church in the earliest days.

Furthermore, Luke stayed at Philip's house in Caesarea together with Paul on their way to Jerusalem after Paul's third missionary journey (Acts 21:8). Thus it is reasonable to assume that Luke visited Philip again while Paul was in prison in Caesarea. At that time he could have collected material for his later accounts, such as the election of the seven 'deacons', Philip's mission in Samaria (Acts 8:5–25) and the conversion of the Ethiopian eunuch (Acts 8:26–40).[63]

Therefore, what F.J. Foakes-Jackson says is true:

> [Luke's] qualifications to write the book [of Acts] are indisputable . . . Thus he was in a position . . . to ascertain the facts of Paul's life . . . Luke fulfils the conditions necessary for a biographer of Paul . . . He was evidently comparatively so unimportant in the Christian community that the ascription of two books to him cannot be purely arbitrary.[64]

Luke's portrait of Paul in Acts is much more reliable than used to be suggested, and it is this thesis which we shall attempt to substantiate in the following chapters.

---

[63] So correctly, Dunn, *Beginning*, 75–6.
[64] Foakes-Jackson, *Acts*, x–xi, though I have added many more reasons in this book as to why Luke could be a reliable author for Acts.

1

Vielhauer and 'Paulinism' in Acts[1]

Now we turn to examine Philipp Vielhauer's extremely influential article which appeared in 1950. He initiated an investigation to discuss 'the question whether and to what extent the author of Acts took over and passed on theological ideas of Paul, whether and to what extent he modified them'.[2] He undertook this examination by paying special attention to Luke's portrayal of four Pauline theological themes, namely, natural theology, the law, Christology and eschatology. His conclusion is straightforward: the Paul of Acts is radically different from the real Paul, and in these major areas, Luke presents no specifically Pauline theology, but rather his own theological doctrine, which is that of early catholicism around the turn of the first century.[3] In this way Vielhauer has highlighted the fundamental differences between the Lucan Paul and the historical Paul.

A similar line of argument had already been presented by Martin Dibelius, according to whom Luke's primary interest in Acts was not to preserve the reliable *history* of the earliest church, but to write the *theology* of his contemporary church towards the start of the second century.[4]

---

[1] The first draft of this chapter was presented at the New Testament Department Seminar, Durham University (9 June 1997).

[2] Vielhauer, '"Paulinism"', 33. This translation of the original article, 'Zum "Paulinismus" der Apostelgeschichte', *EvT* 10 (1950–51), 1–15, was previously published in *Perkins School of Theology Journal* 17 (Fall, 1963). The pages we refer to are from *SLA*.

[3] Vielhauer, '"Paulinism"', 48.

[4] Dibelius, *Studies in the Acts*; especially 'The Acts of the Apostles as an Historical Source' in that volume, pp. 102–8. Dibelius has completely ignored some earlier contributions to the study of Acts by Ramsay, Harnack, Wikenhauer and Meyer. About a century earlier than Dibelius, Baur, *Paul*, questioned Luke as a highly tendentious and fictitious historian, whose material cannot be reliable. It is interesting to note that Dibelius refers to Baur only twice in his book, *Studies in the Acts*, with little description of Baur's position. Cadbury, 'The Speeches in Acts', 402–27, arrived at a similar conclusion to that of Dibelius after comparing speeches in Acts with

Vielhauer's dependence on Dibelius' work is evident,[5] but he has gone on to develop Dibelius' study by providing a method of comparing some specific themes in Acts with those in Paul's own letters. With such a methodological contribution Vielhauer has exercised an extraordinary influence in denying the historical reliability of Acts.[6] For E. Haenchen, Vielhauer has opened a new development for critical studies on Acts.[7] As a result, later scholars have restrained themselves from using the material in Acts to study Paul and his theology. Despite constant attempts to refute this denial, with some success,[8] Vielhauer has been considered, on the whole, correct, and as expressing 'the authoritative statements' on the topic of the reliability of Luke's portrait of Paul.[9] The more recent monograph by John Lentz, *Luke's Portrait of Paul*, largely reaffirms Vielhauer's position.[10]

In the 1960s W.C. van Unnik characterized this academic debate, sparked by Vielhauer, as a 'storm center in contemporary scholarship'. Writing in 2012, D.P. Moessner and other editors added their opinion that 'the sea is barely becalmed. Paul's relation to Luke's writings is still disquieting and

---

those of Greco-Roman historians. More recently this position has been advocated again: Mount, *Pauline Christianity*; Tyson, *Marcion and Luke-Acts*. However, the current consensus on the date of Acts is that it was written in the 80s or early 90s: Dunn, *Beginning*, 67; Sanders, *Paul the Apostle's Life*, 13–14.

[5] Nearly half of Vielhauer's endnotes favourably refer to Dibelius' works.

[6] Those who follow Vielhauer's lead include Käsemann, Lohse, Conzelmann, Haenchen, Harbsmeier, Andersen, Bauernfeind, Marxsen, Klein and Grässer. For bibliographical details see Wilckens, 'Interpreting Luke-Acts', in *SLA*, 62–5, 78–9; also Gasque, *History*, 287 n. 78. For a critical assessment of Vielhauer, see Gasque, *History*, 283–91; Buckwalter, *Character*, 231–72; and Bovon, 'Law in Luke-Acts', 59–73.

[7] Haenchen, *Acts*, 48. See Porter, *Paul in Acts*, 190–99, for a helpful critique on Haenchen, and 199–205, on Vielhauer. In Conzelmann, *Theology of Luke*, who has become a main figure in highlighting Luke's theology in Acts, he concludes, 'These are not abbreviated versions of actual speeches but are literary creations' (*Commentary*, 44). But for criticisms of Conzelmann's view, see Marshall, *Luke: Historian and Theologian*, 77–102; Bovon, *Luke the Theologian*, 13–16.

[8] For example, Ellis, *Luke*, 45–50; Marshall, *Acts*, 42–4; Hanson, *Acts*, 182–3; Gärtner, *Areopagus Speech*, 248–52; Jervell, *Unknown Paul*; Bruce, 'Real Paul?', 282–305; and Gasque, *History*, 283–91.

[9] Porter, *Paul in Acts*, 189. This is the judgement of Barrett, *Acts*, ICC, 1:651, who has written probably the most substantial commentary on Acts in recent years. The judgement of Marshall (*Acts*, 42) that Vielhauer's contention has been 'convincingly destroyed' by Ellis's six-page argument (*Luke*, 45–50), seems too optimistic.

[10] Lentz, *Luke's Portrait*, 23–61, arrives at a sceptical position after questioning Paul's social status as to citizenship, education and profession. Lentz' position, however, cannot stand in the light of Rapske's recent research, *Roman Custody*, 71–114, 245–6. See also Rapske's book review: 'Review of *Luke's Portrait of Paul*', 347–53; also Ascough's book review in *NovT* 36 (1994): 408–10.

debated as ever', and so they launched a volume with sixteen articles on the subject, including Vielhauer's epochal article as its first chapter.[11] Earlier, W. Ward Gasque listed this debate as one of the three areas for further critical study on Acts,[12] and some sixty years after the first publication of Vielhauer's thesis, scholars are still debating it.[13]

The reprinting of Vielhauer's article as the first chapter in a recent monograph, with contributions from fifteen other scholars,[14] indicates the ample interest in and influence of his work which continues today in the scholarly world.

In this chapter we shall attempt to evaluate his thesis in the four areas he chose. An adequate understanding of the theology of the historical Paul and that of Luke's presentation of it are prerequisites for a comparative study such as this. So we shall examine both Paul's theological ideas and Luke's presentation of them so as to determine the extent of the credibility of Vielhauer's thesis.[15] In doing so we shall also pay attention to the fact that the scope of Luke's work in Acts is different from that of Paul in the letters. Then, towards the end, we shall question Vielhauer's methodology, which compares two works of a different character without discerning or taking account of the differences in the scopes of their writings. Our investigation will examine to what extent Vielhauer's thesis on Luke's portrayal of Paul's theology as expressed in his missionary preaching can be sustained.

Natural Theology

Following Dibelius, Vielhauer takes Acts 17:22–31 as a typical Hellenistic

---

[11] Moessner, Marguerat, Parsons, Wolter, eds, *Paul and the Heritage*, xvi. Flichy, 'Paul of Luke', 21, assesses Vielhauer's thesis as being 'a veritable thunderclap'.

[12] Gasque, *History*, 359.

[13] The study of Paul in Acts has constantly attracted scholars. The Society of New Testament Studies took it as their topic in 2008, and the publication of their studies, Moessner, Marguerat, Parsons, Wolter, eds, *Paul and the Heritage*, reprints Vielhauer's article as its first chapter. See Walton, *Leadership*, 6–12, for a survey of critiques of Vielhauer; also Keener, *Acts*, 1:250–52, esp. p. 158; Porter, *Paul in Acts*, 188–206; Phillips, *Paul, His Letters, and Acts*, 30–49. Bovon's book, *Luke the Theologian*, demonstrates the never-ending interest in studying Luke as a theologian. In this nearly 700-page book Bovon offers useful summaries and assessments, and a very extensive bibliography on Luke's theology, history, literature, salvation history and eschatology.

[14] Moessner, Marguerat, Parsons, Wolter, eds, *Paul and the Heritage*.

[15] Longenecker, *Paul, Apostle of Liberty*, 246, rightly points out that proper understanding of Paul's teaching is vital to understand Luke's description of Paul in Acts.

message to Gentiles about God as the Creator and the Lord of heaven and earth (Acts 17:24–25; also 14:15).[16] He notes that the Areopagus speaker does not condemn the Athenians for their idolatry, because it has been done out of 'ignorance' and because God let it pass unpunished (Acts 17:23, 28–30; cf. 3:17; 13:27; 14:15). He perceives, however, that the Paul of Romans, on the contrary, asserts that the Gentiles led themselves into ungodliness and wickedness by suppressing the knowledge of God obtained from the display of his creation. As a result they are without excuse (Rom 1:19–20). He concludes, therefore, that the natural theology of Acts 17 is completely different from that of Romans 1, and to this extent Luke misrepresents Paul.[17]

However, we find that several other elements need to be examined if Vielhauer's conclusion is to be sustained. The Areopagus speaker preaches from the presupposition that the members of his audience do not know God. He mentions that they can be excused because the God whom he is talking about is yet unknown to them. However, Paul's accusation in Romans 1:20 is based on the fact that his unspecified audiences, 'they', do not glorify God but rather are engaged in idolatry *despite the fact that they know him* (note the important *gnontes* in v. 21). In other words, since 'their' knowledge of God is affirmed in Romans 1, their actions are declared inexcusable. For Vielhauer, Paul's audiences for both messages consist exclusively of *Gentiles*. Vielhauer's understanding is based on a long-maintained hypothesis that Romans 1:18–32 represents the characteristic Hellenistic Jewish critique of Gentiles.[18] This general consensus, however, has been questioned by some scholars, who argue that this is Paul's indictment of *humanity* (i.e. Gentiles *and Jews*) in typically Jewish terms.[19] We have supported elsewhere the conclusion of the latter position (albeit presenting a different argument) that Paul includes Jews in his accusation in Romans 1:18–32.[20] The fact that 'they' do know God and his righteous decree (Rom 1:21, 32) suggests that Paul's charge is directed not only to Gentiles but also to *Jews* (cf. Gal 4:8: 'Formerly . . . you [Gentile Galatians] did not know God . . .').

Vielhauer also overlooks Paul's references elsewhere that God disregarded sins committed from ignorance. Although Vielhauer is aware that there is a connection between Acts 17:30 and Romans 3:25, he does not examine these references to consider whether Luke's report in Acts 17:30 is

---

[16] Vielhauer, '"Paulinism"', 34–5; Dibelius, 'Paul on the Areopagus', 26–77.

[17] Vielhauer, '"Paulinism"', 36–7. A similar line of argument was independently presented earlier, though briefly and less forcefully, by McNeile, *New Testament Teaching*, 133–4.

[18] See Chae, *Paul*, 73 nn. 2–3, for bibliographical details.

[19] E.g. Hyldahl, 'Reminiscence', 285–8; Hooker, 'Adam in Romans 1', 297–306; idem, 'Further Note', 181–3; Barrett, *From First Adam*, 17–19; Dunn, *Romans*, 1:60–61.

[20] For a detailed argument see Chae, *Paul*, 73–94.

credible. As Paul refers to Jesus' death using a Jewish sacrificial term, he adds that God 'did this to demonstrate his justice, because in his forbearance he had left the sins committed beforehand unpunished' (Rom 3:25). Here Paul indicates that God's forbearance was applied to all (i.e. Jews and Gentiles), for *all* have sinned (Rom 3:23). So he says that God passed over the sins of Jews and Gentiles committed before the atoning death of Jesus. Later he applies this understanding to himself: 'Even though I was once a blasphemer and a persecutor and a violent man, I was shown mercy because I acted in ignorance and unbelief' (1 Tim 1:13).

God does not punish ignorant sinners instantly, but waits patiently for them to repent (cf. Rom 11:32; 1 Tim 2:4). Paul often refers to God's patience and tolerance as a sign of his kindness in waiting for people's repentance (Rom 2:4; 9:22; 10:21); God does not seek to punish human beings for their sins, but to reconcile them to himself (Rom 4:7–8; 2 Cor 5:18–19). So the notion that God allows sins committed in ignorance to go unpunished is also common to the historical Paul presented in his letters, and thus Vielhauer's view (that Luke presents an utterly contradictory picture of the real Paul) is difficult to maintain.

Nevertheless, Vielhauer further asserts, 'The emphasis upon "ignorance" as an excuse is a constant motif of the missionary preaching in Acts'.[21] Indeed the 'ignorance' motif is common in Acts. Peter tells the Jews that their crucifixion of Jesus was done in ignorance (Acts 3:17; cf. Luke 23:34). The Lucan Paul also preaches a similar message to the Jews at Pisidian Antioch (Acts 13:27), and to the Gentiles at Lystra (14:16) and in Athens (17:30). But it is important to note that Luke does not present the 'ignorance' motif as a type of excuse, as Vielhauer contends, but reports both Peter and Paul acknowledging it as a stepping stone to urge repentance from their hearers (Acts 3:17, 19; 13:27, 40–41).[22]

The Areopagus preacher does the same: 'In the past God overlooked such ignorance, but now he commands all people everywhere to *repent*' (Acts 17:30). The call for repentance is appropriate because the new aeon has dawned with the death and resurrection of Jesus Christ. So the Areopagus speaker introduces a new situation with the emphatic *'but now'* (*ta nun*),[23] implying that from now on God does not overlook their ignorance, and that is why all sinners should repent. The speaker does not approve of their idolatry at all.[24] Paul also makes such a shift in Romans 3. God's patience is

---

[21] Vielhauer, '"Paulinism"', 36.

[22] That God's patience calls for the repentance of all human beings is also expressed in the OT (Gen 18:32; Neh 9:30–31; Jonah 3:10; 4:11). So also Wis 11:23 (RSVA): 'thou dost overlook men's sins, that they may repent'.

[23] The Greek expresses a clear shift, 'in this present instance': see Zerwick and Grosvenor, *Grammatical Analysis*, 411.

[24] Gempf, 'Athens, Paul in', 52; Caragounis, 'L'universalisme moderne', 23–6.

related to his righteousness demonstrated '*at the present time*' (Rom 3:25–26; '*but now*', *nuni de*, in v. 21). Paul urges repentance, obedience and faith (Rom 2:4–5; 10:21; 11:23; 2 Cor 7:9–10; 12:21). Vielhauer's view is, thus, incorrect in saying that the 'ignorance' motif is emphasized as an excuse in Acts 17. Rather, the Areopagus speaker directly connects it to the urgent need for repentance (Acts 17:30). Both the real Paul and the Lucan Paul stress that because of what God has done in Christ, he is no longer unjust even if he punishes those who do not believe. The Lucan Paul does not display substantial differences from the Paul of his letters on this point.

Further points of correspondence can be found when Acts 17 is compared with 1 Thessalonians 1:9–10. From these passages David Wenham notes three features of agreement between Paul's teaching in the letters and that set out in Acts: (1) the urge to turn from idols to the living God; (2) the need to be prepared for the coming judgement; (3) the resurrection of Jesus. The reports of both Paul and Luke convey a common pattern of Christian preaching to Gentiles, and so Wenham is correct to contend that the gap between the Paul of Acts and the Paul of the letters is narrowed.[25]

However, Vielhauer attempts to strengthen his thesis by asserting that some of the most familiar Pauline terms, such as 'sin', 'grace' and 'cross', are lacking in the Areopagus speech. These words do not occur in the speech, but Vielhauer does not seem right to contend that even the *ideas* they convey are lacking here. The speaker's strong appeal for repentance is undoubtedly related to and based on the Athenians' sin of idolatry. According to Luke the greatest sin for the Jews is that they crucified Jesus whom God made both Lord and Christ (Acts 2:22–39), but for the Gentiles, it was idolatry (Acts 17:16, 24–31; 19:26; cf. 20:21). Both ethnic groups sinned in ignorance (Acts 3:17; 17:30), but repentance is strongly required from both groups (Acts 2:38; 3:19; 17:30). The fact that the Judge, who will judge the world with justice, has been appointed is a clear indication that all people will be punished according to their sins.

Neither is the idea of God's grace absent in the speech. The fact that God has overlooked the Gentiles' sin of idolatry (since it is done in ignorance) is an expression of God's grace (Acts 17:30). Luke had already made it clear that God had shown kindness by providing the Gentiles with material blessings (Acts 14:17). That sinners can, and do, have kinship with God is also an expression of God's abundant grace. Most of all, in the death and resurrection of Jesus, God's grace is evidently manifested for sinners to turn to the living God (Acts 17:31; 14:15). Through Christ they can reach out for God and find him.

---

[25] Wenham, 'Paulinism', 54. So also Hemer, 'Speeches of Acts', 85; Barrett, 'Paul's Address', 109–10. See also Drane, *Introducing the New Testament*, 241: Acts 17:22–31 is not much different from what Paul writes in Rom 1:18 – 2:16.

Likewise one cannot say that the idea of the cross is absent.[26] Phrases such as 'a death sentence', 'asked Pilate to have him executed', 'carried out all that was written about him', 'took him down from the tree' and 'laid him in a tomb' (Acts 13:28–29) abundantly proclaim the death of Jesus on the cross. Luke's expression, 'by raising him from *the dead*' (Acts 17:31), echoes almost exactly Paul's own phrases in Romans 6:4; 8:11; 10:9; 1 Corinthians 6:14; 15:15; and Colossians 2:12, and it certainly presupposes Jesus' death on the cross.[27] 'The "word of the cross" seems tactfully omitted, because it was known to be "folly to Gentiles" (1 Cor 1: 23)'.[28] Vielhauer's assertion that Luke deleted Paul's Christological part of his sermon has no ground. He assumes too lightly that Luke is recording a complete speech. It is to be noted that this speech is made in response to the invitation from the philosophers who have heard Paul preaching Jesus and the resurrection (Acts 17:18), and so Paul could have expounded Christology if his speech had not been disturbed (see also Acts 24:25). Nevertheless, the Lucan Paul clearly preaches that God would judge the world through Jesus Christ, the appointed Judge, whose credentials God has proved through his resurrection (Acts 17:31; cf. Rom 1:3–4). Moreover, the concept that God would judge through Christ is exactly what Paul himself says in Romans 2:16: 'God will judge men's secrets through Jesus Christ' (so similarly Rom 14:10; 1 Cor 4:3–5; 2 Cor 5:10; cf. Acts 10:39–42; 2 Tim 4:1, 8).

Our examination above shows that the natural theology of Romans 1 and that in Acts 17 are not 'utterly different' as Vielhauer asserts.[29] He uses limited Pauline references, and compares them with Acts 17. His perception that in Acts 17 Luke records Paul's natural theology is also questionable. Rather, Luke's concentration lies with Paul's introductory speech about the God yet unknown to his Gentile audience. We have found sufficient evidence that Luke's portrayal of Paul's natural theology is not distorted;[30] rather, in substance, Acts 17 contains Pauline themes and theology.[31]

---

[26] *Pace* Maddox, *Purpose*, 68, 83. See Porter, *Paul in Acts*, 168–70, for a helpful argument against Maddox's interpretation of natural theology.

[27] Rom 6:4: 'Christ was raised from the dead'; Rom 8:11: 'he who raised Christ from the dead'; Rom 10:9: 'God raised him from the dead'; 1 Cor 6:14: 'God raised the Lord from the dead'; 1 Cor 15:15: 'he raised Christ from the dead'; Col 2:12: 'who raised him from the dead'.

[28] Bruce, 'St Luke's Portrait', 189.

[29] Vielhauer, '"Paulinism"', 36.

[30] Gärtner, *Areopagus Speech*, 248–52; Hanson, *Acts*, 182–3. Luke's description that Paul was waiting for his fellow workers in Athens (Acts 17:13–16) is supported by Paul's own writing (1 Thess 3:1).

[31] *Pace* Conzelmann, 'Address', 218.

The Law

Vielhauer highlights eight areas in which he notes that, unlike the real Paul, the Lucan Paul is depicted as totally loyal to the law and to Judaism: (1) only after being rejected by the Jews does Paul turn to preach to the Gentiles; (2) he submits to the Jerusalem apostles; (3) he initiates Timothy's circumcision; (4) he accepts and spreads the apostolic decree; (5) he takes a personal vow; (6) he travels to Jerusalem to participate in religious festivals; (7) he participates in a Nazirite vow with others; (8) he stresses his Pharisaic background.[32]

Vielhauer notes that the description of Paul in Acts as going first to the Jews before turning to the Gentiles does not contradict the agreement of the Jerusalem conference, for the demarcation is not of religions but of territory (Gal 2:7–9). In the light of Paul's testimony that he had been lashed five times by the synagogue authorities (2 Cor 11:24), Vielhauer also accepts that Paul participated in worship in the synagogues and lived as a Jew even in the Diaspora to win more Jews (cf. 1 Cor 9:19–23). He also thinks that it would have been possible for Paul to accommodate such practices mentioned above within his understanding of freedom.[33] However, Vielhauer argues that the Paul of Acts is presented as having different attitudes to the law and circumcision, and to the doctrine of justification by faith, from the Paul of the letters.

Paul's attitude to the law and circumcision

Vielhauer offers two main reasons for his contention. First, he states that Paul's *motivation* for participating in the vows of other believers as described in Acts 21 is most unlikely. 'It was Pauline doctrine that the Mosaic Law was not the way of salvation, that circumcision was not a condition of salvation, and that Jewish "customs" were without significance with regard to salvation.'[34] Since such a theological stand was applicable not only for Gentiles but also *for Jews*, if Paul had followed James's advice (Acts 21:23–24, 26), he would have been in direct contradiction to and in denial of his own gospel.[35] Furthermore, it is extremely unlikely that James, knowing Paul's gospel and mission, could have possibly suggested 'such a deception' to him.

Second, he states that Luke's description of the motivation for Jewish hostility towards Paul is different from Paul's own understanding of it. According to Luke, Jews persecuted Paul precisely because of their jealousy and their rejection of the messiahship of Jesus. But Paul says that it is rather be-

---

[32] Vielhauer, '"Paulinism"', 37–8.
[33] Vielhauer, '"Paulinism"', 38–9.
[34] Vielhauer, '"Paulinism"', 39.
[35] So similarly, Pervo, *Mystery*, 134.

cause of his doctrine of freedom from the law and circumcision, which nullifies Jewish supremacy and identity. In this connection, the notion that Paul initiated the circumcision of Timothy is unthinkable, because such an action is contradictory to Paul's theology, and it requires acknowledgement of the saving significance of circumcision.[36] What Paul writes in 1 Corinthians 9:19–23 should not be cited to rationalize these episodes as historical.

So Vielhauer reinforces his assertion that Luke portrays a distorted picture of Paul, and this time with regard to his own understanding and practice of the law. He insists that Luke's overriding concern is to present Paul as one who not only is faithful to the law but also acknowledges the full validity of the law for Jewish believers.[37] So Luke misrepresents Paul, argues Vielhauer, due either to his ignorance of the significance of the debate over the law,[38] or to his attempt to cover up the bitter battle over this issue.

Our argument against Vielhauer's contention is based on the question of methodology in comparing the materials in Acts and in the letters. It is vitally important to perceive that what Luke reports on Paul's thoughts and activities in Acts and what Paul writes in the letters are presented from different perspectives. Acts depicts Paul's view on the law (and thereby circumcision) mostly with regard to the *Jewish* people; but when Paul argues against keeping the law in the letters it is exclusively with regard to *Gentile* believers. Nowhere in his letters does Paul explicitly insist that the *Jews* should not keep the law nor circumcise their children (cf. Rom 2:13–15, 25–29; 7:12, 13, 14, 16; Phil 3:4–7).[39] Paul's polemic against the law and circumcision is mainly derived in the course of defending the legitimacy and sufficiency of the salvation of *Gentile* believers apart from keeping the Jewish law.[40] His forceful argument is made especially in reaction to the vigorous attempt of some Jewish believers to impose such obligations on *Gentile* converts.

However, Acts shows Paul's attitude to the law mainly with respect to the Jews, and so his behaviour as a Jew among Jews is often described. The circumcision of Timothy, the participation in a Nazirite vow, and Paul's defence

---

[36] Vielhauer, '"Paulinism"', 40–41.
[37] Vielhauer, '"Paulinism"', 42.
[38] Similarly, Bornkamm, *Paul*, 25.
[39] The Jerusalem believers received reports that Paul had been teaching *all the Jews* in the Diaspora to turn away from the Mosaic law and not to circumcise their children. James's advice to Paul to participate in the Nazirite vow was to prove that 'there is no truth in these reports' about Paul (Acts 21:21–24). James knew not only that the rumour was false but also that Paul himself was living in obedience to the (ritual) law, and so his advice was appropriate. Above all, Paul's participation in the rite of the Jewish *believers* does not contradict his soteriology because with this act he does not demonstrate that such customs have *salvific* significance, as Vielhauer insists.
[40] For a fuller treatment see Chae, *Paul*, 302–7; see also Bruce, 'St Luke's Portrait', 187.

before the Jewish crowd are to be understood from this perspective. But his letters expose his theological stand that the Jewish law should not be imposed upon *Gentile* Christians, as if it had salvific significance. The different pictures drawn in Acts and in Paul's letters are to be perceived accordingly. We have hardly any examples in Paul's letters of what he testifies in 1 Corinthians 9:20: 'To the Jew I became like a Jew, to win the Jews. To those under the law I became like one under the law . . . so as to win those under the law.' Acts provides us with such examples and occasions.

According to Vielhauer, 'the circumcision of Timothy stands in direct contradiction to the theology of Paul [as shown in Gal 5:2–5]'.[41] Here again Vielhauer implausibly compares Paul's solemn warning to the Gentile believers in response to the Judaizing attempt of some Jewish believers with his missionary tactic to circumcise Timothy who was already regarded as a Jew.[42] This procedure was performed not to obtain the right status or full salvation by fulfilling a legal obligation, but practically and culturally to prepare Timothy for his missionary involvement with Paul (cf. 1 Cor 10:32–33).[43] 'Circumcision is never a matter of indifference [for Paul]', asserts Vielhauer,[44] but he does not note what Paul says in 1 Corinthians 7:17–20 and in Galatians 5:6; 6:15, that circumcision should not be a crucial matter of difference:[45]

> Nevertheless, each one should retain the place in life that the Lord assigned to him and to which God has called him. This is the rule I lay down in all the churches. Was a man already circumcised when he was called? He should not become uncircumcised. Was a man uncircumcised when he was called? He should not be circumcised. Circumcision is nothing and uncircumcision is nothing. Keeping God's commands is what counts. Each one should remain in the situation that he was in when God called him (1 Cor 7:17–20).

It is also significant to note that at the concluding part of his vigorous argument against keeping the law and circumcision, Paul repeatedly indicates that his main point of argument has not really been to attack circumcision itself. 'For in Christ Jesus neither circumcision nor uncircumcision has any value. The only thing that counts is faith expressing itself through love . . . Neither

---

[41] Vielhauer, '"Paulinism"', 40–41.

[42] Marshall, *Acts*, 259; Keener, *Bible Background Commentary*, 366; Bruce, 'St Luke's Portrait', 188.

[43] Bruce, 'St Luke's Portrait', 187: 'this is not at all inconsistent with Paul's own testimony. The following of the customs was an ethically neutral matter in his eyes'.

[44] Vielhauer, '"Paulinism"', 40–41.

[45] So Bruce, *Book of the Acts*, 322 n. 7, seems more accurate in saying that 'even when writing to the Galatians, Paul points out that circumcision *per se* is religiously indifferent'.

circumcision nor uncircumcision means anything; what counts is a new creation' (Gal 5:6; 6:15).[46]

Furthermore, Paul often acknowledges the value of the law and circumcision, especially in his letter to the church in Rome, which consisted of Gentiles *and* Jews. He affirms that the law is holy, spiritual and good, and that he delights in God's law (Rom 7:12, 14, 16, 22). The law is 'the embodiment of knowledge and truth' (Rom 2:20b), and so is to be submitted to and fulfilled (Rom 2:13, 25; 8:7; 13:8, 10). Paul clearly acknowledges circumcision as one of the Jewish advantages that still has value for Jews (Rom 2:25; 3:1–2). Although Paul does not develop these remarks, his lack of elaboration should not be construed as a denial of such value for Jews.

What Paul vigorously opposes in Galatians is the demand for circumcision as a legal obligation and a condition of salvation especially upon *Gentile believers*. Furthermore, what Paul says to Peter during the Antioch incident indicates that Paul assumes that a Jew is to live like a Jew. Paul rebukes Peter because he, in effect, 'force[s] Gentiles to follow Jewish customs' (Gal 2:14). The implication is that Paul accepts that Jewish believers live like Jews, following Jewish customs. It is also important to note that Paul promptly objects to the role of the law in salvation only after his first missionary journey in Galatia (cf. Acts 15:1–2). Only when it has become an issue some years later, through the disturbance of the Judaizers, does the apostle explain his objection forcefully. And yet he does not deny the value of circumcision for the Jews (Rom 3:1–2; 9:4).

In this connection it is important to note Luke's report that Paul vigorously disputed the demand for circumcision and for keeping the law only after they were demanded as a condition for salvation for *Gentile believers* (Acts 15:1–2). Paul indicates his twofold policy: one for Jews and one for Gentiles, or one for the weak and one for the strong (1 Cor 8:4–13; 9:19–23; 10:25–33: 'Do not cause anyone to stumble, whether Jews, Greeks or the church of God – even as I try to please everybody in every way': 1 Cor 10:32–33). James's remark, 'as for the *Gentile* believers', also implies such a twofold practice (Acts 21:25).

The report about the episode in Acts 21 does not seem to be Luke's invention; rather, what he describes here may well reflect what Paul declares in 1 Corinthians 9:20: 'To those under the law I became like one under the law (though I myself am not under the law)'. Vielhauer is right to say that for Paul, the law, circumcision and Jewish customs are not the way to salvation.[47] However, what he misses is the fact that Paul denies the value of those Jewish

---

[46] Likewise, concerning the observation of Sabbath/festivals, Paul advises, 'Each one should be fully convinced in his own mind' (Rom 14:5), and so leaves it open to each believer whether they should eat food sacrificed to idols (1 Cor 8; Rom 14:2–6). Paul's policy of tolerance is extended to evangelism as well (Phil 1:15–18).

[47] Vielhauer, '"Paulinism"', 39.

elements in the course of arguing against those who impose them on the *Gentile believers* who have already been saved by faith. Vielhauer also overlooks the fact that Timothy and the participants in the purification rites in Acts 21 are *Jewish* believers. Paul could have accepted this, as such rites were not for their salvation, but to show that he himself lives in obedience to the law as a Jew (Acts 21:24; 1 Cor 9:20). If this is so, Luke seems to have correctly understood Paul's view of the law and circumcision regarding Gentiles and Jews.

The difference between Luke and Paul is that Luke reports more on Paul's encounters with *Jews*, while in the letters Paul himself deals with these issues primarily in connection with *Gentiles*. So, we find Vielhauer's methodology and interpretation of Paul unconvincing, because he compares two different sets of arguments without discerning their contexts and emphases.

Paul's doctrine of justification by faith

Vielhauer also argues that Luke exhibits his own soteriology, one that is strikingly different from Paul's doctrine of justification by faith.[48] He finds such a difference in Acts 13:38–39: 'Therefore, my brothers, I want you to know that through Jesus the forgiveness of sins is proclaimed to you. Through him everyone who believes is justified from everything you could not be justified from by the law of Moses.' Vielhauer then offers more specific reasons for his contention:

> First of all, justification is equated with the forgiveness of sins and thus is conceived entirely negatively, which Paul never does; again, 'forgiveness of sins' does not occur in his major letters, but rather in Col. 1:14 and in Eph. 1:7, and is used in Acts 13:38 in the same sense as in the speeches of Peter (Acts 2:38; 3:19; 5:31; 10:43). Furthermore, the forgiveness of sins is tied to the messiahship of Jesus which is based on the resurrection (vs. 37), and also 'nothing is said in this connection about the particular significance of his death.' Finally, it is here a question only [of] partial justification, one which is not by faith alone, but *also* by faith.[49]

This argument has two main points: first, Luke's phrase, 'the forgiveness of sins', is not Pauline,[50] but rather Petrine; second, according to Luke justification by faith is only complementary for Jewish believers while Paul absolutely denies the significance of the law for salvation. At this point, Vielhauer quotes Harnack's remark, 'According to Paul the law has absolutely no saving significance . . . [but] according to Luke . . . justification by faith is so to

---

[48] Vielhauer, '"Paulinism"', 41, 42 (and here he follows Dibelius; see Vielhauer's endnote 30).

[49] Vielhauer, '"Paulinism"', 41–2; the inner quotation is cited from de Wette and Overbeck, *Apostelgeschichte*, 205.

[50] Followed by Conzelmann, *Acts*, 106.

speak only complementary for Jewish Christians'.[51] We shall examine these points to assess the validity of his contention.

The phrase 'the forgiveness of sins' rarely occurs in Paul: 'he . . . brought us into the kingdom of the Son he loves, in whom we have redemption, the forgiveness of sins' (Col 1:13–14); and 'In him we have redemption through his blood, the forgiveness of sins' (Eph 1:7). However, these references are significant because in both verses 'the forgiveness of sins' is precisely equated with 'redemption'.[52] The notion that Christ redeemed us is abundantly expressed elsewhere in Paul (Rom 3:24; 4:25; 1 Cor 1:30; 2 Cor 5:19; Gal 3:13–14; cf. Titus 2:14). In Romans 3:23–24, Paul relates forgiveness of sins to redemption and justification: 'for all have sinned and fall short of the glory of God, and are justified freely by his grace through the redemption that came by Christ Jesus' (cf. Heb 9:12, 15; 10:10–12). Moreover, when Paul attempts to substantiate his point by highlighting 'the blessedness of the man to whom God credits righteousness [justification] apart from works', he quotes what David said about the blessedness of the person who experiences the forgiveness of sins (Rom 4:6–7; Ps 32:1–2).

It is to be noted that although Paul does not use the phrase 'the forgiveness of sins' in Romans 3:23–25, the language certainly echoes that of Leviticus where making atonement is precisely for the forgiveness of sins.[53] Both Paul and Jewish believers would obviously have known Leviticus. It is therefore arguably more appropriate for Paul to use the phrase when speaking or writing to Jews (as in Acts 13) than when writing to Gentile and Jewish believers (as in Romans 3).

Furthermore, the concept and language of 'God forgave our sins' is abundant in Paul. He relates the forgiveness of sins with justification. He reminds the Corinthians that he preached that Christ died 'for our sins' as one of the most important parts of his missionary message. This shows that they believed that Christ died for their sins, and by implication, they experienced the forgiveness of sins (1 Cor 15:3–8; cf. 2 Cor 5:19). He says the same thing in Galatians: 'the Lord Jesus Christ . . . gave himself for our sins' (Gal 1:4; cf. 2:20: '[He] gave himself for me'). The same language that 'God forgave our sins' is used elsewhere as well (Col 2:13–14; 3:13; Eph 4:32). Paul often conveys the concept of forgiveness of sins: 'Christ died for the ungodly' (Rom 5:6); 'While we were still sinners, Christ died for us' (Rom 5:8; also 1 Thess 5:10), then he adds, 'we have now been justified by his blood' (Rom

---

[51] Vielhauer, '"Paulinism"', 42.

[52] So does the author of Ephesians: 'In him we have redemption through his blood, the forgiveness of sins' (Eph 1:7).

[53] E.g. Lev 4:20, 26, 31, 35; 5:10, 13, 16, 18; 6:7; 14:19–20; 19:22; so also Num 15:25, 28.

5:9). Paul often says that believers have been *justified from sins* (Rom 6:7),[54] or have been *set free from sins* (Rom 6:18, 22). Paul connects the forgiveness of sins with justification as we have seen, and so does the Lucan Paul here in Acts 13 and later in 26:18.

That Luke does not use Paul's exact vocabulary or phrase does not necessarily indicate that he misrepresents Paul and his theology. The terms and phrases are 'scarcely to be distinguished here'.[55] Our examination shows that Luke fairly represents Paul on this point, because Paul uses the concepts of justification, redemption and forgiveness without making such a sharp distinction. Therefore Vielhauer is incorrect in asserting that Luke has deliberately distorted Paul in order to convey his own theology.

Now we turn to examine the role of the law expressed in Acts 13:38–39: 'Through him everyone who believes is justified from everything you could not be justified from by the law of Moses.' Here the Lucan Paul says two things. First, *everyone who believes in him* (whom God raised from the dead, and through whom the forgiveness of sins is proclaimed) is justified. Second, faith in him is the (only) condition, and the Lucan Paul offers justification for *everyone* (whether Jew or Gentile). This theme is very much in line with what Paul says in the letters (Rom 1:16; 3:22; 4:11; 10:4, 11–13).

More difficult is the ambiguity in Acts 13:38b; it may mean either 'Jews *could* be justified by the law not from all things but from something',[56] or 'Jews could *not at all* be justified by the law from all things'. One cannot be sure, as Vielhauer asserts, that the Lucan Paul is speaking about 'a partial justification ... *also* by faith', because it is also possible for him to be talking about the salvific *impotence of the law* for the Jews. Both Paul and Luke state the impotence of the law for salvation.[57] In the light of this ambiguity, we need to take Bauernfeind's warning not to put Acts 13:39 'under the theological microscope',[58] because Luke may have simply conveyed the general fact that Paul preached justification by faith.

Nevertheless, it is true that the Lucan Paul speaks of the impotence of the law much less frequently than the Paul of the letters. This may indicate that either by the time when Luke wrote Acts, 'the acuity of the debate regarding

---

[54] The same Greek verb used in Luke 18:14 is correctly rendered as 'justified' (e.g. KJV, RV, RSV, NRSV, NIV, NASB, NJB, NAB, PHILLIPS); and it is also to be noted that this verb is often translated as 'acquitted of his sins' (REB, NEB).

[55] So correctly, Haenchen, *Acts*, 412.

[56] This view has been rejected by Haenchen, *Acts*, 412; Conzelmann, *Acts*, 106; Marshall, *Acts*, 228; but what Paul writes in Rom 2:6–7 – 'God "will give to each person according to what he has done". To those who by persistence in doing good seek glory, honour and immortality, he will give eternal life' – suggests that Paul may have preached such an idea to the Jews in Pisidian Antioch.

[57] Rom 3:20, 21, 28; 4:14; 10:4; Gal 2:16, 19; 3:10, 11; 5:2–4; Phil 3:9; Acts 10:34–35; 13:38–39; 15:9–11.

[58] As cited in Vielhauer, '"Paulinism"', 50 n. 27.

the validity of the law is no longer Luke's concern',[59] or the validity of the law was not the real issue for Paul during his missionary period, which Luke writes about. We would contend that the latter was the case. Luke seems to say that Paul preached justification by faith during his initial missionary preaching, but its force was much less stressed than it is shown to be later in the letters. Unlike Vielhauer's contention, the doctrine of justification by faith *apart from the law* might not have yet come to the fore in 'its central significance and absolute importance'[60] during Paul's missionary endeavour in Pisidian Antioch. The doctrine, therefore, was not as strongly argued as in Galatians, for example.

Rather, Paul preached 'justification by faith in *the death and resurrection of Jesus*' during his missionary work in the region of Galatia, which includes Pisidian Antioch. However, his emphasis has been transferred to 'justification by faith *apart from the law*', in his letter to the Galatian churches, as he defends the legitimacy and sufficiency of the salvation of the Gentiles in reaction to the Judaizers.[61] If we are right, it is probable that Luke is rather appropriately portraying the degree of Paul's emphasis on justification by faith during the early years of his missionary work.

One thing is clear, however, from Paul's speech in Pisidian Antioch: what Luke records as the main point of Paul's sermon is about the death and resurrection of Jesus, who is both the Son of David and the Son of God, in fulfilment of prophecies (Acts 13:26–37). Luke does not record the statement on justification by faith as the most crucial part of Paul's speech. Only later does Paul expound the meaning of the gospel he preached in the light of the new situation caused by the Judaizers, and now in some letters, he explains the implications of the gospel in relation to the law for Gentile believers.

Christology

Vielhauer acknowledges some similarities between the account of Acts and that of Paul on the two points of Jesus being a descendant of David, and of his death and resurrection as the fulfilment of the Scriptures (Acts 13:34–37; 26:22–23; Rom 1:3–4; 1 Cor 15:3–4). But he quickly dismisses such correspondence by asserting that 'the Christological statements of Paul in Acts 13:16–37 and 26:22f. are neither specifically Pauline nor Lucan but are [the]

---

[59] Marguerat, 'Paul After Paul', 73.
[60] *Pace* Vielhauer, '"Paulinism"', 42.
[61] I have expounded this point in Chae, *Paul*, 302–7; and also in 'From Preaching the Gospel to Expounding Its Implications: Rediscovering Paul's Missionary Preaching and Its Development', an unpublished paper presented at the Paul Seminar, British New Testament Conference, Aberdeen (13 Sept. 1996).

property of the earliest congregation'.⁶² Thus he concludes that Luke's presentation of Christology in Paul's speeches is closer to that of the Jerusalem church than to Paul's own Christology.

Vielhauer also argues that although the title 'Saviour' in Acts 13:23 appears to echo the title in Philippians 3:20, they are not true parallels, because Luke uses it for the *earthly* Jesus while Paul uses it for the *returning* Lord. A crucial weakness in Vielhauer's approach is to compare a verse in Acts with a Pauline verse that contains only the same vocabulary or phrase. This method can be adopted only when both passages are talking about or reporting the same event (and even then, two authors may employ different terms). Since Acts 13 and Philippians 3 are not talking about the same incident, if the comparison is to be attempted it should be taken from wider contexts. If Paul says that the Saviour in Acts 13:23 is the earthly Jesus, he certainly continues to say that he is the exalted Jesus (Acts 13:32–37). Luke himself does not distinguish the earthly Jesus from the exalted Lord (cf. Luke 2:11–12); neither does Paul (cf. Phil 2:6–11).

Furthermore, the Lucan Paul and the Paul of the letters not only use the title 'Saviour' for Jesus but also convey the same message about the condition for believers to be saved by Jesus the Saviour. The Lucan Paul says to the jailer at Philippi, 'Believe in the Lord Jesus, and you will be saved' (Acts 16:31). Paul also writes to the Romans: 'if you confess with your mouth, "Jesus is Lord," and believe in your heart that God raised him from the dead, you will be saved' (Rom 10:9). In both references, faith in Jesus the Saviour is depicted as the condition for salvation.

Vielhauer also notes that the Paul of Acts affirms that Jesus is a descendant of David and is the Son of God just as Paul does in his letters (Acts 13:23, 33; Rom 1:3, 4, 9; 5:10; 8:3, 29, 32; 1 Cor 1:9; 15:28; Gal 1:16; 2:20; 4:4, 6; Col 1:13; 1 Thess 1:10). But he dismisses this correspondence by arbitrarily insisting that the Pauline references are based on 'a pre-Pauline formulation'. However, the question whether they are Pauline or pre-Pauline should not be the issue. Although Paul may have adopted them from earlier sources, it is clear that he used them as *his* Christology, and so Luke perceived it as *Paul's* Christology.

According to Vielhauer, more decisive evidence for differences between the Paul of the letters and the Lucan Paul is found in the concept of the work of the cross. He asserts that for Paul 'in the cross of Christ *salvation [for all humanity] is wholly realized*' (Gal 1:4), but in Acts 13:37–39 especially, 'nothing is said of the saving significance of the cross of Christ; and consequently also nothing of the reality of "in Christ" and of the presence of the whole of salvation'.⁶³ It is true that Luke presents the saving significance of the cross less prominently in Paul's speeches than he does in the earlier part

---

⁶² Vielhauer, '"Paulinism"', 44.
⁶³ Vielhauer, '"Paulinism"', 45, his emphasis.

of Acts (Acts 2:23; 3:13–15; 4:10–12). However, this does not endorse Vielhauer's assertion. In the same speech Luke records Paul's sermon: 'they asked Pilate to have him executed. When they had carried out all that was written about him, they took him down from the tree and laid him in a tomb. But God raised him from the dead' (Acts 13:28–30). He preaches that *Jesus was executed on a tree*, and thus clearly talks about Jesus' death on the cross. The cross is mentioned together with the resurrection of Jesus as the fulfilment of the Scriptures (Acts 13:27, 29).

Furthermore, the Lucan Paul proves 'that the Christ had to suffer and rise from the dead' (Acts 17:3), and is recorded as saying that the message of the cross and resurrection of Jesus was to be proclaimed to Jews and Gentiles (Acts 26:23); and this is totally in line with what the real Paul writes in 1 Corinthians 15:1–4. I.H. Marshall emphasizes this by pointing out that the statement in Acts 20:28, 'Be shepherds of the church of God, which he bought with his own blood', is equivalent to Mark 10:45b. As Marshall rightly says, Luke assumes the sacrifice, redemption and forgiveness as the effect of the cross.[64] Luke knows that Paul preached and expounded the cross of Jesus during his missionary work in Ephesus. In this follow-up speech Luke does not need to expound it, but rather to connect it more appropriately to the protection of the church, which is now the duty of the elders.

Finally, it seems odd that Vielhauer does not compare how Paul and Acts use Christological titles such as Christ and Lord. According to Acts, Paul strove to prove that Jesus is the Christ (Acts 9:22; 17:3; 18:5, 28); Luke records Paul as frequently referring to Jesus as the 'Lord', the 'Christ', 'Jesus Christ', 'Christ Jesus', or 'the Lord Jesus Christ'. In fact Luke uses all these Christological titles for Jesus as Paul uses them in the letters: the Son of God, the Judge, and especially 'Christ', 'Lord'. In Paul's letters, certainly, these are also the favourite Christological titles, whose references are too many to give here. Our study shows that Vielhauer appears to be tendentious and at times selective in his choice of material.

Eschatology

On this last topic Vielhauer asserts that the real Paul expected the imminent Parousia, but the Lucan Paul does not; rather he expects the world to continue by emphasizing a 'continuous redemptive historical process'.[65] Thus Vielhauer argues that Luke portrays the central Pauline theme of eschatology as a peripheral matter. Space does not allow us to respond in detail to the many

---

[64] Marshall, 'Place of Acts 20.28', 154–70.
[65] Vielhauer, '"Paulinism"', 45–7; thus he asserts that Luke's writing does not belong to primitive Christianity; also endorsed by Schoeps, *Paul*, 263.

points he asserts, and so we confine ourselves to evaluating two points: first, whether the imminent Parousia is Paul's central theme in the letters as well as in his missionary preaching, and second, whether Luke presents redemptive history in order to undertake, in Vielhauer's words, 'an enormous prolepsis, which antiquated the apologetically intentioned portrayals of church history in the second century even before they appeared'.[66]

The imminent Parousia: the central Pauline theme?

Vielhauer's assertion is based on the assumption that just like the Jerusalem apostles, Paul 'expected the return of Christ, the resurrection of the dead, and the end of the world in the immediate future', and it was this conviction which motivated his mission to the Gentiles.[67] Vielhauer does not really substantiate his assertion, except by arguing that Paul believes that the new aeon has arrived because the '"fullness of time" is already fulfilled' in the saving act of Christ. He bases such Pauline eschatological understanding primarily on 1 Corinthians 15:20, 22–24: 'in Christ all will be made alive. But each in his own turn: Christ, the firstfruits; then, when he comes, those who belong to him. Then the end will come'. He asserts that here Paul ignores the intervening redemptive history of the world by linking the resurrection of Christ and that of the believers with a simple particle 'then'. Vielhauer claims that the imminent Parousia is the central theme in Pauline eschatology. We shall examine this issue by asking three questions.

Does the pronoun 'we' indicate the imminent Parousia?

The references such as 1 Corinthians 15:12–57 and 1 Thessalonians 4:13 – 5:11 are often taken as evidence that Paul expected an imminent Parousia. Paul writes, 'Listen, I tell you a mystery: *We will not all sleep, but we will all be changed* . . .'[68] For the trumpet will sound, the dead will be raised imperishable, and *we will be changed*' (1 Cor 15:51–52). Also in 1 Thessalonians 4:15: 'we tell you that *we who are still alive*, who are left till the coming of the Lord, will certainly not precede those who have fallen asleep.' The pronoun 'we' is often taken as referring to Paul and his converts, and thus indicating the expectation of the Parousia in their lifetime.[69] But these verses do not seem to support such an interpretation with certainty, and so require

---

[66] Vielhauer, '"Paulinism"', 47.

[67] Vielhauer, '"Paulinism"', 45–6.

[68] The existence of at least five textual variations testifies to the complexity of this clause. See Fee, *First Corinthians*, 796; but the Editorial Committee of the UBS accepts the text, *ou koimēthēsometha, pantes de allagēsometha*, as virtually certain: see Metzger, *Textual Commentary*, 569.

[69] E.g. Collins, 'First Letter to the Thessalonians', 778.

an exegetical scrutiny.[70]

We note, first of all, that the two occurrences of the pronoun 'we' in verse 51 do not refer to the same group of people. 'We will not all sleep' means 'some of us will sleep and others will not',[71] and the 'we' in 'we who will all be changed' are those who will be alive and be changed at the event of the Parousia.[72] They are the same group as 'we who are still alive', as in 1 Thessalonians 4:15, 17. And this 'we' does not necessarily refer to 'you Corinthians/Thessalonians and I, Paul',[73] because in this case he would have said, 'some of us will be changed'. So what he conveys here is rather a general sense of 'those who are still alive [like us]'.[74] The present participle (zōntes) does not necessarily carry the temporal value of the present tense.[75]

Furthermore Paul uses 'we' (hēmeis) in 1 Corinthians 15:52 in order to draw a comparison with 'the dead (who believed and died)' in general, rather than to imply that Paul expects to be alive together with all of his readers in Corinth.[76] In other words, this 'we' denotes those who will still be alive and will be changed at the time of the Parousia.[77] As A.T. Robertson points out, the 'we' in 1 Corinthians 15:49[–52] merely associates the Corinthians with Paul without specifically including them. More probably Paul used the pronoun 'we' here 'in a representative manner as one of a class',[78] because 'the use of the first person plural in Greek is no guarantee that the speaker or writer included himself'.[79] Paul's primary concern in both 1 Corinthians 15:12–57 and 1 Thessalonians 4:13–5:11 is to give assurance of the certainty of the resurrection of the dead to those who are ignorant about, or even doubt,

---

[70] Following Dick and Deissmann, Moulton, *Grammar of New Testament Greek*, 1:86–7, notes that Paul's use of the first-person pronouns (I/we) does not maintain any regular format, and leaves the grammatical issues to the exegete of particular passages.

[71] Robertson, *Grammar*, 423: '[1 Cor 15:51] means "all of us shall not sleep," not "none of us shall sleep"'; so again in p. 753

[72] The first 'we' in 1 Cor 15:49 refers to humanity in general who 'have borne the likeness of the earthly man', and the second 'we' refers to the believers who shall 'bear the likeness of the man from heaven'.

[73] *Pace* Robertson and Plummer, *1 Corinthians*, 377.

[74] Ridderbos, *Paul*, 492, is correct to say, 'This "we" can accordingly signify nothing other than a general designation that has a facultative thrust'. Earlier Lightfoot, *Notes*, 66, paraphrased the phrase, *hoi zōntes hoi perileipomenoi* (1 Thess 4:15), as 'When I say "we," I mean those who are living, those who survive to that day.'

[75] See Porter, *Verbal Aspect*, 377–80; Porter, *Paul in Acts*, 204.

[76] Orr and Walther, *1 Corinthians*, 350.

[77] So similarly, Fee, *First Corinthians*, 802 n. 27; but his designation of the second 'we' in v. 51 as the living and the dead does not seem correct. Paul uses the term 'being changed' in relation to the living, but 'being raised' in relation to the dead.

[78] Robertson, *Grammar*, 677–8.

[79] I am grateful to Prof. C.C. Caragounis, whose mother tongue is Greek, for supporting my position by making this remark in a letter (22 March 1998).

The Historical Paul in Acts

the resurrection of those believers who died without seeing the Parousia.

Is the imminent Parousia Paul's central issue?

Vielhauer accuses Luke of presenting Paul's central theme of the imminent Parousia as a peripheral subject. However, we find his assertion unconvincing. The issue which prompted Paul to expound his teaching in 1 Corinthians 15:12–52 was the uncertainty among the Corinthians concerning the resurrection of the dead, because some of them said that 'there is no resurrection of the dead' (1 Cor 15:12). Paul is not responding to questions such as, 'Why hasn't the Lord come back yet?', or 'When will the Lord come back?' During his missionary work in Corinth Paul emphasized the resurrection and the second coming of the Lord. And so the Corinthians were eagerly waiting for the Parousia (1 Cor 1:7–8; so also 1 Thess 1:10), and Paul reaffirms this in the letter (1 Cor 4:5). However, the fact that the Corinthians are not sure about the resurrection of *the dead* seems to suggest that he did not teach (at least, not clearly enough) the implications of the resurrection of Jesus with regard to the believers. So Paul now explains the mystery of the resurrection of the dead in Christ and of the physical body when the Lord comes.[80] As he expounds this important issue, he adds a further teaching concerning those who will still be alive at the time of the Parousia.

This is also one of the concerns of the Thessalonians. Paul says that they know perfectly well that the manner and timing of the Parousia is sudden and unexpected. And so he makes it clear that he does not need to write anything more because what he taught during his missionary work was sufficient (1 Thess 5:1–3; cf. Matt 24:36). Here again his topic is not so much concerned with the imminence of the Parousia, as with the certainty of the resurrection of the dead. Even here Paul does not say that the Thessalonians, as is often assumed, first raised the question. Rather he takes the initiative to explain the 'mystery' (i.e. 'the word of the Lord'). The most important concern for Paul is to explain the mystery about the resurrection of those who have fallen asleep in the Lord.

The imminence of the Parousia seems suggested in the course of Paul's further explanation concerning those who are still alive, but it is not his crucial issue here. The main concern in both 1 Thessalonians 4:13 – 5:11 and 1 Corinthians 15:12–57 is to re-emphasize both the certainty of the return of the Lord and the resurrection of those who have fallen asleep in Christ, rather than to explain *how soon* it will happen or why it has been *delayed*. The remarks concerning 'we who are still alive' are made to explain the subsequent event after the resurrection of those who have fallen asleep in Christ. Paul's

---

[80] The fact that Paul praises the Corinthians for remembering and holding everything which he taught them (1 Cor 11:2) seems to strengthen our view that Paul seems to expound something new here in addition to that which he has already taught.

explanation is not intended to address the imminence of the Parousia. The fact that he expounds this issue only now in the letters, not during his missionary preaching, also suggests that the imminent Parousia was not a central theme for Paul during his missionary preaching.

Does Paul indicate that the Parousia has been delayed?

Vielhauer's understanding that Paul believed in an imminent Parousia is based on the prevailing scholarly view of his day that Paul preached the imminent Parousia, but later Paul changed his position as reflected, for example, in 2 Corinthians 5:1–10 and in Philippians 1:21–24, and so the delay of the Day of the Lord caused problems among the earliest believers as well as for Paul. His words in 2 Corinthians 5:1–10 are often regarded as an alternative explanation to what he wrote in 1 Corinthians 15:12–56, and indicate his belief that the bodily resurrection of the believers is now postponed until the Parousia that will occur in the indefinite future.[81] However, it is to be noted that Paul does not write 2 Corinthians 5:1–10 in order to explain (even indirectly) the problem of the delay of the Parousia, but to give his converts heavenly hope and assurance in the light of current hardship. Paul applies this hope and assurance to himself in Philippians 1:21–24.

Another passage which is often regarded as an explanation of the delay of the Parousia is 2 Thessalonians 2:1–12: 'that day will not come until the rebellion occurs and the man of lawlessness is revealed' (v. 3); 'you know what is holding him back, so that he may be revealed at the proper time' (v. 6). It is crucial, however, to note that Paul is not 'qualifying his doctrine of the speedy and unexpected coming of Christ',[82] but is teaching the same message that he had already taught *during his missionary work in Thessalonica*: 'Don't you remember that when I was with you I used to tell you these things?' (v. 5). Paul's reminder clearly indicates that he has not changed his mind; he simply re-emphasizes what he told the Thessalonian church earlier: that there would be a time of rebellion by a man of lawlessness before Christ returns (cf. 2 Thess 2:1–5). In his first letter to the Thessalonians he also clearly states that he does not need to write about the timing and manner of the Parousia because they already know this so well from his missionary preaching (1 Thess 5:1–2).

However, the believers at Thessalonica were confused concerning those who had fallen asleep, and so they grieved over them like those who had no hope (1 Thess 4:13). They also had 'become easily unsettled or alarmed by some prophecy, report or letter' asserting that 'the day of the Lord has already

---

[81] See Kreitzer, 'Eschatology', 260–61, for a brief treatment of the questions concerning the delay of the Parousia and the development of Paul's thought.

[82] *Pace* Goodspeed, *Paul*, 98.

come' (2 Thess 2:1–2). Such misapprehension by the Thessalonians may suggest that Paul did not give a clear and comprehensive teaching on every important aspect of his eschatology. This may, in turn, imply that the imminent Parousia, to be realized in his lifetime, was not his core message during his missionary work there.

It is also to be noted that Paul stresses the nearness of the Parousia in the later letters as well, but his emphasis is strongly connected to his exhortation to live up to the Christian ethical standard, or to endure persecution and hardship (Rom 8:19, 23; 13:11–14; Phil 3:20; 4:5; cf. 2 Pet 3:11–14). Paul's earlier teaching concerning the Parousia was also related to such pastoral concerns (cf. 1 Thess 5:6–11). Our findings suggest that Paul did not change his eschatology.[83] Rather, it seems more probable that Paul *unfolds* the different facets of the mystery as different issues arise (1 Cor 15:12–56; 1 Thess 4:13–5:11; 2 Thess 2:1–12). So, what he shares later does not contradict his earlier position, but reveals a fuller explanation.[84]

Redemptive history in Paul

We now turn to examine Vielhauer's claim that 'Luke replaces the apocalyptic expectation of the earliest congregation and the christological eschatology of Paul by a redemptive historical pattern of promise and fulfillment in which then eschatology *also* receives its appropriate place.'[85] According to Vielhauer, Luke's intention to portray history as 'a continuous redemptive historical process' is shown in at least two areas.

First, he claims that Luke stresses that the gospel is what God promised to the fathers and is now fulfilled in Christ (Acts 13:27, 29, 32–36), and that for Luke the mission to the Gentiles is part of the redemptive process (Acts 13:46–47). By means of writing the 'history' of the earliest church – regardless of its reliability – Luke demonstrates his expectation that the world will continue, and so makes a missionary appeal. Second, Luke reports the establishment of the churches, which not only will continue to survive but also will carry out missionary functions. We will attempt to evaluate Vielhauer's contentions as we examine Paul's own views in these two areas, so as to determine the extent of Luke's departure from Paul.

---

[83] So similarly, Guthrie, *New Testament Theology*, 809–10. If Paul's teaching seems incoherent on this point, it is because he does not write a systematic exposition on the eschatological events (cf. Kümmel, *Theology*, 235).

[84] Cf. the author of 2 Peter who testifies that Paul indicated in his letters that the Lord would not return immediately so that more people might be saved (2 Pet 3:15–16).

[85] Vielhauer, '"Paulinism"', 47, his emphasis.

The promise-fulfilment motif in Paul

It is to be noted that Paul also stresses that the death and resurrection of Christ is the fulfilment of God's promise for humanity, and so the mission to the Gentiles is the process of redemptive history. Right at the beginning of his letter to the Romans, Paul defines the gospel as what God 'promised beforehand through his prophets in the Holy Scriptures regarding his Son' and now fulfilled in the death and resurrection of Jesus Christ (Rom 1:2–4). Later Paul says that the promise was first given to Abraham: 'Through a son from your own body, your offspring shall be as numerous as the stars in the sky'. Abraham believed this promise, and God credited his faith as righteousness (Gen 15:4–5, 6; Rom 4:5). In Romans, Paul insists that God has fulfilled his promise by saving those (Jews and Gentiles) who are of the faith of Abraham (Rom 4:9–12), and so the promise that he would be the father of many nations is fulfilled in the death and resurrection of Jesus (Rom 4:13–16, 23–25; Gal 3:16; 4:28).

Paul also reminds the Corinthians that the gospel he preached during his missionary work among them was the message of fulfilment: 'For what I received I passed on to you as of first importance: that Christ died for our sins *according to the Scriptures*, that he was buried, that he was raised on the third day *according to the Scriptures*' (1 Cor 15:3–4). With the frequent usage of the phrase, 'as it is written', Paul also intends to convey that his argument or teaching is based on the promises or predictions in the Scriptures, which are now fulfilled in Christ. Especially in the thematic conclusion of his letter to the Romans, Paul indicates that the equal inclusion of the Gentiles into God's salvific blessing is also the fulfilment of his promises through the prophets (Rom 15:8–12),[86] and this theme is also abundantly clear in the Lucan Paul (Acts 13:27–37; cf. Luke 24:44–48).

Furthermore, Paul also portrays the redemptive history as a process. He declares that God predestined and called a people not only from the Jews but also from the Gentiles (Rom 8:28–30; 9:24; 2 Thess 2:13; cf. Eph 1:4). Although God has carried out the process of his salvific plan for the world, it remained a mystery whose true meaning had been hidden for generations (Rom 16:25–27; Col 1:25–27; cf. Eph 3:7–12). God sent his Son to the Jews when the time had fully come according to his plan (Gal 4:4; cf. Mark 1:15; Rom 5:6). His salvific blessing was intended for the Jews first, yet the Gentiles were also equally included in it (Rom 1:16). But when the Jews refused to believe in Jesus as the Messiah, God shifted the main thrust of mission to the Gentiles 'first'.[87]

In Romans 9:6–29 Paul argues for God's rationale in reaching the Gentiles with his salvation amidst the background of rejection by the Jews. The

---

[86] See Chae, *Paul*, 58–68.
[87] See Chae, *Paul*, 250–53.

hardening of Israel will be continued 'until the full number of the Gentiles has come in'. He understands that his ministry is 'saving some of Israel' (see Rom 11:14), and the mystery of the salvation of 'all' Israel is to be realized after him. The salvific drama of massive turning to Jesus Christ as the Messiah will take place among the Jews (Rom 11:25–26). Paul's doxology in Romans 11:33–36 is based on his understanding of God's redemptive plan in history for Jews and Gentiles. Paul's 'then' (*epeita*) in 1 Corinthians 15:23 certainly has a temporal significance. In using this word, however, Paul neither hints at the imminence of the Parousia nor indicates that 'during this interval nothing more of significance can happen, especially no redemptive history', as Vielhauer contends.[88]

The planting and organizing of the churches in Paul

Vielhauer surprisingly contends that in his belief in the imminent Parousia Paul never preached in support of the establishment of churches;[89] but Luke often highlights the gathering of the believers and their establishment as congregations, and thus implies that the world and the churches would continue. We find Vielhauer's understanding of Paul at this point highly unconvincing. Luke is often perceived as indicating the delay of the Parousia by reporting historical church plants, while Paul emphasizes the imminent Parousia. However, the facts that Paul planted these churches, and that he writes them letters, indicate that he wanted to build them up as communities of Christ through their witness in words and deeds.

Paul sends his greetings to the churches, recognizing their establishment as legitimate and desirable (Rom 16:4–5, 16; 1 Cor 1:2; 2 Cor 1:1; Gal 1:2; 1 Thess 1:1). Paul has deep concern for the churches, not only for their purity in faith and Christian life but also for their growth so as to become powerful witnesses to the world (1 Cor 5:9–13; 6:12–20; 2 Cor 7:12; 11:28; 12:20; 1 Thess 3:10). He often makes ethical exhortations for unity within a church (e.g. Rom 12:9–16; 14:1 – 15:7), and so he emphasizes the concept of one body (Rom 12:4–8; 1 Cor 12:12–26) and warns against division within the churches (Rom 16:17; 1 Cor 1:11–13; 3:3–4; 6:6; 12:25; 2 Cor 12:20; Phil 4:2).

More importantly, Paul declares in 1 Corinthians 3:10–15 that he laid the foundations of the local churches as an expert; and he certainly expects others to continue to build them up. He knows that he established the churches according to God's will and grace (1 Cor 1:2; cf. Rom 1:7). Paul clearly says not only that God starts the churches but also that he establishes them by providing different gifts and leadership over the congregations (1 Cor

---

[88] Vielhauer, '"Paulinism"', 46.
[89] Vielhauer, '"Paulinism"', 47: 'the establishment of congregations was never the subject of sermons or of catechetical instruction'.

12:28).⁹⁰ He expresses that his greatest struggle besides all hardship was to establish his churches as mature and strong communities (2 Cor 11:28). So Butticaz is right to argue that 'both [Luke and Paul] promote a missionary eschatology – that is, both transpose eschatology into the realm of mission history'.⁹¹

We have found not only that the eschatology of the imminent Parousia is not as central in Paul's theology as Vielhauer claims, but also that Paul, too, explains redemptive history in his letters. To this extent Vielhauer's charge that Luke has distorted Paul, so as to convey his own theology, is not well grounded. Due to his misinterpretation of Pauline letters, he has made incorrect assumptions, and so unduly tainted the reliability of Acts.⁹² When we understand *Paul's* eschatology adequately, we can conclude that *Luke's* portrayal is sufficiently credible.

Questioning Vielhauer's Methodology

In the course of this investigation we have noted that the weakness of Vielhauer's thesis is largely connected to the methodology he adopts. The first problem is that his investigation is, in most cases, based on assumptions. To be sure, hardly anyone can write a paper totally free from presuppositions, but assumptions should be justified first. However, as R.B. Hays points out, Vielhauer fails to use the narrative-critical approach.⁹³ Rather, he starts his investigation with the 'generally acknowledged' assumption that Paul's speeches in Acts are Luke's own compositions.⁹⁴ In so doing Vielhauer uses a logical fallacy: Luke cannot have known Paul because the Paul whom he is reporting is so different from the real one, but Luke as a Thucydidean reporter would have changed Paul's speeches whether he had heard them or not. If Vielhauer's view of the speeches is correct, he cannot use them to prove that

---

⁹⁰ 1 Cor 12:28: 'in the church God has appointed first of all apostles, second prophets, third teachers, then workers of miracles, also those having gifts of healing, those able to help others, those with gifts of administration, and those speaking in different kinds of tongues.'

⁹¹ Butticaz, 'Salvation', 161.

⁹² So correctly, Wilckens, 'Interpreting Luke-Acts', 76–7. If Paul was expecting an imminent Parousia, and if Luke was not, as many scholars contend, are they saying that Luke was right and Paul was wrong in their expectations, as human history shows that the end is not here yet? Neither Paul nor Luke had an imminent apocalyptic expectation. The problem is not with Paul or Luke, but with the scholars who have misinterpreted Paul's eschatology.

⁹³ Hays, 'Paulinism of Acts', 36.

⁹⁴ Vielhauer, '"Paulinism"', 33; but see Gasque's protest in *History*, 284, that Vielhauer's assumption is not 'generally acknowledged'.

Luke did not know Paul.[95]

Vielhauer's understanding of Paul's theology is also often based on assumptions. For example, he presupposes that Romans 1:18–32 is Paul's indictment exclusively of the Gentiles, and so compares this account with the Lucan Paul's speech to the Gentiles in Acts 17. But it is crucial to perceive that in Paul's argument in Romans 1 he includes Jews also in his indictment, so as to establish the equality of Jew and Gentile in sinfulness.[96]

Vielhauer also presupposes that Paul preached the doctrine of justification by faith during his initial missionary work with the same intensity and emphasis of argument as he does in Galatians and Romans. He does not note that although Paul presents the same doctrine, his emphasis has shifted from justification by faith *in the death and resurrection of Jesus Christ* to justification by faith *apart from the law* in reaction to the Judaizers' teaching.[97] Thus, Luke's less emphatic presentation of this doctrine in Acts 13:38–39 seems a plausible description of Paul's position during the first missionary journey. Vielhauer has also asserted that Paul preached the Parousia as imminent, to be realized in his lifetime. Without substantiating this hypothesis, and upon this assumption, Vielhauer has established his thesis that 'the eschatology disappears' in the Lucan Paul, and that redemptive history never exists in the real Paul. We have attempted above to demonstrate that his contentions are not well grounded.[98]

The second major weakness of Vielhauer's thesis is with his methodology in comparing at face value the Pauline theology of the letters with that presented in Acts. This is, at best, superficial because the nature and the scope of these writings are different. Luke's first concern in Acts is to present the evangelistic progress of the earliest church from Jerusalem to Rome, as he sets out in Acts 1:8. As far as his portrait of Paul is concerned, his primary interest is to describe Paul's *missionary* activities, including the gospel message he preached to *convert* the Gentiles, and to convince the Jews that Jesus is the awaited Messiah. Paul's main interest in the letters, however, is to strengthen the *converted* believers as he addresses the specific situations of the churches concerned by providing practical and theological teaching.[99] In this respect Paul's address to the Ephesian elders (Acts 20:17–38) is, methodologically, the most appropriate passage in Acts to compare with Paul's

---

[95] I am indebted to Dr C.H. Gempf on this point.

[96] See Chae, *Paul*, 73–94, for a detailed treatment.

[97] We have demonstrated such a shift of emphasis elsewhere, and reconstructed Paul's *missionary* preaching from his epistles: see my unpublished paper, 'From Preaching the Gospel'.

[98] Gasque, *History*, 287, also notes that Vielhauer's essay is 'full of unwarranted assumptions, question-begging exegesis, and false inferences'.

[99] So correctly, Moule, 'Christology of Acts', 173.

thoughts expressed in the letters; and they are very similar in many respects.[100]

In general, therefore, describing Paul's role as pastor or theologian does not belong to Luke's main scope in Acts. This is most probably why Luke writes almost nothing about Paul's activities or the content of his teachings, for example, during his long stay in Corinth and in Ephesus (Acts 18:11; 19:10). On the other hand, the Paul of the letters is primarily concerned with practical and doctrinal teachings to help the believers to grow into Christian maturity as individuals and as churches.[101] In most letters Paul expounds the *implications* of the gospel that he preached during his missionary work. Sometimes he shifts the emphasis within the same substance from an earlier message, or he unfolds further the teachings which he did not teach fully while he was with his readers.

It is important to note that even within the Pauline corpus Paul sometimes writes differently depending on the situation he is addressing. For example, he argues for 'freedom' in Galatians while he urges 'restraint' of freedom and rights to the Corinthians. Paul presents the Abraham story differently to the Romans as compared to the Galatians, and also presents the Parousia differently to the Thessalonians (1 Thess 4:13–5:11) as compared to the Corinthians (1 Cor 15:12–57). In view of this, Vielhauer ought also to allow room to permit Luke to present Paul from his own perspective and observation, provided he maintains Paul's tradition and focus.

It is almost a universal consensus that Paul's letters are *follow-up letters addressing certain situations* rather than simply doctrinal expositions. Yet Dibelius, Vielhauer, Haenchen and more recent scholars regard Luke's account as his exposition of Paul's theology, and Paul's writings as theology irrespective of local situations. They then attempt to compare the theological positions of the two authors. That explains in part why they often misapprehend Paul's theology, Luke's theology and Luke's portrayal of Paul's theology. One is in a position to interpret Paul's letters and Acts more adequately if one grasps the situational dependence of the letters, and allows a similar measure of missionary situations in reviewing Paul's speeches in Acts.

So these apparent differences do not necessarily suggest the unhistorical character of Luke's account as Vielhauer asserts. Luke has legitimate freedom to report Paul's speeches using his own expressions. On the other hand,

---

[100] See below, pp. 76-77, 138-40; so correctly, Walton, *Leadership*, for adopting this methodology to compare Paul's speech in Acts 20 with 1 Thessalonians. So also Marguerat, 'Paul After Paul', 72; Bruce, *Speeches*, 26; cf. Chase, *Credibility*, 234–88.

[101] This point has been already expressed by Marshall, *Acts*, 43 n. 4; so similarly Drane, *Introducing the New Testament*, 241. But neither of them offers a critical alternative on the basis of this insight.

the differences can also be explained when we note that Paul has used different terms according to the different *contexts* of the audience/recipients to which the speeches and the letters are given or directed. In this respect it is no coincidence that the Levitical phrase 'forgiveness of sins' is found in the speech to the Jews. Nor is it surprising that the epistle-like but non-Lucan idea of Christians 'bought with his own blood' is found in Paul's only speech in Acts that is given to *believers* (Acts 20:28; Eph 1:7).[102] Vielhauer's view of Luke as a historian cannot stand because it is presented without considering these different *scopes* and *contexts*, while at the same time looking for the same vocabulary and phrases to compare the two accounts.[103]

Vielhauer's third shortcoming is uneven handling of different evidence. His tendentiousness is obvious, for he highlights the differences but undervalues some important correspondences between the real Paul and the Lucan Paul. Both claim Jesus as the Lord, Christ, the Son of God, Judge and Saviour. Both declare that the gospel is what God promised in the Old Testament; and so the death and resurrection of Jesus is the fulfilment of the Scriptures,[104] and this is the core of the gospel message.[105] Both also convey that Paul was called to preach to Jews and Gentiles, though more specifically to Gentiles.[106] Paul says that the gospel is for the Jew first and equally also for the Gentile (Rom 1:16), and Luke shows Paul putting this into practice by preaching to Jews first. Both perceive that until the return of the Lord the mission to the Jews and Gentiles is the mandate of the church, and so both show fundamental concern for the inclusion of the Gentiles in the people of God. Both report that Paul made visits to Jerusalem in order to get acquainted with the leading apostles, to settle the issue of the validity of Gentile salvation, and to deliver the relief fund from the Gentile believers.[107] Both mention the Damascus road experience as decisive in his Christian thought and career.[108] Both experience the unbelief of the Jews and the faith of the Gentiles as general phenomena in response to Paul's preaching.[109] Both show that Paul was a missionary apostle and church planter. Paul says his missionary work has been accompanied by miracles through the power of the Holy

---

[102] Paul uses the same language in 1 Cor 6:20; 7:23; similarly in Rom 3:24; 5:9; 1 Cor 1:30; Gal 3:13; Col 1:14, 20.

[103] See Gasque, *History*, 288–91, for different points of criticism of Vielhauer's methodology.

[104] Rom 1:2; 4:13; 1 Cor 15:3–5; Acts 13:27–35; 24:14–15; 28:23b.

[105] Rom 4:24–25; 8:31–34; 10:9; 14:9; Acts 24:21; 25:19; 26:6–8.

[106] Rom 1:5; 15:15–21; Gal 1:15–16; Acts 9:15; 13:2–3, 46–47; 16:6–10; 18:6; 20:20–24; 22:17–21.

[107] Gal 1:18; Acts 9:26–28; Gal 2:1–10; Acts 15:1–21; Rom 15:25–31; Acts 24:17; cf. Gal 2:10.

[108] 1 Cor 9:6; 15:8; Gal 1:11–12, 15–16; Acts 9:1–19; 22:6–16; 26:12–23.

[109] Rom 2:12–15, 25–29; 9:25–33; 10:19–21; 1 Thess 2:14–16; Acts 9:29; 13:40–41, 48–50; 14:19; 18:6–17; 28:21–28.

Spirit, and Luke provides us with some of these details.[110]

Conclusion

We have attempted to examine the selected Pauline theological themes Vielhauer chose as presented in Paul's letters as well as in the Lucan accounts of those topics. We have done this so as to evaluate Vielhauer's thesis that Luke passes on no specifically Pauline theology, but rather presents the theological ideas of the early catholic church (around AD 90).[111] Our investigation suggests that Vielhauer's thesis is difficult to sustain. In most cases his interpretation of Paul's theology is incorrect.[112] His study is based on a presumption that Paul's (developed) theology is necessarily expressed in his evangelistic speeches in Acts. He misunderstands the character of the summarized speeches in Acts, and thus misinterprets the theology of the speeches. So, D. Marguerat's overall assessment of Vielhauer's thesis is right: 'Now in its entirety, Vielhauer's position proves to be untenable.'[113]

A proper understanding of Paul's theology, not based on assumptions but on careful consideration of the context and rhetoric, is crucial for a comparative study such as Vielhauer's.[114] Despite the fact that there appear to be some differences between the two, the differences are neither because Luke is presenting his own theology under the veil of writing history about Paul, nor because he stands within the early catholic church.[115] Some differences are there because Luke is writing Paul's theology as shown during his *missionary* work, while Paul is writing follow-up letters on the basis of his previous missionary message. We have also seen above that Paul's letters confirm (though indirectly) that the accounts of Acts are largely trustworthy.[116]

S. Porter's conclusion, after examining the contention of both Haenchen

---

[110] Rom 15:19; 1 Cor 2:4; 1 Thess 1:5; Acts 13:9–12; 14:8–18; 16:23–34.

[111] Vielhauer does not date Acts in the article we are concerned with here, but dates it at about AD 90 in his later work, *Geschichte der urchristlichen Literatur* (Berlin, 1975), 407.

[112] Keener, *Acts*, 1:251: 'Vielhauer has misread Paul on the basis of traditional theological assumptions'. Gasque, *History*, 287–8, assessed Vielhauer's position earlier: 'it is doubtful whether his understanding of "the real Paul" is anything other than the product of the imagination of existentially dominated exegesis.'

[113] Marguerat, 'Paul After Paul', 72.

[114] So also Ellis, *Luke*, 47; Gasque, *History*, 287–8.

[115] Gasque, *History*, 287 n. 78, notes that this is the only major area which even some of Vielhauer's advocates reject.

[116] So also Munck, *Paul*, 120.

and Vielhauer, is right: 'There may well be differences of emphasis and focus, but the evidence is far from substantiating contradictions.'[117] Vielhauer has not made a sufficient effort to compare the real Paul and the Lucan Paul with the same scope of their writings, and the contexts of Paul's message. When comparing the apostle's missionary preaching (e.g. Acts 13) and his theological presentation of it in the later writings (e.g. Romans), Vielhauer does not allow room for Paul to emphasize different points or to grow in his understanding of the gospel. He does not accept that it was natural for Paul to place new emphasis on certain points as the years went by, or that he dealt with particular issues according to the need of the churches. To this extent Vielhauer's thesis must be judged, on the whole, as unsustainable.

However, until we provide an alternative methodology with which we can legitimately compare Paul's account and Luke's, our main task remains. We propose to rediscover the main points of Paul's *missionary* message from his letters, and compare it with the Lucan Paul's *missionary* preaching as summarized in Acts. We will then be in a better position to measure the reliability of Luke's description of Paul in Acts, because we can then compare them on the basis of the common nature and scope of these two accounts of Paul's *missionary* preaching. So first we must turn to reconstruct the core of Paul's missionary message from his letters.

---

[117] Porter, *Paul in Acts*, 206.

2

Rediscovering Paul's Missionary Preaching

Paul was fully conscious that he had been set apart for the gospel (Rom 1:1; Gal 1:15–16; 1 Thess 2:4; Col 1:23; cf. Acts 9:15; 1 Tim 1:12; Titus 1:3), and that accordingly his first and foremost responsibility was to preach the good news. So he declares, 'Christ did not send me to baptise, but to preach the gospel' (1 Cor 1:17); 'I am compelled to preach. Woe to me if I do not preach the gospel' (1 Cor 9:16). He was not ashamed of the gospel (Rom 1:16), and so he devoted his life to preaching it from Jerusalem to Rome. What then was the main content of his preaching and teaching during his church-planting missionary work? The sermons attributed to him in the book of Acts are often considered as a secondary witness at best,[1] and so the Pauline letters must be the primary source for such an enquiry. His letters, however, do not contain his missionary proclamation. Rather, they are primarily intended to offer further pastoral teaching to meet the specific needs of those who have already responded to his earlier preaching. So it may seem rather complicated to reconstruct his *missionary* preaching from the material written some years later in the course of defending and expounding the truth of the gospel.[2]

Nevertheless, some scholars have attempted to rediscover the core of Paul's missionary preaching from his letters. In general, as we shall show, they tend to reconstruct this preaching from the letters (written some time later) without considering that Paul's thoughts might have developed in later times. Some have said that the attempt to rediscover Paul's *missionary*

---

[1] Cf. Mounce, 'Preaching, Kerygma', 735; Keck, *Paul*, 33.
[2] The difficulties in rediscovering Paul's missionary preaching from his letters are recognized by Dodd, *Apostolic Preaching*, 11, and Caird, *Apostolic Age*, 37. However, both are optimistic about the task; see esp. Bussmann, *Themen*. A more pessimistic view is expressed by Jervell, *Unknown Paul*, 52–3: 'Vanished almost completely is . . . the Pauline missionary preaching'. Thus he suggests that we should not restrict the use of other NT writings which could help us to discover the unknown Paul.

preaching in this way seems methodologically inappropriate.[3] We shall therefore propose an alternative method, namely, to reassemble the essential parts of Paul's missionary proclamation by paying special attention to Paul's *reminder formula* which he uses to remind his converts of the content of his preaching and teaching given them during his initial missionary work.

Rediscovering Paul's *missionary* message seems important for various reasons. It can shed light on other disputed issues, such as the development of Pauline theology,[4] the reliability of the speeches attributed to Paul in Acts,[5] the unity or diversity of his kerygma in relation to that of the Jerusalem apostles,[6] and so on. There has been much misunderstanding concerning these issues largely because the developed theological thoughts which Paul expresses in his letters are compared with the primitive preaching attributed to him and to the Jerusalem apostles in Acts. In this chapter we shall attempt to rediscover the *content* of Paul's *missionary* preaching,[7] proclaimed during the church-planting stage, and to discern its development and the implication of his missionary preaching, as expounded in his letters. This investigation to compare the missionary preaching of the two Pauls will assist us in discerning the reliability of Luke's portrayal of Paul.[8]

The Question of Methodology

One of the first modern scholars who tried to rediscover this missionary message was J. Weiss.[9] He assumed that Paul's letters contain almost the same message as his missionary preaching (though condensed), and so suggested using all the details written in Paul's letters. Weiss also set out to discern the

---

[3] Walton, *Leadership*, 212: 'compar[ing] the epistles as a whole with Paul's speeches in Acts as a whole is mistaken'.

[4] Cf. Sanders, *Palestinian Judaism*, 444–7, does this so as to demonstrate that Paul's anthropology is only an implied development of his theology, Christology and soteriology, because Paul does not preach about the plight of humanity but about salvation offered by God.

[5] Cf. Vielhauer, '"Paulinism"', 33–50; but a more affirmative view is expressed by Longenecker, *Paul, Apostle of Liberty*, 246; Stanton, *Jesus of Nazareth*, 110.

[6] Cf. Dodd, *Apostolic Preaching*, 22–30; for a different view, see Dunn, *Unity*, 11–32.

[7] See Porter, *Paul in Acts*, 129–50, for a form-critical examination of Paul's *argumentative style* in his missionary preaching.

[8] Walton, *Leadership*, 214, suggests that comparing the two Pauls' *missionary* preaching is one of the two areas worth pursuing in the effort to discern the reliability of Luke's portrayal of Paul.

[9] Weiss, *Earliest Christianity*, 1:219–57. See Bussmann, *Themen*, 3–12, for a brief survey of German scholars who studied Paul's missionary preaching before and after 1920 when Oepke's monograph, *Missionspredigt*, was published.

difference between Paul's missionary preaching to the Jews and that to the Gentiles. He asserted that, for example, the passages which are now recorded in Romans 2:17–24 and the scriptural quotation in Romans 3:10–18 were the message which Paul preached to accuse the self-righteous Jews.[10] Likewise, passages such as Romans 1:18–32 and 1 Thessalonians 1:9–10 show 'certain fundamental features of the mission preaching to Gentiles'.[11]

C.H. Dodd's attempt to reconstruct Paul's missionary message from his letters has had considerable influence.[12] Although his primary concern is to rediscover the actual content of the gospel preached by the apostles, he starts the investigation with Paul. His methodology is to isolate certain recurrent phrases (although they are mostly brief) which indicate the content of Paul's preaching. He suggests that 'what Paul was accustomed to preach as Gospel [is] clearly distinguished from the theological superstructure of his thought'.[13] He also goes on to deduce the content of Paul's gospel from the phrase 'my gospel', because it contains 'a high degree of originality in his presentation of the Gospel'.[14]

Having paid attention to Paul's statement, 'faith comes from hearing' (Rom 10:17), H. Conzelmann recommends a method to reconstruct the preached kerygma by focusing on the usage of the verbs 'confess' and 'believe' (Rom 10:9; cf. 1 John 5:5).[15] He also proposes reassembling the early proclamation from the confessional formulae (i.e. Jesus as the Messiah, as the Son of God and as the Lord) and from statements on the work of Christ (i.e. the death and resurrection of Jesus). Following Lietzmann, Conzelmann maintains that each confessional formula implies the whole of the creed: for example, through the confession of 'Jesus is Lord', believers clearly confess the whole belief.

J.D.G. Dunn examines Paul's kerygma in the course of investigating whether there was 'one single, normative expression of the gospel' (*kerygma*)

---

[10] Weiss, *Earliest Christianity*, 1:222–3.

[11] Weiss, *Earliest Christianity*, 1:239–40; so also Elliott, *Rhetoric*, 108.

[12] Dodd, *Apostolic Preaching*. The importance of Dodd's work is well recognized: Hunter, *Unity*, 22: Dodd's work (1936) is 'one of the most important and positive contributions to New Testament science in our generation' as cited in Mounce, *Essential Nature*, 60. Mounce himself says that 'it is inevitable' that one should start from examining Dodd's work (p. 60).

[13] Dodd, *Apostolic Preaching*, 13.

[14] Dodd, *Apostolic Preaching*, 12; his summary of Paul's kerygma is as follows (p. 21): 1. The prophecies are fulfilled, and the new Age is inaugurated by the coming of Christ. 2. He was born of the seed of David. 3. He died according to the Scriptures, to deliver us out of the present evil age. 4. He was buried. 5. He rose on the third day according to the Scriptures. 6. He is exalted at the right hand of God, as Son of God and Lord of quick and dead. 7. He will come again as Judge and Saviour of men [i.e. humankind].

[15] Conzelmann, *Outline*, 60–71; so also Bultmann, *Theology*, 1:87–92.

or whether there were 'many different expressions of the gospel' (*kerygmata*) in the early church.¹⁶ His method is to survey 'the most important proclamations of the gospel in the NT, concentrating on picking out the characteristic features of each kerygma rather than attempting a fully balanced treatment of the whole'.¹⁷ He then examines the kerygmata of Jesus, in Acts, of Paul and of John, concluding that there is one common kerygma seen throughout the sermons in Acts, in Paul and in John.¹⁸ As far as Paul's initial missionary proclamation is concerned, Dunn suggests reconstructing it from the 'various kerygmatic or confessional formulae which Paul preserves' and from 'the great distinctives of his message as a whole' expressed in his letters.¹⁹ In his opinion, the most prominent feature of Paul's kerygma is the death and resurrection of Jesus,²⁰ together with the imminent Parousia (1 Thess 1:10; 2 Thess 2:5). He then goes on to claim that the most distinctive expressions of Paul's gospel are Christological, and that this core of Paul's message is expressed differently according to the different situations of those he addressed. He also notes that Paul's expression of his message (especially of the Parousia) has been developed over the years; and so Paul's proclamation did not have 'any final or fixed form'.²¹

To a certain extent, one may be able to rediscover Paul's missionary message using the methods proposed by the scholars above. With these methods, however, one cannot be certain whether what has been rediscovered is Paul's core message preached during his church-planting stage or the message developed later in the course of defending and expounding his earlier proclamation. In this regard, Weiss's suggestion, to reassemble Paul's missionary kerygma with his ideas before the Jerusalem conference,²² seems plausible. However, it is an uncertain, if not impossible, task to discern which of Paul's thoughts emerged before or after the conference, and we could end up with questionable results. Weiss himself reconstructs Paul's missionary preaching

---

¹⁶ Dunn, *Unity*, 11.

¹⁷ Dunn, *Unity*, 13.

¹⁸ According to Dunn, the components of this essential kerygma are the proclamation of Jesus' resurrection, the call to respond in faith and the promise in relation to faith exercised. He also notes 'the considerable diversity of the different kerygmata', and so he asserts, '*If we insist on the unity of the kerygma in the NT, we must insist also on the diversity of kerygmata in the NT*' (*Unity*, 30, 31). And so he concludes that although there is a distinctive core of the gospel that runs through all the NT kerygmata, the actual gospel proclaimed was different in different situations, even to the point, in some cases, where the different situations have the effect of altering the character of the kerygma (p. 32).

¹⁹ Dunn, *Unity*, 22.

²⁰ Rom 1:3–4; 3:24–25; 4:24–25; 8:34; 10:9; 1 Cor 1:23; 2:2; 15:3–11; 2 Cor 5:14–21; Gal 3:1; 1 Thess 1:10.

²¹ Dunn, *Unity*, 26.

²² Weiss, *Earliest Christianity*, 1:256.

from numerous passages written after the conference without identifying such chronological connections. The passages such as Romans 1:18–32; 2:17–24; 3:10–18 do not seem to represent his *missionary* preaching; rather, they are rhetorically constructed to undermine the complacency of Jews in his attempt to establish the equality of Jew and Gentile.[23]

C.H. Dodd uses only a handful of references to rediscover Paul's missionary kerygma (Rom 1:1–4; 2:16; 8:34; 10:8–9; 1 Cor 15:1–7; Gal 3:1–4; 4:6; 1 Thess 1:9–10), which do not seem sufficient.[24] We may also question whether his sharp distinction between *kerygma* and *didache* can be so rigidly drawn.[25] He has suggested rediscovering Paul's preaching from the phrase 'my gospel', which contains 'a high degree of originality in his presentation of the Gospel'.[26] But he seems to be preoccupied with the attempt to establish that Paul's gospel is not fundamentally different from that of the Jerusalem apostles, and that there is almost no element of the apostolic kerygma whose origin is in Paul. And so he concludes, 'There is, indeed, very little in the Jerusalem *kerygma* which does not appear, substantially, in Paul'.[27] It is furthermore difficult to prove with certainty from the early stage of his missionary work that Paul preached 'a high degree of originality' (Dodd), or 'the great distinctives of his message' (Dunn). Paul's 'my gospel' seems to have become distinctive (as compared to the common gospel: 1 Cor 15:11) at a later stage in the course of defending the gospel he preached among the Gentiles.[28] Neither is Conzelmann's methodology satisfactory. It is a kind of guesswork: believers confess Jesus as the Son of God; therefore, Paul must have preached that Jesus is the Son of God. This may be true, but it does not adequately reveal the kind of message which assured Paul's audience that Jesus was indeed the Son of God. We find, therefore, that these methods are not fully satisfactory for rediscovering Paul's missionary message.

---

[23] See Chae, *Paul, passim*.

[24] Dodd, *Apostolic Preaching*, 11–21.

[25] Dodd, *Apostolic Preaching*, 10, argues: 'It was by *kerygma*, says Paul, not by *didaché*, that it pleased God to save men'. He maintains this view in a later writing, *Gospel and Law*, 10: 'This order of approach, first the proclamation, then the beginning of instruction in morals, first *kerygma*, then *didaché*, seems to have been thoroughly characteristic of the Christian mission; it is precisely this order, first *kerygma*, then *didaché*, which we have seen to be general in the New Testament writings.' Dodd's distinction, however, has been considered as too rigid: cf. Hunter in the Foreword to Mounce's *Essential Nature*, 5; Worley, *Preaching*; Stanton, *Jesus of Nazareth*, 9.

[26] Dodd, *Apostolic Preaching*, 12.

[27] Dodd, *Apostolic Preaching*, 20–21, 30–33; the quotation is taken from pp. 32-3.

[28] See Chae, *Paul*, 302–7.

The 'Reminder Formula' and Paul's Missionary Preaching

Hardly anyone would expect any missionary to repeat the actual words of his/her missionary preaching in follow-up letters, such as Paul's.[29] Such letters naturally assume certain knowledge held by the recipients, and are a continuation of the earlier teachings. Therefore, if the converts do not follow the earlier instructions, the missionary would remind them rather than repeating the message all over again. When the missionary wants to build on previous preaching, a few words of reminder would suffice before expounding its implications or presenting further teaching. So some New Testament authors use the reminder formula in their writings.[30] Among them Paul adopts this formula the most to *remind* his readers of what he preached and/or taught while he was with them.[31] These reminders are, in most cases, very briefly formulated, yet they provide us with *Paul's own testimony* to what he actually preached and taught during his missionary endeavour. It is also important to note that Paul usually builds up his arguments by drawing on reminders to his earlier teachings. From this point of view we propose to rediscover Paul's missionary preaching by examining the passages where Paul uses the reminder formula.[32] Once our task is completed, from his letters we will be able to reconstruct the main components of the gospel Paul preached.

---

[29] So correctly, Stanton, *Jesus of Nazareth*, 113; cf. Dodd, *Apostolic Preaching*, 11–12.

[30] For example, the author of the Pastorals often reminds Timothy (1 Tim 1:18, 4:14; 2 Tim 1:6, 13; 2:2, 8; 3:10–14). Peter reminds his Gentile Christian readers: 'This is the word that was preached to you' (1 Pet 1:25; cf. 1:12, 18; 2 Pet 3:2). The author of 2 Peter uses a typical reminder formula: 'So I will always remind you of these things, even though you know them . . . I think it is right to refresh your memory as long as I live' (2 Pet 1:12–13, and again in 3:1). Jude uses almost identical wording (Jude 5). John also reminds his addressees to love one another on the basis of 'the message [they] heard from the beginning' (1 John 2:24; 3:11). Since his letters relate so much to previous teaching, John writes: 'I am not writing you a new command, but one we have had from the beginning . . . As you have heard from the beginning his command is that you walk in love' (2 John 5–6; very similarly and repeatedly, 1 John 2:7, 21).

[31] E.g. 1 Thess 5:1–2; 2 Thess 2:5; 2 Cor 13:2; similarly, 1 Cor 4:17; 5:9–11; 11:2, 23–26; Gal 5:21; 1 Thess 1:4–6; 2:8–9; 4:1–2, 6b, 11; 2 Thess 2:15; 3:4, 6, 10. Since our overall focus for this study is on Luke's portrait of Paul, it is worth noting that Luke also describes Paul using the reminder formula ('you know . . .' or 'remember . . .') when he speaks to those whom he had previously taught: Acts 20:18, 20, 31, 34).

[32] See my earlier treatment in Chae, 'Paul', 276–7, and also in Chae, *Paul*, 305–6.

The reminders of his preaching to the Corinthians

The testimony about God and Christ

The fact that Paul praises the Corinthians that 'our testimony about Christ was confirmed in you' (1 Cor 1:6) clearly indicates that he testified about Christ during his pioneering work. He also reminds them that he was determined to proclaim the testimony about God during his missionary work. 'When I came to you, brothers, I did not come with eloquence or superior wisdom as *I proclaimed to you the testimony about God*' (1 Cor 2:1). Then he continues to say that his preaching was devoted to prove that Jesus is Christ: 'I resolved to know nothing while I was with you except Jesus [being] Christ and him crucified' (1 Cor 2:2). He also reminds the Corinthians that he preached to them that Jesus is the Son of God, the Christ and the Lord (2 Cor 1:19; 4:5). Paul recalls that he *'testified about God* that he raised Christ from the dead' (1 Cor 15:15).

The death and resurrection of Christ

One of the most outstanding examples is in 1 Corinthians 15:1–2a: 'Now, brothers, I want to *remind [gnōrizō]*[33] *you of the gospel I preached to you, which you received and on which you have taken your stand. By this gospel you are saved*'. Here Paul reminds the Corinthians of the gospel which he preached during his pioneering ministry. He points out that, 'with top priority' (*en prōtois*),[34] he passed on the gospel which he had also received.[35] His kerygma was about the death, burial and resurrection of Christ as the fulfilment of the Scriptures.[36] Paul also says that he passed on the teaching about the sacrament of the Lord's Supper, which itself is the reminder of the death of Jesus (1 Cor 11:23).[37]

---

[33] The English translations that render this verb as 'remind' include NIV, PHILLIPS, RSV, JB, NEB and TEV.

[34] The rendering of the Anchor Bible. Cf. for various renderings: 'the greatest importance' (TEV); 'as essential' (PHILLIPS); 'first and foremost' (NEB); 'as of first importance' (NIV, RSV); 'among the things to be stated first' (Edwards, *Commentary*).

[35] The verb *parelabon* can refer to a direct revelation from Christ (Gal 1:12), but probably refers to tradition; so also Orr and Walther, *1 Corinthians*, 319–20. For a survey on the discussion on this issue, see Schütz, *Paul*, 54ff.

[36] 1 Cor 15:3–8; cf. Matt 26:24; Luke 24:25–27, 45–47; John 2:21–22; Acts 2:25, 30–31; 17:2–3; 26:22–23. Bultmann, *Kerygma and Myth*, 1:112, who regards the kerygma only as the act of preaching, and thus excludes 1 Cor 15:3–8 from the Pauline kerygma. But see the opposite view in Dodd, *Apostolic Preaching*, 11ff. For an examination of 1 Cor 15:1–11 as Paul's missionary preaching, see Pak, *Paul as Missionary*, 115–41.

[37] Paul teaches about this sacrament in three stages: (1) during his missionary work, (2) more in 1 Corinthians, and (3) further instruction is intended (1 Cor 11:34c).

Likewise Paul's emphasis is certainly on the resurrection. He writes that the success of his preaching depended upon whether he clearly preached the resurrection or not (1 Cor 15:12–15). For him, the resurrection of Jesus was the most essential part of his preaching, and also of the believer's faith and justification: 'If Christ has not been raised, our preaching is useless and so is your faith' (1 Cor 15:14, 17; Rom 4:25).[38] He clearly states that 'we have testified about God that he raised Christ from the dead' (1 Cor 15:15, 20).

At the beginning of the letter Paul has already recalled his determination to preach the death of Jesus on the cross as well as Jesus being the Christ: 'For I resolved to know nothing while I was with you except Jesus Christ and him crucified' (1 Cor 2:1–2). Paul also affirms, 'we preach Christ crucified', for that message is the power of God for salvation for both Jews and Gentiles (1 Cor 1:21–25). He mentions crucifixion only in two references; 'cross and resurrection constituted a single meaning-complex'.[39] However, '[t]he death on the cross and the resurrection of Christ cannot in Paul be isolated as two distinct facts: rather in his view they are inseparably united.'[40] By preaching the death and resurrection of Christ, the apostle laid the foundations for the church in Corinth (1 Cor 3:10–15).

The Parousia

Right at the beginning of the first letter Paul praises the Corinthians 'because our [earlier] testimony about Christ was confirmed in you' (1 Cor 1:6). Then he connects it straight away to the fact that they are eagerly waiting for the Lord Jesus Christ to be revealed, and this clearly indicates that he preached about the Parousia to them while he was there (1 Cor 1:7). The fact that he encourages them to 'wait till the Lord comes' (1 Cor 4:5), and that he often uses the phrase 'the Day of the Lord' without explaining it, indicates that he taught about the return of the Lord (1 Cor 1:7–8; 5:5; 2 Cor 1:14). After affirming the certainty of the resurrection of the dead, Paul moves on to give a long answer to the question, 'How are the dead raised?' (1 Cor 15:35). Here Paul does not talk about the return of the Lord, but the entire explanation is based on the presupposition that it will all happen when the Lord comes. Paul takes the Corinthians' understanding of the Parousia of the Lord as a *fait accompli*, because he has taught his converts about it already in person.

Godly life

'I already gave you a warning [about orderly Christian life] when I was with you', Paul clearly recalls, and then reiterates in a further instruction: 'I now repeat it while absent' (2 Cor 13:2). The apostle passed on a set of teachings

---

[38] Cf. Sanders, *Palestinian Judaism*, 444.
[39] Keck, *Paul*, 36.
[40] Deissmann, *Paul*, 197.

concerning the Christian manner of life, which '[he taught] everywhere in every church' (1 Cor 4:17; cf. 7:17–19). Now Paul sends Timothy in order for him to remind the Corinthians of the Christian way of life which Paul lived among them (1 Cor 4:16–17). Sexual immorality is especially to be avoided, as he has previously written, and now Paul repeats it with some added items (1 Cor 5:9, 11). 'Your body is a temple of the Holy Spirit, who is in you, whom you have received from God . . . Therefore honour God with your body' (1 Cor 6:19–20). The Galatians were warned by being reminded ('I warn you, as I did before') that those who engage in the fifteen acts of the sinful nature listed in Galatians 5:19–21 will not inherit the kingdom of God. Paul uses the same phrase, 'will not inherit the kingdom of God', twice in 1 Corinthians 6:9–10 by listing the similar items mentioned in Galatians 5:19–21 (1 Cor 6:9–20). This seems to indicate that Paul gave a similar set of teaching to the Corinthians as well during his missionary work there.

The reminders of his preaching to the Galatians

The testimony about Jesus

Paul briefly states to the Galatians that he had simply preached 'the gospel' (Gal 2:2; 4:13), or the gospel of Jesus Christ (Gal 1:7, 11). He preached Christ (Gal 1:8). 'God . . . was pleased to reveal his Son in me so that I might preach *him* among the Gentiles' (Gal 1:15–16). Paul preached and proved that Jesus was the Son of God. That Jesus is the Christ and the Son of God was an essential part of Paul's missionary message.

The death and resurrection of Jesus

Paul does not describe in detail the content of his preaching which he proclaimed in the region of Galatia. By asking a series of questions, however, he refreshes the Galatians' memory concerning what he preached, and what and how they believed:

> You foolish Galatians! Who has bewitched you? Before your very eyes Jesus was clearly portrayed as crucified. I would like to learn just one thing from you: Did you receive the Spirit by observing the law, or by believing what you heard? Are you so foolish? After beginning with the Spirit, are you now trying to attain your goal by human effort? Have you suffered so much for nothing – if it really was for nothing? Does God give you his Spirit and work miracles among you because you observe the law, or because you believe what you heard? (Gal 3:1–5)

With the statement, 'Before your very eyes Jesus was clearly portrayed as crucified', Paul indicates that he preached the death of Jesus on the cross in his proclamation to the Galatians. Furthermore, his declaration that his only boast is in the cross of Jesus Christ reaffirms that he had preached the fact and significance of Jesus' death there (Gal 6:14; also 1 Cor 2:2). He reminds the Galatians that they had received the Spirit by believing his message of the cross, not by observing the law. Paul's overall concern in writing this letter was to uphold the cross of Christ through which (and through belief in which) they had become new creations in Christ (cf. Gal 6:12–15). He reaffirms the legitimacy and sufficiency of their salvation by reminding them of their experience of the Spirit when they first believed in his message of the cross.

Although only the cross of Jesus is mentioned here (as in 1 Cor 1:23; 2:2), we can safely assume that he mentioned the resurrection of Jesus as well.[41] Paul reminds the Galatians of his previous way of life in Judaism. How the risen Christ had appeared to him was a part of his story (Gal 1:13–16). The fact that Paul simply mentions the statements such as 'God the Father, who raised him from the dead' (Gal 1:1), without any explanation, indicates that he previously preached and explained the resurrection of Jesus Christ.

Godly life

After mentioning the fifteen acts of the sinful nature, Paul solemnly declares: 'I warn you, *as I did before*, that those who live like this will not inherit the kingdom of God' (Gal 5:19–21). Here he apparently reminds the Galatians that he had specifically and emphatically taught that they should live a godly life by repudiating such sinful works (cf. Phil 3:17–19). Because he previously warned them while he was in Galatia, he does not elaborate each item of the sinful nature in the letter but simply lists them.

The reminders of his preaching to the Thessalonians

The living and true God

Jesus was preached as God's Son from heaven, as risen Lord and as the Deliverer from the coming judgement (1 Thess 1:10). Paul reminds the Thessalonians that thus they 'turned to God from idols to serve the living and true God' (1 Thess 1:9; 2:2).[42] We may safely assume that he preached against idolatry, as Galatians 5:20–21 shows. There he reminds the Galatians that he preached against idolatry (among others) during his initial missionary preaching in Galatia. From a Christian perspective, Paul has presented a major theme of Jewish missionary preaching, namely, urging the Gentiles to turn from idols to the true and living God.[43]

---

[41] See above, pp. 30–31, 52.

[42] For a detailed study of 1 Thess 1:9–10 as Paul's missionary preaching, see Pak, *Paul as Missionary*, 3–26.

[43] Senior and Stuhlmueller, *Foundations*, 185–6.

The death and resurrection of Jesus

Paul's earlier teaching on the Parousia presupposes that he preached the death and resurrection of Christ (cf. 1 Thess 2:15; 4:14). Jesus died for us so that believers may live with him (1 Thess 5:10). The statement that the Thessalonians were 'wait[ing] for his Son from heaven, whom he raised from the dead' indicates that Paul preached to them the death and resurrection of the Son of God (1 Thess 1:10).

The Parousia

Paul clearly says that he preached about the Parousia of Jesus during his missionary preaching in Thessalonica (1 Thess 1:10; cf. 4:16; 5:2; 2 Thess 1:7). In his further teaching (2 Thess 2:1ff.), Paul explicitly reminds the perplexed Thessalonians, by asking: 'Don't you remember that when I was with you I used to tell you these things?' (2 Thess 2:5). This reminder is placed in the middle of his reinforced teaching, but it is intended to exhort confused believers 'to hold to the teachings we [previously] passed on to you' (2 Thess 2:15). In the first letter Paul had already refreshed their memory concerning his teaching on the Parousia. As a result they had waited for God's Son from heaven (1 Thess 1:10), and so the apostle could say: 'We do not need to write to you, for you know very well that the day of the Lord will come like a thief in the night' (1 Thess 5:1–2; cf. 4:16; 5:23).

Godly life

Paul writes, 'we instructed you how to live in order to please God, as in fact you are living', and urges them by saying, 'do this more and more. For *you know what instructions we gave you*' (1 Thess 4:1–2). The apostle continues, 'Now about brotherly love we do not need to write to you, for *you yourselves have been taught* . . . Yet we urge you . . . to do so more and more' (1 Thess 4:9–10). He also recalls his earlier warning: '*We have already told you and warned you*' to avoid sexual immorality (1 Thess 4:6b, 11: 'just as we told you'). He reminds them of his own lifestyle as an example (1 Thess 2:5–12; 2 Thess 3:6–10). He also stresses the rule 'If a man will not work, he shall not eat' by reminding them twice of the fact that he has already instructed them in person concerning the rules on Christian living (2 Thess 3:6, 10).

Persecution

Paul reminds the Thessalonians that he faced strong opposition in preaching the gospel (1 Thess 1:6; 2:2; cf. Acts 17:1–9). He also tells them that he had warned them to be prepared for the coming persecution: 'In fact, *when we were with you*, we kept telling you that we would be persecuted' (1 Thess

3:4); and his warning certainly prepared them to persevere well in all persecutions from their own countrymen (1 Thess 2:14; 2 Thess 1:4).

The reminders/reports of his preaching to the Romans and the Colossians

Both Romans and Colossians were letters sent to believers to whom Paul had never preached face to face (cf. Rom 1:9–14; 15:23–24; Col 1:6–9), and so there seems to be nothing for Paul to remind them of. Romans contains, however, various references which are similar to his earlier missionary preaching, because he is now writing the gospel which he intended to preach in person (cf. Rom 1:15). Several references, expressed in a *reminder* or *report formula*, reflect what Paul preached elsewhere during his missionary work.

The testimony about Christ

In Romans and Colossians, Paul seems to write a fuller account of the gospel than he usually does in other letters, because the readers would need more explanation as they 'hear' him for the first time. For example, Paul writes in some detail about the supremacy of Christ (Col 1:15–23). Then he says that this is the gospel the Colossians heard from 'Epaphras, our dear fellow-servant . . . on our behalf' and 'I, Paul, have become a servant [of this gospel]' (Col 1:7, 23). Though his words are coloured by his own immediate purpose in writing to the Colossians, Paul indicates that both Epaphras and he proclaimed the same content of the gospel. So also in Romans: Paul expounds more about who Jesus is in Romans 1:3–4, and about the content of the gospel of justification and reconciliation in Romans 5 – 8.

The death and resurrection of Christ

Paul declares that belief in the resurrection of Jesus and confession of the lordship of Christ are two vital elements for saving faith. 'The word of faith we are proclaiming' (note the present *kēryssomen*): 'That if you confess with your mouth, "Jesus is Lord," and believe in your heart that God raised him from the dead, you will be saved' (Rom 10:8–9).[44] This shows that Paul preached the lordship of Christ and the resurrection of Christ. Through the resurrection Jesus was declared to be the son of David, the Messiah and the Son of God (Rom 1:3–4). He also preached Jesus' death as well: 'Christ died and returned to life so that he might be the Lord of both the dead and the living' (Rom 14:9). Paul frequently mentions Jesus' death[45] and resurrection.[46] The death, resurrection and exaltation of Jesus constitute an essential

---

[44] Cf. Dodd, *Apostolic Preaching*, 14.
[45] Rom 5:6, 8; 6:10; 14:9, 15; Col 2:12, 20.
[46] Rom 1:4; 4:24–25; 6:4, 5, 9; 7:4; 8:11, 34; 10:9; Col 1:18; 2:12, 3:1.

part of his preaching (Rom 4:24–25; 8:31–34; 10:9; 14:9). Then he challenged people to respond to Christ in confession and faith.

Paul also reminds the Colossians: 'Once you were alienated from God and were enemies . . . But now he has reconciled you by *Christ's physical body through death . . . This is the gospel that you heard and that has been proclaimed to every creature under heaven,* and of which I, Paul, have become a servant' (Col 1:21–23). Paul affirms that the gospel the Colossians heard from Epaphras was the same common gospel he (Paul) also preached all over the world (Col 1:5–7). The content of the common gospel was the reconciliation between God and humankind through the physical sacrifice and the resurrection of Jesus Christ.

Godly living

Unlike in the case of the Galatians, Paul writes to the Colossians in some detail when giving his instructions for godly living (Col 3:1–17). He does the same in his letter to the Romans. The apostle expounds in much detail on the loving relationship with fellow believers (Rom 12:9–21; 13:8–14; 14:1–23). This is most probably because he has not taught them previously in person, and these details can provide us with a clue as to what kind of message he might have preached when he exhorted his converts face to face. He must have given them an exhortation to live a life worthy of the Lord, as his followers, and also to love one another, as fellow believers.

The summary of Paul's missionary preaching

We have attempted to rediscover the core of Paul's missionary message by analysing his reminder formula as expressed in his letters, and now we sum up our findings. The main core of his preaching is certainly the death and resurrection of Jesus: he was crucified for our sins, was buried and was raised again on the third day. The fact that Paul preached these events as 'according to the Scriptures' indicates that from the Old Testament itself he testified to the Christ-event as the fulfilment of the Scriptures. Thus, for Paul, the crucifixion was not a miscarriage of justice, but the accomplishment of God's salvific purpose.[47]

The word of the cross was the heart of the earliest missionary proclamation. Paul emphasized that Jesus died[48] 'for our sins to rescue us from the

---

[47] Rom 1:2–3; 1 Cor 15:3–7; Acts 13:26–31; 17:2; 18:28; 28:23; Luke 24:44–48.

[48] It seems almost impossible for Paul to preach the death of Jesus without mentioning his life and ministry. Therefore, Stanton, *Jesus of Nazareth*, 113, seems correct in concluding that 'the possibility must be allowed that Paul laid greater emphasis on the pre-crucifixion events and the character of Jesus in his preaching than he does in his epistles'. The statement is affirmatively cited in Mounce, 'Preaching', 736. So also Hengel, *Earliest Christianity*, 83; Kim, 'Jesus, Sayings of', 474–92. Most

present evil age'.⁴⁹ Paul stressed the historicity and certainty of the resurrection of Jesus by expounding the promises in the Old Testament and by listing many eyewitnesses (1 Cor 15:5–8). His preaching of Jesus as the Son of God, Christ, the Lord and the Judge[50] was based on the significance of his resurrection (2 Cor 1:19; Rom 1:4).[51] The message of the resurrection of Christ is the central part of the kerygma of both Paul and the apostles.[52] In fact Peter's preaching in Acts[53] and Paul's in the letters[54] are very much of the same content. G. Bornkamm is right to say that 'Paul's gospel and theology are the exposition and development of the primitive Christian kerygma', whose content includes the death, resurrection and Parousia of Jesus.[55] Paul's proclamation of the exaltation and the Parousia of Jesus was also probably derived from the implications of his resurrection (cf. Phil 2:8–9).

When Paul preached the significance of Christ's death as 'for our sins', he also urged people to respond in repentance.[56] 'Paul's message was gospel, good news, only for the person who believed it. Consequently Paul, like every early preacher, called for faith. Apart from faith, Paul's word brought no salvation.'[57] His preaching had an objective: it anticipated the salvation of his listeners through repentance of their sins, faith in Jesus' death and resurrection, and confession of Jesus as Lord. As Paul's audience believed and accepted his message, they experienced the manifestation of the Holy Spirit

---

affirmatively, Klausner, *From Jesus to Paul*, 315–16. For a thorough treatment of Paul as a follower of Jesus, see Wenham, *Paul*.

[49] Gal 1:4; 1 Cor 15:3; Rom 5:8; Gal 3:13; Eph 5:2; Titus 2:14; cf. 1 Pet 2:24.

[50] Bultmann, *Theology*, 1:75–9.

[51] Sanders, *Palestinian Judaism*, 447: the resurrection of Jesus 'implies Christ's *lordship*, his *return*, the *judgment* and the *salvation of those who believe*'.

[52] Rom 1:4; 4:25; 8:19ff.; 1 Cor 15:20ff.; 1 Thess 4:14; Acts 2:36; 4:12; 10:42; 24:15; Ladd, *Theology*, 317.

[53] Acts 2:14–39; 3:13–26; 4:10–12; 5:30–32; 10:36–43.

[54] Rom 1:2–4; 2:16; 8:34; 9:5; 10:8–9; 1 Cor 15:3–4; cf. Acts 13:17–41; 17:22–31; 23:6; 24:21; 25:19; 26:6–8.

[55] Bornkamm, *Paul*, 110, 114. He continues at p. 113: 'In his own view, Paul was one in a succession and accordingly – especially in the matter of his Christology, although it does have its own special features – we should not raise the question of any particular "originality" he may possess. This shows that the nature of the apostle's theology is completely misconceived when he himself is viewed as a "religious genius" and his theology regarded simply as the direct result of his own personal and individual experiences.'

[56] Although the language of repentance is not frequent in Paul's letters (cf. only in Rom 2:4; 2 Cor 7:9, 10; 12:21), he is surely implying this meaning when using other expressions such as 'turning away from idols' (1 Thess 1:9–10), 'renewing of your mind' (Rom 12:2) and 'unrepentant heart' (Rom 2:5).

[57] Keck, *Paul*, 49.

(1 Cor 2:4–13; Gal 3:1–5; 1 Thess 1:4–6), which was taken as the clear evidence of God's salvific grace.[58]

In his missionary message Paul included his exhortation to the believers to live godly lives as new creations in Christ. He also warned new converts to be prepared for persecution for the cause of their new faith in Christ Jesus (1 Thess 3:4). Paul could have used a different approach and emphasis according to the different backgrounds of his audience (cf. 1 Cor 9:19–23). To the Jews, he might have addressed the death and resurrection of Jesus as the fulfilment of the promises in the Old Testament, from which he explained that Jesus was the promised Messiah. To the Gentiles, Paul might have included the message about the true knowledge of the living God, and about the uselessness of idols (cf. 1 Thess 1:9; 2 Cor 6:16). He often included his own testimony of how he believed in the Lord even though he had, at first, a hostile attitude towards Jesus and his followers (Gal 1:13–14; Phil 3:4–11). However, whenever he preached, he would always include the message of the cross and resurrection as it was the heart of his preaching. Many other teachings and instructions were given on the basis of this essential and consistent message.

Earlier we have contended that Vielhauer's method is not plausible in comparing, at face value, the evangelistic preaching of the Lucan Paul (given to *unbelievers* to convert them) with the pastoral message of the real Paul (delivered to *believers* to strengthen them in faith). For too long, scholars have wrongly compared the missionary sermons attributed to Paul in Acts with the more developed implications of the gospel expounded in Paul's letters. That is why their studies often arrived at wrong conclusions. Our study above has now identified the *missionary* preaching of Paul derived from his letters, and thus we are now in a better position to determine the reliability of the account of the *missionary* sermons attributed to him in Acts.

Comparing the Lucan Paul with the Real Paul in Their Missionary Preaching

Our task now is to identify the missionary proclamation of the Lucan Paul from what is recorded in Acts. In this way we will be able to assess the level of compatibility of the *missionary* message of the real Paul and the Lucan Paul. Then we shall undertake two more examinations in order to determine Luke's credibility in describing Paul as a missionary preacher. We shall attempt to examine whether there are some evangelistic topics which correspond in Acts and in the letters. Then we shall study whether there are any

---

[58] Turner, *Holy Spirit*, 135: 'Christian "life" begins by the Spirit'.

specific corresponding elements between Paul's initial mission to particular cities as described in Acts (e.g. Corinth) and his follow-up letters sent to the churches in those cities (1 and 2 Corinthians). This multilateral examination will further assist us in ascertaining the level of reliability of Luke's portrayal of the apostle.

Paul's missionary preaching in Acts

In the section above we recovered the core of Paul's missionary preaching from his letters. Its core contains the person of Christ, the death and resurrection of Christ, the Parousia and his exhortation to live a godly life. It is significant to note that among these topics Luke also presents the person of Christ and the death and resurrection of Christ as the most important subjects. This seems natural because Luke's focus in recording Paul's ministry is Paul the missionary evangelist, rather than Paul the pastor or theologian. Now we will compile the core of the evangelistic sermons in Acts attributed to Paul, and then compare them with these two topics we have recovered from the letters by employing the reminder formula.

The person of Christ

Luke writes that straight after his conversion, Paul preaches in the synagogues in Damascus that Jesus is the Son of God, and also argues with the Jews by proving (from the Scriptures) that Jesus is the Christ (Acts 9:20, 22). In the course of talking about his Damascus experience, Paul writes that God 'revealed his Son to me' (see Gal 1:16). In Pisidian Antioch, he preaches from the Old Testament to prove that Jesus is not only the Son of David, the promised Saviour Messiah, but also God's Son on the basis of his resurrection (Acts 13:22, 33). This is what the real Paul also says in Romans 1:2–4: 'the gospel he [God] promised beforehand through his prophets in the Holy Scriptures regarding his Son, who as to his human nature was a descendant of David, and who through the Spirit of holiness was declared with power to be the Son of God, by his resurrection from the dead'. So for Paul the gospel is the gospel of God's Son (Rom 1:9). More clearly Paul reminds the Corinthians that 'the Son of God, Jesus Christ . . . *was preached among you by me and Silas and Timothy*' (2 Cor 1:19). It is to be noted that the Lucan Paul is the only speaker in Acts who refers to Jesus with the familiar Pauline title, the Son of God.

Luke also describes Paul as preaching Jesus as the Christ in the synagogue in Thessalonica by reasoning and proving from the Scriptures the death and resurrection of Christ, and declaring, 'This Jesus I am proclaiming to you is the Christ' (Acts 17:2–3). Furthermore, Luke writes, 'Paul devoted himself exclusively to preaching, testifying to the Jews [in the synagogue in Corinth] that Jesus was the Christ' (Acts 18:5; cf. earlier in 17:3; so did Peter and

Apollos: 5:42; 18:28). Here it seems significant to note that Paul also reminds the Corinthians that 'I resolved to know nothing while I was with you except Jesus Christ and him crucified' (1 Cor 1:23; 2:2). The Lucan Paul also testifies before King Agrippa and the Jewish leaders that he has been 'saying nothing beyond what the prophets and Moses said would happen' (Acts 26:22; 24:14–15; 26:6–7; cf. Luke 24:27, 44–47), and then continues, 'that Christ would suffer and . . . rise from the dead' (Acts 26:23). His attempt to prove Jesus is the Christ is continued in Rome as well (Acts 28:31). This indicates that he has been using the Scriptures to prove the death and resurrection of Christ as the fulfilment of the Scriptures, especially to his Jewish audience (Rom 1:2–4; 1 Cor 15:3–4; Gal 1:15–16; Acts 28:23). It seems clear that both Paul and Luke present similar accounts: the essential part of Paul's preaching was to prove from the Scriptures that the crucified and risen Jesus is Christ and the Son of God.

The death and resurrection of Christ

The Lucan Paul constantly preaches the death and resurrection of Jesus. He emphasizes this in his sermon in the synagogue in Pisidian Antioch (Acts 13:28–30). It is especially interesting to note the Lucan Paul saying, 'But God raised him from the dead, and for many days he was seen by those who had travelled with him from Galilee to Jerusalem. They are now his witnesses to our people' (Acts 13:31). This content is supported and echoed by what Paul writes in 1 Corinthians 15:5–8 about numerous witnesses of the resurrection of Christ, 'most of whom are still living'. In the sermon in Pisidian Antioch, the Lucan Paul stresses the resurrection of Jesus by citing an Old Testament passage to prove it (Acts 13:30–37).[59] He does this also in Athens: a group of philosophers invited him to speak 'because Paul was preaching the good news about *Jesus and the resurrection*' (Acts 17:18). It seems he would have continued to talk about the resurrection of Jesus if he had not been interrupted (Acts 17:31–32). The Lucan Paul contends that the resurrection is the proof that God had appointed Jesus Christ to be the Judge of the world (Acts 17:31), just as he says in Romans 1:4 that God declared and proved the sonship of Jesus by raising him from the dead.

Later the Lucan Paul repeatedly asserts that he stands on trial because of his preaching of the resurrection (of Jesus) (Acts 23:6; 24:15, 21; 26:6–8, 22–23). In fact, the resurrection is the central theme of the speeches in Acts.[60] Governor Festus sums up how Paul claimed that Jesus had been raised from the dead and was alive (Acts 25:19). The centrality of Jesus' resurrection in

---

[59] See Steyn, *Septuagint Quotations*, 169–94.
[60] Ladd, *Theology*, 317: 'resurrection': 1:22; 2:31; 4:2; 17:18, 32; 23:6; 24:21; 'raised up': 2:24, 30; 3:15, 26; 4:10; 5:30; 10:40; 13:30, 33, 34, 37; 17:3, 31; 25:19, 26:8, 23.

Paul's missionary preaching is also clearly stressed in 1 Corinthians 15:12–15:

> But if it is preached that Christ has been raised from the dead, how can some of you say that there is no resurrection of the dead? . . . And if Christ has not been raised, our preaching is useless and so is your faith. More than that, we are then found to be false witnesses about God, for we have testified about God that he raised Christ from the dead.

The most crucial content of Paul's preaching, and of the faith of the believers, is the resurrection of Jesus.[61]

Just as Paul sums up how he preached the gospel of the death and resurrection of Jesus as the fulfilment of the Scriptures (1 Cor 15:3–4; Rom 1:2–4), the Lucan Paul does the same. In his sermon in the synagogue in Pisidian Antioch, he argues that the condemnation of Jesus by the Jewish authorities was a fulfilment of the Scriptures. Moreover, he surveys the Old Testament to prove Jesus' sonship, messiahship and his death and resurrection by quoting verses from the Old Testament as proof (Acts 13:23–37). In Thessalonica, he again 'reasoned with [the Jews] from the Scriptures, explaining and proving that the Messiah had to suffer and rise from the dead. "This Jesus I am proclaiming to you is the Messiah," he said' (Acts 17:2–3). In Corinth, the Lucan Paul does the same: 'Every Sabbath he reasoned [from the Scriptures] in the synagogue, trying to persuade Jews and Greeks [about Jesus Christ and his death and resurrection]' (Acts 18:4; and also 18:19).

In the course of his defence later, the Lucan Paul repeatedly says that his preaching was based on the Scriptures. Before Felix, he testifies, 'I believe everything that agrees with the Law and that is written in the Prophets, and I have the same hope in God . . . that there will be a resurrection of both the righteous and the wicked' (Acts 24:14–15). To King Agrippa, he also explains that he said 'nothing beyond what the prophets and Moses said would happen – that the Christ would suffer and [be] the first to rise from the dead' (Acts 26:22b–23). Luke records that Paul was consistent in his presentation of the gospel based on the Old Testament from the beginning in Damascus till the end in Rome (Acts 9:22; 28:23). Here we see the Lucan Paul preaching the death and resurrection of Jesus by reasoning and proving it from the Scriptures, just as the real Paul precisely testifies in 1 Corinthians 15:3–4.

The Lucan Paul does not appear to have said much to his converts about living godly lives. However, it is significant to note how he sums up his entire missionary life in obedience to God's call before King Agrippa: 'I preached that they should repent and turn to God and *prove their repentance by their deeds*' (Acts 26:20; Gal 6:10; Col 3:1–17; 1 Tim 6:18). Thus we can conclude

---

[61] Rom 1:4; 4:25; 6:4; 8:11; 10:9; 1 Cor 6:14; 15:4, 15; Gal 1:1; Eph 1:20; Col 2:12; 1 Thess 4:14, etc. So correctly, Sanders, *Palestinian Judaism*, 444.

that there is a high level of probability that Luke's portrayal of Paul corresponds with what the real Paul has preached: that Jesus was crucified for our sins and was raised from the dead, and thus that Jesus is the Christ and the Son of God.

The Parousia of Christ

Paul writes to the Corinthians: 'you eagerly wait for our Lord Jesus Christ to be revealed' (1 Cor 1:7; 4:5; 6:5). To the Thessalonians, he assures them that he 'will glory in the presence of our Lord Jesus Christ when he comes' (1 Thess 2:19; 3:13; 4:15–16; 5:23; 2 Thess 1:7–10). Both Lucan Paul and the real Paul present the Jesus of the Parousia as the Judge of the living and the dead.[62] Luke also bears witness to the second coming of Jesus as he records the ascension of Christ: 'This same Jesus, who has been taken up from you into heaven, will come back in the same way you have seen him go into heaven' (Acts 1:11). Furthermore, the fact that Paul writes to the Corinthian church in so much detail about the resurrection of the dead indicates that he did not teach about it in detail during his missionary work in Corinth (1 Cor 15:20–28). Set against this, it is interesting to note that the Lucan Paul also talks about the resurrection of the dead at a later stage of his ministry (Acts 26:6–8).

The corresponding evangelistic topics in Acts and in the letters

The kingdom of God

The kingdom of God is a prominent theme in Paul's letters. However, he does not explain or expound this important subject. It seems probable that he does not do so because he has already taught about it during his missionary journeys. The fact that in most cases in the letters he talks about *inheriting* the kingdom of God reinforces our understanding (e.g. Rom 14:27; 1 Cor 4:20).[63] Luke also conveys that the kingdom of God was an overall theme of Paul's preaching. He writes that Paul spoke boldly in Ephesus for three months, arguing persuasively about the kingdom of God (Acts 19:8). The Lucan Paul reminds the Ephesian elders that he preached the kingdom to them, which was related to 'the whole will of God' (Acts 20:25, 27). Later he taught the Jews in Rome about the kingdom of God by explaining about Jesus from the Scriptures (Acts 28:23, 31). The real Paul teaches about the kingship of Jesus (1 Cor 15:22–25; cf. Eph 5:5; 1 Tim 6:15), and likewise the Lucan Paul was accused of preaching the kingship of Jesus (Acts 17:7).

---

[62] Rom 2:16; 14:9–12; 1 Cor 4:5; 2 Cor 5:10; 2 Thess 1:8–10; 2 Tim 4:1; Acts 17:31.

[63] Also 1 Cor 4:20; 6:9–10; 15:24, 50; Gal 5:21; Eph 2:2; 5:5; Col 1:12–13; 4:11; 1 Thess 2:12; 2 Thess 1:5; 2 Tim 4:1, 18.

Call to turn away from idols

Paul reminds the Thessalonians that they were like 'the heathen, who do not know God' (1 Thess 4:5), but now they have 'turned to God from idols to serve the living and true God' as the result of his preaching against idolatry (1 Thess 1:9; 2:2). He also reminds the Corinthians of their idolatrous past: 'You know that when you were pagans . . . you were influenced and led astray to mute idols' (1 Cor 12:2). Now they have turned away from idols, but Paul repeatedly urges them not to become idolaters or associate with them (1 Cor 5:10–11; 6:9; 10:7, 14; 2 Cor 6:16). He thus reinforces his earlier teaching with regard to idols: '[*You*] *know* that an idol is nothing at all in the world and there is no God but one' (1 Cor 8:4; also in 10:19–20). To the Romans Paul also strongly condemns idolatry (Rom 1:22–25; 2:22).

Furthermore, what Paul writes to the Galatians is most noteworthy, because it can be compared with the accounts in Acts. Paul implies that the Galatians turned to God from idol worship in response to his preaching of the gospel: 'Formerly, when you did not know God, you were slaves to those who by nature are not gods' (Gal 4:8). Paul urges the Galatians to avoid idolatry, as he warned earlier ('I warn you, *as I did before* . . .') together with fourteen other acts of the sinful nature (Gal 5:19–21). This indicates clearly that he preached against idolatry while he was in Galatia.

Luke writes that Paul urged the Gentiles of Lystra in the Galatia province to turn away from idols: 'We are bringing you good news, telling you to turn from these worthless things to the living God, who made heaven and earth and sea and everything in them' (Acts 14:15). Luke also reports that in Athens Paul was greatly disturbed to see that the city was full of idols. When an opportunity was given to him to speak at the Areopagus, he started his speech by mentioning the subject of idol worship, and concluded, 'Therefore . . . we should not think that the divine being is like gold or silver or stone – an image made by man's design and skill. In the past God overlooked such ignorance, but now he commands all people everywhere to repent' (Acts 17:29–30). According to Luke, the idol-making silversmith in Ephesus had complained that Paul had convinced large numbers of people that 'man-made gods are no gods at all', including the goddess Artemis (Acts 19:26–27).

Call to repentance

The term 'repent/repentance' does not frequently occur in Paul's letters; probably he did not need to call the recipients to repentance *so as to be saved*, because they were already believers. The term 'repentance' is used rather in relation to their living as Christians. Talking about his stern letter that caused the Corinthians sorrow, Paul points out that they rightly repented: 'your sorrow led you to repentance . . . Godly sorrow brings repentance that leads to salvation' (2 Cor 7:9–10). However, when he has unbelievers in mind he makes a strong challenge for repentance. 'Or do you show contempt for the riches of his kindness, tolerance and patience, not realising that God's kindness leads you towards repentance? But because of your stubbornness and your unrepentant heart, you are storing up wrath against yourself for the day of God's wrath' (Rom 2:4–5).

The Lucan Paul reminds the elders of the Ephesian church: 'I have declared to both Jews and Greeks that they must turn to God in repentance and have faith in our Lord Jesus' (Acts 20:21).[64] Here he recalls his urge to repentance for salvation as the right response to his preaching, but he does not demand that the elders repent. Later he sums up the account of his missionary work: 'I preached that they should repent and turn to God' (Acts 26:20). To the idol-worshipping Gentiles in Athens, the Lucan Paul declares, 'Now [God] commands all people everywhere to repent' (Acts 17:30). Earlier in Lystra he is reported as urging the Gentiles to turn from idols to the living God in repentance (Acts 14:15; cf. 1 Thess 1:9–10).

Responses to Paul's preaching

Paul proclaimed the gospel to both Jews and Gentiles, for he believed it is the power of God for salvation for the Jew first and also equally for the Gentile (Rom 1:16). Both Paul and Luke agree on the response to Paul's preaching from the two ethnic groups: overall, the Gentiles welcomed the gospel message, but the Jews rejected it.[65] Luke especially makes note of the good response from Paul's mission in Galatia, and Paul himself also alludes to such a welcome when he arrived in Galatia (Acts 13:43, 49; 14:1, 21; Gal 4:12–15). According to Acts, Paul goes into the synagogues as was customary for him.[66] Some scholars understand that Paul stood against the Jews and the Jewish law, and therefore they suspect that he did not approach them. However, the fact that he was disciplined five times by the synagogue authorities (2 Cor 11:24) indicates that such discipline happened due to his attempts to witness to the Jews, probably in the synagogues. Furthermore, Paul testifies that he is passionate in proclaiming the gospel to his own people, the Jews (1 Cor 9:19–20; Rom 9:1–4; 11:14), and such passion may well have led him to preach in the synagogues.

The fact that all the churches Paul planted were predominantly Gentile indicates that it was predominantly the Gentiles who accepted his gospel message, as Luke describes. Paul reports an open door in the Gentile regions of Ephesus and Troas: 'I will stay on at Ephesus . . . because a great door for

---

[64] Walton, *Leadership*, 161–2: the *epistrephō* in 1 Thess 1:9 is equivalent to the *metanoia* in Acts 20:21.

[65] Rom 9:27–33; 10:21; 11:7–8, 17–24; Acts 13:44–47; 14:19; 18:6, 12; 19:9–10; 28:28.

[66] Acts 9:20; 13:5, 14; 14:1; 17:2, 10, 17; 18:4, 18; 19:8; 28:17–29.

effective work has opened to me' (1 Cor 16:9); and, 'Now when I went to Troas to preach the gospel of Christ [I] found that the Lord had opened a door for me' (2 Cor 2:12). Probably Paul is referring to his experience of openness among the Gentiles when he visited Troas and Philippi (Acts 16:8, 11–15). In Romans, Paul affirmatively describes the Gentiles as having faith in Christ (Rom 2:14–15, 26–29; 9:25–26; 10:20; 11:20).

On the other hand, using the imagery of an olive tree, Paul explains to the Romans that Jews were broken off because of their unbelief (Rom 11:20, 25). In Romans, Paul repeatedly accuses the Jews of unbelief (Rom 9:30–33; 10:21; 11:7–10, 25) and affirms the faith of the Gentiles. Quoting Deuteronomy 32:21, he explains that the Jews are made jealous by the Gentiles who, though once outside God's blessing, now enjoy the blessing of salvation (Rom 10:19; 11:11, 14).

The accounts in Acts give us a similar picture. Luke also contrasts the faith of the Gentiles and the unbelief of the Jews (Acts 13:44–50; 14:2, 14–19; 17:4, 12; 18:8, 16; 19:9). The Lucan Paul also proves the unbelief of the Jews from the Scriptures, and makes harsh comments (Acts 13:41, 46, 51; 18:6; 28:25–29), just as Paul does in Romans (Rom 2:17–29; 9:27–29; 10:21; 11:7–9). As Paul does in Romans, so Luke writes that the Jews became jealous: 'When the Jews saw the [Gentile] crowds, they were filled with jealousy and talked abusively against what Paul was saying' (Acts 13:45; Rom 10:19; 11:14). When a large number of Gentiles believed Paul's preaching in Thessalonica (1 Thess 1:6), the Jews again became jealous and agitated the crowds, not only in Thessalonica but also in Berea (Acts 17:4–5, 13). It is a common occurrence in Acts that the Jews opposed Paul's message, and often it was these circumstances that led him to turn to the Gentiles (Acts 13:46–48; 16:6–10; 18:6; 22:21; 26:20; 28:28). On the other hand, the Gentiles welcomed the message, and the Lucan Paul reports the conversion of the Gentiles as a very special work of God (Acts 14:27; 15:3; 21:19; so also Paul: 1 Cor 16:9; 2 Cor 2:12; Col 4:3). Likewise the real Paul affirms that the priority of the soteriological direction in mission has been reversed, so that the fullness of the Gentiles will be accomplished before the salvation of 'all Israel' (Rom 11).[67]

Paul the preacher of the gospel

Now we turn to compare the descriptions of Paul and Luke in their presentation of Paul as the preacher of the gospel. We will pay attention to Paul's confidence in his call, to his mission to the Jews, despite a very clear awareness of his call to the Gentiles, and to some other minor topics.

---

[67] See Chae, *Paul*, 251–3, for further explanation.

Confidence in his call to preach the gospel

Paul was fully aware that he had been specifically called and sent to preach the gospel: 'For Christ did not send me to baptise, but to preach the gospel' (1 Cor 1:17); 'I am compelled to preach. Woe to me if I do not preach the gospel [*euangelizomai*]' (1 Cor 9:16; also Gal 1:16). So he had devoted himself to the preaching of the gospel wherever he went (1 Cor 15:1–2; Gal 1:6–9, 11, 23), and he was still planning to do so (Rom 1:15; 15:23–24; 2 Cor 10:16). Luke also frequently uses the verb *euangelizomai* to describe Paul's missionary work.[68] Both Paul and Luke also employ the verb *kēryssō* to describe Paul's evangelistic ministry.[69] Another term that is common to Paul and Luke is *katangellō*.[70] Luke uses these three verbs, which are the most important terms which Paul uses to describe his apostolic ministry.

Luke also portrays Paul as clearly conscious of his call to preach the gospel: 'I consider my life worth nothing to me, if only I may finish the race and complete the task the Lord Jesus has given me – the task of testifying to the gospel of God's grace' (Acts 20:24; cf. 9:15; 22:15; 26:16–18). And the gospel of God's grace is a main theme of Paul's letter to the Romans.[71] The Lucan Paul was aware that the vision of a Macedonian was given to him to preach the gospel to the Macedonians, and so he spoke the word of the Lord in that region (Acts 16:10, 13, 32).

A Jewish apostle to the Gentiles

Paul was aware of his specific task to preach the gospel to the Gentiles: he was an apostle to the Gentiles.[72] At the same time he had a fundamental concern for his own people (Rom 9:1–5; 10:1; 11:14), and so he worked hard to be like a Jew in order to preach the gospel to the Jews (1 Cor 9:19–23). Although he insists on the equality of Jew and Gentile,[73] he was conscious that the gospel was 'to the Jew *especially*, but equally to the Gentile' (Rom 1:16, JNT).[74] Paul affirms that the people of Israel were the first fruits, the root of the olive tree (Rom 11:16, 17–20, 24), and so acknowledges their advantages (Rom 3:1–2; 9:1–5). Paul often stresses his own Jewishness (2 Cor 11:22;

---

[68] Rom 1:15; 10:15; 15:20; 1 Cor 1:17; 9:16, 18; 15:1, 2; 2 Cor 10:16; 11:7; Gal 1:8, 9, 11, 16, 23; 4:13; Acts 14:7, 15, 21; 15:35; 16:10; 17:18.

[69] Rom 16:25; 1 Cor 1:23; 9:27; 15:11–12; 2 Cor 1:19; 4:5; 11:4; Gal 2:2; 5:11; Col 1:23; 1 Thess 2:9; Acts 9:20; 20:25; 28:31.

[70] 1 Cor 2:1; 9:14; Phil 1:17–18; Col 1:28; Acts 15:36; 16:17; 17:3, 13; 26:23.

[71] So correctly, Wright, *Was Paul of Tarsus*, 110.

[72] Gal 1:15–16; 2:7–8; Rom 1:5; 11:13; 15:15–16; 1 Cor 1:17; 9:16; cf. Acts 9:15; 13:46–47; 18:6; 22:17–21; 26:16–18; 28:28; 1 Tim 2:7.

[73] Rom 3:9–20, 22; 10:12–13; 1 Cor 12:13; Gal 3:28; Col 3:11.

[74] Rom 1:16; 2:9, 10; Acts 13:26, 46; cf. Acts 3:26. See Chae, *Paul*, 46–51, for the support of this translation of Rom 1:16.

Phil 3:6), and calls the Jews 'my people', 'my brothers', 'my fathers', 'my own race', 'my kinsmen', and refers to 'our father' Abraham/Isaac (Rom 4:1; 9:3, 10; 11:1; 16:7, 11, 21; Gal 1:14).

The Lucan Paul also underlines his Jewish roots, and addresses the Jews as 'my brothers', 'our fathers' and 'our people'.[75] According to Luke, it was Paul's custom to go first into the synagogue in towns he visited, where he preached the gospel by expounding the Scriptures.[76] Paul also emphasizes that the gospel is the fulfilment of the Scriptures (Rom 1:1–4; 1 Cor 15:1–4; Gal 3:8). It seems obvious then that he should go first to those Jews who knew the Scriptures, and that the good news of the arrival of the Messiah should be proclaimed first to those who had been waiting for him to come. In Romans alone Paul makes fifty-three citations from the Old Testament in order to persuade both the Jews and the Gentiles in Rome of his presentation of the gospel, but the Jews should be impressed most, for they would know and accept the authority of the Scriptures.

One should not assume therefore that Luke is incorrect in portraying Paul the apostle to the Gentiles as going into the synagogues first. 'Of all the New Testament writers, it is Luke who offers the closest parallels to the Pauline formula "the Jew first (*prōton*), then the Greek"'.[77] The *prōton* in Acts 3:26 and 13:46 is often understood as referring to the priority of presenting the gospel to the Jews, and to Paul's missionary principle of reaching Jews first before he approached Gentiles.[78] Of course, Paul knew from the Old Testament, especially from his understanding of Abraham's justification (Rom 1:16–17; 4:1–25; 9:15, 25–26; 10:11–13, 20; Gal 3:15–25), that it was legitimate to turn to the Gentiles. 'Understand, then,' writes Paul, 'that those who believe are children of Abraham. The Scripture foresaw that God would justify the Gentiles by faith, and announced the gospel in advance to Abraham: "All nations will be blessed through you"' (Gal 3:7–8). It seems most probable that Paul maintained that he had to speak the word of God to the Jews first, but when they rejected it, he turned to the Gentiles, as Luke records (Acts 13:46–47; 18:6; 28:23–28; Isa 49:6; cf. Eph 3:6).

Nevertheless, Paul does not condone or rationalize the unbelief of the Jews. Some have argued that for Paul the hardening of the Jews is not in vain; rather it serves God's salvific plan for the blessing of salvation to reach the Gentiles: 'Israel's blindness is not in vain, but participates in the divine project of universally manifesting the riches of the divine glory (cf. [Rom] 9.23) . . . If Israel is temporarily "disobedient and rebellious" (10.20), it is for the

---

[75] Acts 13:26, 31, 32, 38; 22:1; 23:1, 6; 26:4, 17; 28:17, 19.
[76] Acts 13:5, 14; 14:1; 17:1–3, 10, 17; 18:4, 19; 19:8; 28:17, 23.
[77] Butticaz, 'Salvation', 160.
[78] Butticaz, 'Salvation', 160.

benefit of the gentiles'.[79]

The use of the Old Testament

Paul reminds the Corinthians that the gospel he preached was 'that Christ died for our sins according to the Scriptures, that he was buried, that he was raised on the third day according to the Scriptures' (1 Cor 15:3–4). The Lucan Paul preaches:

> The people of Jerusalem and their rulers did not recognise Jesus, yet in condemning him *they fulfilled the words of the prophets* that are read every Sabbath. Though they found no proper ground for a death sentence, they asked Pilate to have him executed. When they had carried out *all that was written about him*, they took him down from the tree and laid him in a tomb. But God raised him from the dead . . . *What God promised our fathers he has fulfilled for us*, their children, by raising up Jesus (Acts 13:27–30, 32–33).

Then he quotes Psalm 2:7, Isaiah 55:3 and Psalm 16:10 to prove and affirm the resurrection of Jesus Christ (Acts 13:33–37).

Luke also writes that after arriving in Rome Paul 'explained and declared to them [the Jews] the kingdom of God and tried to convince them about Jesus *from the Law of Moses and from the Prophets*' (Acts 28:23). Luke shows that Paul quotes the Scriptures to them to explain the gospel to the Jewish audience. On the following occasions when he preaches in the synagogues, he just briefly mentions, 'he reasoned . . . from the Scriptures, explaining and proving [from the Scriptures] that the Christ had to suffer and rise from the dead' (Acts 17:2–3, 10, 17; 18:4–5; 19:8). In this regard it is to be noted that the real Paul also quotes the Scriptures most in Romans as he presents his argument primarily to Jews.[80]

In further correlation, both the Paul of Acts and the Paul of the letters use the Old Testament to describe the Jewish rejection, and the Gentile welcome, of the gospel. After seeing the rejection of his message by the Jews, the Lucan Paul condemns the unbelief of the Jews by quoting Isaiah 6:9–10. Then he declares, 'Therefore I want you to know that God's salvation has been sent to the Gentiles, and they will listen!' (Acts 28:28). The rejection by the Jews and the welcome by the Gentiles are general patterns when the Lucan Paul preaches the gospel (Acts 13:40–41, 48–49; 14:2, 19; 17:5, 12; 18:6; 19:9), and he understands this phenomenon as the fulfilment of the Scriptures (Acts 13:46–47; 18:6; 28:28). In his first and last recorded sermons to the Jews, the

---

[79] Butticaz, 'Salvation', 160–61; so also Wright, *Messiah*, 173, 308 n. 21; Watson, *Paul*, 169; see my critique in Chae, *Paul*, 260–62.

[80] Out of Paul's 88 quotations, 53 of them are cited in Romans alone: see Chae, *Paul*, 13–14, 30–32, and many more.

Lucan Paul uses four quotations to explain the gospel, and one more to legitimize his turning to the Gentiles (Acts 13:33–47; 28:26–28). His use of the Old Testament 'only makes sense in the light of a concern to justify Gentile mission'.[81] He is convinced that his gospel and mission to the Gentiles are nothing beyond what the Scriptures said (Acts 24:14–15; 26:22–23; 28:23).

The real Paul explains the same response by citing many Old Testament passages, especially in Romans.[82] He sets out that the gospel he preaches is the good news that God had 'promised beforehand through his prophets in the Holy Scriptures regarding his Son' (Rom 1:2–3: cf. Luke 24:44–47).

He then quotes the passages which favourably affirm that the Gentiles are included in God's salvation as they welcome the gospel message (Rom 9:25–26; 10:20). He also cites the Old Testament to explain the rejection of the Jews as the fulfilment of the Scriptures (Rom 9:27–29; 10:21). In Romans 11:8 Paul quotes Deuteronomy 29:4 and Isaiah 29:10 to affirm the unbelief of the Jews, and the Lucan Paul does the same with a very similar accusation from Isaiah 6:9–10 (Acts 28:25–27). Paul also says that because of this transgression in rejecting the gospel, salvation has come to the Gentiles (Rom 11:11). For Paul, the inclusion of the Gentiles in the salvific blessing of God is the fulfilment of the Scriptures (Rom 15:9–12), and it is to be noted that the one word that appears in all four quotations is 'Gentiles' ($ethn\bar{e}$).[83] Both the Paul of Romans and the Paul of Acts are in agreement that the gospel should be preached to the Jews first but that when it was rejected by them it had gone to the Gentiles (Rom 11:25–26). In this regard Luke's portrayal of Paul's use of the Old Testament is highly reliable.

R.B. Hays also arrives at the same conclusion. Adopting a method of '*hermeneutical* comparison', he investigated the cited passages in Acts intertextually to see whether the Lucan Paul and the real Paul cite the Old Testament texts similarly or divergently. Hays does not offer textual comparisons but rather comparison of the way the two writers are interpreting the OT Scriptures. After investigating some key passages, Hays concludes: 'The theology of Acts can be seen as an organic outgrowth of the Pauline tradition that maintains its roots in at least some of Paul's characteristic themes and concerns.'[84]

Paul's missionary work as the activity of God

Luke often writes that the missionary work of Paul is the activity of God or of the Holy Spirit.[85] Paul's conversion and call to missionary work were

---

[81] Bock, 'Use of the Old Testament', 510.
[82] Chae, *Paul, passim*.
[83] See further Chae, *Paul*, 58–66.
[84] Hays, 'Paulinism of Acts', 36, 37, 47.
[85] Walton, 'The Acts – of God?', 291–306; Turner, *Holy Spirit*, 38, 172-174, 204.

clearly initiated by the Lord Jesus (Acts 9:3–16). Luke also records that it was the Holy Spirit who spoke to the church in Antioch to 'set apart for me Barnabas and Saul for the work to which I have called them' (Acts 13:2), and who continues to guide Paul's steps (Acts 22:17–21). Paul performs miracles by the power of the Spirit, who opens the hearts of people to believe (Acts 13:9–12; 14:8–18). The Lucan Paul's message is what God has done in Christ Jesus: 'God has brought to Israel the Saviour Jesus, as he promised' (Acts 13:23). Although the Jews and Romans crucified him, 'God raised him from the dead' (Acts 13:30, 32, 34, 37). 'What God promised our fathers, he has fulfilled for us' (Acts 13:32). Paul reports that his missionary work is 'all that God had done through them and how he had opened the door of faith to the Gentiles' (Acts 14:27; 15:4, 12). Luke perceived that Paul's missionary work had been carried out by God through the missionaries.

Luke continues to report that during the second missionary journey the Holy Spirit actively intervened to guide Paul by closing the doors of ministry, and then eventually led them to Macedonia through a vision (Acts 16:6–10). Thus Luke writes, 'The Lord opened her [Lydia's] heart to respond to Paul's message' (Acts 16:14). The Lord appears to Paul in a vision to strengthen him to keep on preaching in Corinth and in Rome (Acts 18:9–10; 23:11; 27:23–24). The Lucan Paul says that, compelled by the Spirit, he goes to Jerusalem (Acts 20:22).

The real Paul also says that it is God who is actually at work in his missionary endeavour. He is conscious that it was God who called him to be an apostle, and that it is God who saves people through the foolishness of what he preaches, and so any boasting can only be in the Lord and within the limits which the Lord has assigned (1 Cor 1:1, 21, 31; 2 Cor 10:13). The gospel is what '[God] promised beforehand through his prophets in the Holy Scriptures regarding his Son' (Rom 1:2). Now God has revealed a righteousness apart from the law as the Law and the Prophets testify (Rom 3:21–22). It is God who poured out his love into our hearts by the Holy Spirit (Rom 5:5). 'It is God who justifies', and God who hardens some people or has mercy on others (Rom 8:33; 9:10–29; 11:8–10). God called Paul and gave him the ministry to preach the gospel to the Gentiles (Rom 15:15–16; 1 Cor 3:10), and he testifies, 'I will not venture to speak of anything except what Christ has accomplished through me in leading the Gentiles to obey God by what I have said and done' (Rom 15:18; cf. Acts 14:27).

So Paul acknowledges God as the main agent of his missionary work. Only God makes the seed grow, and 'we are God's fellow-workers; you are God's field, God's building, God's temple' (see 1 Cor 3:5–9, 16; 2 Cor 6:1; 1 Thess 3:2). God revealed Christ to Paul to call him, and gave him more 'visions and revelations from the Lord' (Gal 1:15–16; 1 Cor 9:1; 2 Cor 12:1–4; Acts 9:1–9; 16:6–10; 18:9–10; 22:6–11, 17–21). He begins a good work in those who trust in him (Phil 1:3–6). Paul has experienced God giving his

Spirit to new believers when they believe and working miracles among them (Gal 3:5). Even from this brief examination it is clear that Luke presents a compatible account with Paul's own in describing Paul's missionary work as the activity of God.

Miracles accompanied Paul's preaching

That Paul's preaching was accompanied by miracles is abundantly shown in both accounts.[86] E. Haenchen lists the miracles as the first of his three items in dismissing the credibility of the accounts in Acts. He contends that Luke portrays Paul as a miracle worker[87] when the real Paul is not really, and he gives only one reference, 2 Corinthians 12:12. Haenchen unduly ignores Paul's summarizing statements about his ministry accompanied by signs and miracles. Paul reminds the Corinthians: 'My message and my preaching were not with wise and persuasive words, but with a demonstration of the Spirit's power' (1 Cor 2:4; also 2 Cor 12:12). 'Our gospel came to you not simply with words, but also with power, with the Holy Spirit and with deep conviction' (1 Thess 1:5). In Galatia, too, God worked miracles when the Galatians believed what they heard (Gal 3:1–5). So Paul sums up to the Romans that his missionary work was done 'by the power of signs and miracles, through the power of the Spirit' (Rom 15:18–19). Paul portrays himself as a miracle worker.

Luke portrays the apostle in the same way, and even provides us with some specific stories of the miracles demonstrated during Paul's missionary work. Right at the beginning of his first missionary journey, Paul made Elymas the sorcerer blind (Acts 13:9–11). Luke reports that the Lord confirmed Paul's message by enabling him to do miraculous signs and wonders (Acts 14:3, 8–10). So the Lucan Paul reports at the Jerusalem conference the miracles that God has done among the Gentiles (Acts 15:12). Paul cast out an evil spirit from a slave girl in Philippi, and he and Silas were released from prison by a violent earthquake (Acts 16:16–18, 25–36). Luke simply reports that God did extraordinary miracles through Paul in Ephesus (Acts 19:11–12).

Comparing Paul's missionary preaching in specific regions

Finally, we now turn to examine Paul's missionary preaching in Corinth, Thessalonica and Galatia as recorded in Acts 13 – 20 by comparing it with the material written in Paul's letters to the churches in those regions. Luke describes Paul's missionary preaching in these regions, while Paul writes the letters to the churches in those regions to provide them with further teaching or to resolve particular issues. Thus it may shed light for us to discern the compatibility of Paul's preaching as recorded in the respective letters and in

---

[86] *Pace* Haenchen, *Acts*, 113–14.
[87] Acts 13:6–12, 14; 14:8–10, 19–20; 19:12; 20:7–12; 28:3–6, 7–9.

Acts. We shall then compare the Lucan Paul's speech to the elders of the Ephesian church with what Paul writes in the letters.

Paul's preaching in Corinth

From Paul's letters to the Corinthians we can note that the death and resurrection of Christ was the main topic of his preaching. 'Now, brothers, I want to remind you of the gospel I preached to you . . . as of first importance,' writes Paul to the Corinthians, 'that Christ died for our sins according to the Scriptures, that he was buried, that he was raised on the third day according to the Scriptures' (1 Cor 15:1–4). He preached the death and resurrection of Christ, giving this top priority as the most important message of all. He explained the fact and significance of Christ's death, burial and resurrection as the fulfilment of the Scriptures (1 Cor 15:3–8). He also points out that during his missionary work in Corinth he testified that God raised Christ from the dead (1 Cor 15:15, 20). However, Paul does not give even a summary of his messages revealing how he presented the death and resurrection of Christ *according to the Scriptures*. What the Lucan Paul presents in Pisidian Antioch is something very close to it. Here he preaches and proves the death, burial and resurrection of Jesus as the fulfilment of the Scriptures, by quoting the relevant verses of the Old Testament (Acts 13:27–36).

The Lucan Paul often reasons with the Jews in Corinth, trying to persuade them that Jesus is the Christ (Acts 18:4–5, 19). Paul also reminds them that he has been preaching the crucified Christ as the power and the wisdom of God (1 Cor 1:23–25), and as the Son of God and Lord (2 Cor 1:19; 4:5). He preached this gospel first to the Jews and also to the Gentiles (1 Cor 1:23–25; 9:19–23). Luke briefly sums up Paul's ministry in Corinth for a year and a half with a short statement that 'Paul devoted himself exclusively to preaching, testifying to the Jews that Jesus was the Christ' (Acts 18:5–6). The real Paul also testifies that he 'resolved to know nothing while I was with you except Jesus Christ and him crucified' (1 Cor 2:1–2).

According to Luke the Jews opposed Paul for 'persuading the people to worship God in ways contrary to the law' (Acts 18:13). From Paul's letters to the Corinthians, we find some references that indicate that Paul may have caused trouble among the Jews in Corinth. For example, Paul makes it clear that he himself was not under the law, although to those under the law he became like one under the law. Rather, he became like one not having the law in order to win the Gentiles (1 Cor 9:20–21). Furthermore, he had this principle made applicable to all the churches: Gentile converts were not to be circumcised, for circumcision is nothing, just as uncircumcision is nothing (1 Cor 7:17–19). It is most probable that if the law-observing Jews saw this attitude and practice, they would have certainly opposed him.

Paul's preaching in Thessalonica

Although Luke's record of Paul's missionary work in Thessalonica is very brief, he sums up that Paul reasoned in the synagogue 'from the Scriptures, explaining and proving that the Christ had to suffer and rise from the dead' (Acts 17:3). Since expounding the death and resurrection of Jesus from the Scriptures was Paul's most important way of explaining the gospel (1 Cor 15:1–8), it seems most probable that Paul preached during his missionary work in Thessalonica just as Luke sums up. Just as he would do later in Corinth, he was determined to know nothing except Jesus Christ and him crucified (1 Cor 2:1–2). The Christological title 'Christ' occurs nineteen times in the letters to the Thessalonians. The fact that Paul uses it without explanation in his letters to the Thessalonians suggests that he has sufficiently explained it during his missionary work there. 'This Jesus I am proclaiming to you is the Christ' (Acts 17:3), declares the Lucan Paul in Thessalonica. Thus one can accept Luke's summary of Paul's preaching in Thessalonica as credible, or, at the very least, compatible with Paul's own statements.

Both Paul and Luke report that the apostle was severely persecuted in Thessalonica. Paul reminds the converts that 'With the help of our God we dared to tell you his gospel in spite of strong opposition' (1 Thess 2:2, 8, 9), and the gospel was that 'he died for us', so that we might 'receive salvation through our Lord Jesus Christ' (1 Thess 5:9–10). Paul reminds the Thessalonians that he faced strong opposition in preaching the gospel (1 Thess 1:6; 2:2), and what Luke describes is most probably the nature of the opposition (Acts 17:1–9).[88]

Paul's preaching in Galatia

In his letter to the Galatians, Paul makes a few brief statements that he preached the gospel of Jesus Christ, or Christ, or Jesus as the Son of God (Gal 1:7, 8, 11, 16, 20). In Galatians 3:1–5 Paul refreshes their memory concerning what he preached, and there he writes, 'Before your very eyes Jesus was clearly portrayed as crucified' (Gal 3:1). Furthermore, he declares that he would never boast except in the cross of Christ (Gal 6:14; so also in 1 Cor 2:2). These statements clearly indicate that Paul was, just as in Corinth, determined to know nothing except Jesus Christ and him crucified.

We have already argued that the fact that Paul writes so vigorously about the implications of the law-free gospel in Galatians suggests that he did not explain it clearly while he was in Galatia. That was one of the reasons why the agitators persuaded his converts so quickly (cf. Gal 1:6). Now in the letter his emphasis is shifted to the gospel of justification by faith *apart from the law* (cf. Gal 2:16; 3:11), but while he was in Galatia he preached the gospel

---

[88] See Riesner, *Paul's Early Period*, 337–51, for an excellent treatment of Luke's credibility in his account of the founding of the church in Thessalonica.

of justification by faith in the death and resurrection of Jesus Christ (cf. 1 Cor 6:11).

We find that Luke's report on Paul's evangelistic work during his first missionary journey seems compatible with Paul's own.[89] Luke also writes that Paul proclaimed the word of God (Acts 13:5, 8; 15:35, 36). The Lucan Paul was persuading the Jews by explaining the death and resurrection of Jesus from the Scriptures: 'yet in condemning him they fulfilled the words of the prophets'; 'when they had carried out all that was written about him, they took him down from the tree and laid him in a tomb. But God raised him from the dead' (Acts 13:27, 29–30). The Lucan Paul quotes the Scriptures in an attempt to prove the resurrection of Jesus (Acts 13:33–35). Then he concludes: 'Therefore, my brothers, I want you to know that through Jesus the forgiveness of sins is proclaimed to you. Through him everyone who believes is justified from everything you could not be justified from by the law of Moses' (Acts 13:38–39).

Certainly the Lucan Paul mentions here justification by faith, and that the law was impotent to bring forgiveness of sins. However, he is not stressing justification *apart from the law*. Rather, it is justification by faith *in the death and resurrection of Jesus* that is stressed in this particular preaching as a whole. As we noted above, this might well be the better emphasis in conveying the true tone and nature of Paul's preaching during the first missionary journey, visiting Antioch, Iconium, Lystra and Derbe.[90] Later in the letter the real Paul stresses that in Christ everyone is equal, because justification is open to everyone, regardless of ethnic or social background (Gal 3:26–29; Rom 1:16–17). The Lucan Paul's vocabulary in Acts 13:38–39 is quite similar to what Paul uses in Romans 3:20–26 and Galatians 2:15–16.[91] The Lucan Paul preaches the same thing: 'Through him *everyone* who believes is justified' (Acts 13:39; 16:31), and this was why he preached to both the Jews and the Gentiles, as we read in Acts. Justification through faith in Jesus is certainly fundamental in Paul's preaching.[92]

The brief survey above shows that (1) both Paul and Luke portray the apostle as a prominent preacher of the gospel with a clear sense of calling and determination to fulfil his task, and that (2) Paul's most important message during his missionary work in the regions of Corinth, Thessalonica and Galatia was the death and resurrection of Jesus, a message which he preached boldly to Jews and Gentiles. Furthermore, the key point of Paul's preaching is to reveal

---

[89] Here we follow the South Galatian theory; see below, pp. 126–30.
[90] *Pace* Schweizer, 'Concerning the Speeches', 214, who asserts that the remark on justification described in Acts 13:38–39 is given 'in a very un-Pauline way'.
[91] Bruce, 'St Luke's Portrait', 189.
[92] Rom 3:20–21, 28; 5:1; 9:33; 10:9, 13; 1 Cor 6:11; Gal 2:16; 3:11; Eph 2:8–9; Phil 3:9.

the long-hidden mystery that all Gentiles might believe and obey Christ Jesus (Rom 16:25–26). Paul writes to different churches, proclaiming that the salvation of the Gentiles is the nature of this mystery (Eph 3:5–12; Col 1:25–27). This mystery was revealed to him not only by knowledge but also through the experience of leading Gentiles to believe in Jesus and teaching them to obey him. Luke, therefore, seems to identify accurately that the main source of excitement in Paul's ministry was the salvation of the Gentiles: he repeatedly mentions that Paul 'reported [how God] had opened the door of faith to the *Gentiles*' (Acts 14:27; so also 15:3, 12). This corresponds to what the real Paul says: 'I will not venture to speak of anything except what Christ has accomplished through me in leading the *Gentiles* to obey God by what I have said and done – by the power of signs and miracles, through the power of the Spirit' (Rom 15:18–19).

Paul's follow-up speech to the Ephesian elders

Finally, we turn to compare the Lucan Paul's speech to the Ephesian elders in Acts 20:17–38 with the letters. It is the only speech in Acts that clearly has the same character and content as Paul's letters. Like the letters, it takes the form of a piece of pastoral follow-up teaching given to the Christians.[93] In this respect this passage might contain some of the characteristics of the letters, which may affirm Luke's credibility. So S. Walton is methodologically right in his attempt to compare the Lucan Paul's speech to the Ephesian elders in Acts 20:18–36 with Paul's letters, as that speech has the same purpose as a *follow-up* address to the *Christians*.[94]

The Lucan Paul starts his speech by reminding them of his lifestyle: 'You know how I lived the whole time I was with you' (Acts 20:18). This reminder style is typical of Paul, as seen in the letters when he addresses those whom he taught previously.[95] Then, from his own examples, he makes an indirect exhortation. We can find numerous cross-references from Paul's letters. He reminds them of his humility, tears, Jewish persecution, and hard work.[96] He

---

[93] The speech is often claimed as historical. Gardner's claim (1909) is affirmatively quoted in Bruce, *Acts: Greek*, 437: The speech 'at Miletus has the best claim of all to be historic'; similarly, Marshall, *Acts*, 330; Barrett, 'Paul's Address', 111. For the genre and the purpose of the speech, see Dibelius, *Studies in the Acts*, 155–8, but see Hemer, 'Speeches of Acts', 78–82, for an opposite view. See also Hemer's *Book of Acts*, 425–6, for a discussion of Pauline linguistic, biographical and theological features in the speech.

[94] Walton, *Leadership*, 1, 140–85; also Hemer, 'Speeches of Acts', 77; Marshall, 'Luke's View of Paul', 47; Keener, *Acts*, 1:313–16.

[95] See above, pp. 50–59.

[96] Humility: Acts 20:19; 1 Cor 2:3; 2 Cor 10:1; 11:7; Phil 2:3; Col 3:12; 1 Thess 2:6–9; Eph 4:2; tears: Acts 20:19, 31; Rom 9:2; 2 Cor 2:4; Phil 3:18; persecution:

further mentions his life goal (Acts 20:24; 2 Cor 5:14–15; Gal 2:20) and his planned journey to Jerusalem (Acts 20:22–23; 21:4, 11; Rom 15:30–32; 1 Cor 16:4). Most of all, the Lucan Paul reminds his hearers of his fervent evangelism among both Jews and Gentiles (Acts 20:20–21; 1 Cor 9:19–23; 10:32) by preaching the gospel of the grace of God (Acts 20:24; Rom 3:24; 4:16; 5:15–21; Eph 2:4–9).[97]

Then Paul turns to direct exhortations on pastoral care. The congregation is described as a flock (Acts 20:28–29; 1 Cor 9:7), and as the church of God (Acts 20:28; 1 Cor 1:2; 10:32; 11:16, 22; 15:9; Gal 1:13) which is purchased with the blood of Jesus (Acts 20:28; Rom 3:25; 5:9; 1 Cor 6:20; Eph 1:7).[98] He warns of fierce wolves even from their own number (Acts 20:29; 2 Cor 10 – 13), and thus he gives them a solemn charge to be on their guard (Acts 20:30–31; 1 Cor 10:12; 16:13; 1 Thess 5:6). From this speech we can detect many Pauline themes, languages and tones, which, in turn, indicate that Luke's account of this speech displays a high degree of accuracy.[99]

Conclusion

Despite the different nature and scope of the two accounts, they show overwhelming correspondence when comparing Paul's missionary preaching in Acts and the letters. That Paul was very conscious of his role as a preacher of the gospel of Christ to both Jews and Gentiles is absolutely clear in the letters and Acts. Both the real Paul and the Lucan Paul are shown as preaching the same content of the gospel, and the details of his preaching, especially in Corinth, Thessalonica and Galatia, and of the responses from Jews and Gentiles, are highly compatible in both accounts.

It is not plausible, therefore, to deny the reliability of Luke's account by underestimating such a vast volume of correspondence, and then by highlighting the 'differences' which are inferred largely due to the silence on

---

Acts 20:19b; 1 Cor 16:9; 2 Cor 11:24–26; 1 Thess 2:14–16; hard work: Acts 20:33–34; 1 Cor 4:12; 9:6; 2 Cor 2:17; 11:7–11; 12:13–17; 1 Thess 2:9; 2 Thess 3:7–10.

[97] So correctly, Wright, *Was Paul of Tarsus*, 110, who understands *the gospel of the grace of God* as a main theme of Romans.

[98] Conzelmann, *Theology of Luke*, 201, is of the opinion that this phrase reveals Luke's effort 'to give the speech a Pauline stamp'. But for an opposite view, see Moule, 'Christology of Acts', 171, and Bruce, *Acts: Greek*, 434.

[99] Witherington, *Acts*, 610–11; Barrett, 'Paul's Address', 116–17. Both Witherington and Barrett have compiled their own catalogue of numerous parallels between Paul's letters and the Miletus speech, and both of them notice a high level of compatibility between the two accounts. However, Witherington rightly finds a typical Pauline pastoral speech here, whereas Barrett asserts that the speech was composed by a later Paulinist.

Paul's part on certain matters in the letters. Again we must remember that most of Paul's letters were from the second chronological part of his teaching; the first part was given orally during his missionary work in the cities. We must also remember that Luke is covering Paul's initial *missionary* work to convert his audience, and that in his letters Paul is concerned with *pastoral* issues for the converted, without repeating much of what he had taught earlier. Despite these elements, the compatibility of the two accounts is much more justified than some modern sceptical scholarship has allowed. We have demonstrated that the degree of their correspondence is sufficient for us to contend that Luke's portrayal of the apostle Paul is highly reliable.[100] This also can mean, in turn, that Luke's accounts can be used to fill in gaps in the letters,[101] and that they witness to the true credibility of Paul's accounts as well, despite rhetorical and retrospective elements.[102]

---

[100] So also Witherington, *Acts*, 430–438. *Pace* Goodenough, 'Perspective', 58, who asserts that 'no one in the Galatian or Corinthian churches would have recognized in the pages of Acts the Paul they had heard preach or had read in his letters'.

[101] For example, Acts 10 – 11 provides an explanation for how Peter could be accustomed 'to eat with . . . Gentiles' in the first place (Gal 2:12).

[102] Sometimes the testimony of a witness carries more weight than that of the person concerned. The retrospective and rhetorical nature of Paul's letters does not serve well in reconstructing his life and ministry: Gager, 'Some Notes', 699; Watson, *Paul*, 53–6; Taylor, *Paul*, 62; Betz, *Galatians*, 81; Räisänen, *Paul and the Law*, 232.

3

Understanding the Discrepancies

Now we shall look at certain apparent discrepancies which seem to undermine the correspondence between Paul as presented in his letters and Paul as portrayed by Luke in the book of Acts. While some scholars have compared Paul's letters and Acts by using a theological approach, others have adopted a literary approach. Both have concluded that there are discrepancies in the accounts. They assert that the information Paul provides in his letters must present an accurate portrayal of Paul, and therefore question the accuracy of the account given by Luke in Acts.

The first discrepancy is based on those topics on which, separately, Luke and Paul are silent. Luke is silent about Paul's visit to Arabia and does not mention him as a letter–writer. He hardly writes anything on the collection of gifts for the saints in Jerusalem, unlike Paul who writes at length about it.[1] Luke does not say that Paul saw the Lord at his encounter with the risen Jesus but says that Paul *heard* a voice, while the real Paul repeatedly claims that he has *seen* the Lord. Equally, Paul is silent on some points: he does not acknowledge the Jerusalem decree in his letters, while Luke reports its full text and context, stating that Paul actively uses it to support his cause. Furthermore, unlike the Paul of Acts (Acts 16:37; 22:25–29; 23:27; 25:10), the real Paul does not comment on whether he has Roman citizenship or not.

The second discrepancy is related to Paul's Jewishness. Luke portrays Paul as a law-observing Jew, who preaches to the Jews first even during his mission in the Gentile world. The Paul of the letters, however, is seen as upholding the law-free gospel as he is clearly conscious of his mission to the Gentiles. The third discrepancy relates to chronology. Luke writes that Paul visited Jerusalem three times up to the time of the apostolic council, while Paul mentions only two visits. The fourth discrepancy concerns Paul's relationship with Jerusalem. Knox's critical judgement of Luke's account as unreliable is largely based on the nature of Paul's relationship with Jerusalem. So we shall investigate each of these discrepancies.

---

[1] Johnson, *Acts*, 6.

The Silent Topics of Luke and of Paul

In his letter to the Galatians Paul says that he went to Arabia immediately after his conversion and later returned to Damascus (Gal 1:17). He does not say anything about the reason for this journey or about his activity during his time in Arabia. He writes, '*later* [I] returned to Damascus. *Then after three years* I went up to Jerusalem' (Gal 1:17–18). Although it is not clear whether he means that he stayed in Arabia for three years, it is often understood this way. Luke, however, is completely silent about Paul's sojourn in Arabia. The exact location of 'Arabia' in the first century is uncertain, but is commonly believed to be the Nabatean territory south-east of Damascus.[2] Paul may have gone to Petra, the capital of the Nabatean kingdom, if he went there to preach the newly found gospel, or to the wilderness if he went to meditate on the implications of the revelation he had received from the risen Christ.[3] The total silence from both Paul and Luke on Paul's activity in Arabia suggests that preaching was not the main activity there.[4] Luke's silence about 'Arabia' does not necessarily prove his unreliability as an author since the omission of some information is normal in any biography,[5] just as one cannot argue that Luke's account is unreliable because he does not mention Titus at all in Acts.

What is more likely is that Paul had an extended time of solitude, meditation and study on God's plan for the redemption of humanity prompted by his unexpected encounter with the risen Christ.[6] Paul had heard Stephen's speech surveying the history of Israel from the new perspectives gained from the events of Christ's life, especially his death and resurrection, and it might have stimulated him to reread the Old Testament. However, the fact that the Nabatean authorities wanted to arrest him (2 Cor 11:32) suggests that he caused some trouble there, and preaching the gospel may have been the reason. It is likely, therefore, that Paul spent most of his time in Arabia in a state of solitude, and that towards the end of this period he began to preach the gospel. Luke's silence should not be taken as disproving his credibility in portraying Paul, as Paul himself hardly says anything about his time in Arabia (cf. Gal 4:25). Furthermore, if Jerusalem is the starting point of Paul's mission to the Gentiles (Rom 15:19), Luke's description of the vision in the

---

[2] Murphy-O'Connor, *Paul*, 81; Kuntz, 'Arabia/Arabians', 63; Wessel, 'Arabia', 86; cf. Riesner, *Paul's Early Period*, 256–9.

[3] Longenecker, *Galatians*, 34; Taylor, *Paul*, 73; Deissmann, *Paul*, 247.

[4] See Riesner, *Paul's Early Period*, 260, 263, who asserts that Jerusalem is the starting point of Paul's mission to the Gentiles (Rom 15:19; Acts 22:17–21).

[5] Hengel and Schwemer, *Paul Between Damascus and Antioch*, 106.

[6] Bowers, 'Studies', 33 n. 1; Riesner, *Paul's Early Period*, 260; Robinson, *Life of Paul*, 59; Burton, *Galatians*, 55–7.

temple in Jerusalem carries more weight (Acts 22:17–21).[7]

Luke is also silent about Paul's letters. Paul was a prolific letter-writer by ancient standards. No fewer than thirteen letters bear his name, but Luke does not mention them at all. Was he unaware of the letters? F.F. Bruce is of the opinion that the epistles, because they were handwritten on parchment, could not be easily copied for the benefit of Paul's companions, and so Luke did not possess copies of the letters and had not read them when he wrote Acts. Paul's letters were collected, copied and canonized only much later.[8] Other scholars contend that Luke, as a companion of Paul, from the second missionary tour until near the end of Paul's time in Rome, must have known that he wrote letters or seen him doing so. Those who take this view offer at least four explanations for Luke's silence on the matter. First, the Tübingen School asserted that Luke knew Paul's letters, but used them as a basis for his narrative only when they contradicted or neutralized whatever did not fit into his own theology and motives. Second, R.I. Pervo contends that Luke knew Paul's letters and used many specific words, phrases and concepts in Acts, but refused to mention Paul as a writer of letters due to the potentially divisive nature of these letters in certain groups.[9] Third, Luke deliberately does not mention or use them since they do not belong to the scope of Acts, that is, presenting Paul's initial missionary work in various cities. In his letters Paul deals with theological and pastoral issues, and gives the churches new teachings, corrections and exhortations. As Luke focuses on the birth, expansion and development of the early churches from Jerusalem to the Gentile regions, he does not need to mention, for example, the theological controversies between Paul and Peter during the Antioch incident. Fourth, Luke may not have seen the need to use Paul's letters, for as a travelling companion he had sufficient material to write Acts.[10]

Of these four suggestions, the first seems the most unlikely. It is surely not correct to infer from Luke's silence an intention to depict Paul differently from how he really was. Though the second seems possible, the third and the fourth ones seem more plausible. Luke may have thought that he had derived sufficient material to write the accounts of Paul's missionary preaching. He collected this material from the apostle himself as he travelled with him and worked with him, and also from Paul's co-workers, such as Timothy and Silas.[11] Just as Paul did not intend to present his own self-portrait, Luke was not writing a biography of Paul.

---

[7] Following Hengel, Riesner, *Paul's Early Period*, 260, 263.
[8] Bruce, 'St Luke's Portrait', 186; similarly Knox, *Chapters*, 23.
[9] Pervo, *Dating Acts*, 51–147, esp. 55, 58; and also Pervo, *Mystery*, 36, 125, 162.
[10] Keener, *Acts*, 1:235.
[11] See Richards' invaluable two volumes, *Paul* and *Secretary*, on the public nature of longer letters in first century letter writing. He asserts that Paul's letters would have been done in as 'public' a forum of his associates as possible.

Luke's relative silence on the money collection which Paul brought to Jerusalem has been noted and compared with the strong emphasis placed on it by the real Paul (1 Cor 16:1–4; 2 Cor 8–10). F.F. Bruce gives a reason for Luke's brief allusion to it: 'Luke knew in retrospect that the collection failed disastrously to achieve Paul's purpose for it in Jerusalem, and deemed it wisest to say as little as possible'.[12] However, this seems unlikely because Luke records that the Jerusalem apostles welcomed Paul and advised him, and that Paul accepted their recommendation (Acts 21:17, 20a, 26). L.T. Johnson notes that there is no word of appreciation from James.[13] One needs to note, however, that Luke does not mention the response of the apostles after receiving the famine relief fund earlier (Acts 11:30; 12:25). It seems quite probable that Luke wanted to let his readers know that the donation was well received by recording the fact that James endeavoured to remove the grave rumours circulating about Paul at that time; James did this by advising him to take part in a purification rite, and Paul followed his recommendation. At any rate, for our immediate purpose, it is to be noted that both Paul and Luke do mention the delivery of the collection for Jerusalem (Rom 15:31; Acts 24:17).

Luke writes that Paul *heard* a voice in all three accounts of the Damascus road experience (Acts 9:4; 22:7; 26:14), while the real Paul insists that he has *seen* the Lord Jesus (1 Cor 9:1; 15:8; cf. Gal 1:12, 16; 2 Cor 12:1–5). For M.S. Enslin, this is 'the most serious difficulty in believing that the picture of Paul drawn in Acts was produced by a friend and companion' of Paul.[14] One needs to notice, however, that the Lucan Paul also *saw the light*: 'suddenly a bright light, brighter than the sun, from heaven flashed around him' (Acts 9:3; 22:6; 26:13). Because of this bright light from heaven he fell to the ground and became blind (Acts 9:8, 12, 17–18; 22:11, 13). In the Bible, light often signifies the presence of the holy God (Pss 4:6; 27:1; 89:15; Isa 9:2). For example, light shines from the face of God (Pss 44:3; 104:1–2), he is surrounded by glowing, radiant and brilliant light (Ezek 1:27–28), and God *is* light (1 John 1:5). God dwells 'in unapproachable light' (1 Tim 6:16). Paul writes that the light and glory of God was 'in the face of Christ' (2 Cor 4:6; cf. John 1:4).

From Paul's perspective, when he sees the light from heaven, especially when it is accompanied by the identified voice of Jesus, he knows he has *seen* the risen Lord Jesus. The fact that Luke mentions that the men travelling with Paul did not see anyone implies that Paul did see someone (Acts 9:7). After all, the Lucan Paul testifies elsewhere that he has *seen* the Lord, who said to him: 'I have appeared to you to appoint you as a servant and as a witness of what you have *seen* of me and what I will show you' (Acts 26:16; cf. 22:14).

---

[12] Bruce, *Acts: Greek*, 52.
[13] Johnson, *Acts*, 6.
[14] Enslin, *Literature*, 418.

Understanding the Discrepancies

This aspect of Luke's description of Paul's Christophany experience should not be used to disprove the reliability of Acts. On the contrary, it shows that the accounts in Acts and those in Paul's letters are compatible, and too much has been made by other writers of the voice-versus-vision dichotomy; in reality the contrast is not as complete as they claim. Paul often talked about his previous life in Judaism and his experience on the Damascus road (Gal 1:13–16; Acts 22:2–16; 26:4–23; cf. Phil 3:4–11; 1 Tim 1:12–14), and so it is most likely that Luke heard Paul's Damascus road testimony from the apostle himself. The correspondences among the accounts within Acts, and also with the information in the letters, outmatch the differences.

Paul is also silent about the decree of the Jerusalem Council, which Luke writes about in some detail. Luke describes Paul delivering this decree vigorously (Acts 15:30; 16:4). It is often argued that the best way for Paul to counter-attack and silence the Judaizers was to produce the Jerusalem decree, or at least to refer to it, as it did not demand that the Gentile believers should keep the Jewish law and practise circumcision. Then why does he not talk about this decree? F.F. Bruce is of the opinion that Paul could not use it because he was not keeping one of the four conditions, namely, to 'abstain from food sacrificed to idols' (Acts 15:29; but see 1 Cor 8:1–13; 10:14–30; Rom 14:14, 20).[15] Bruce's second inference seems to suit better: Paul might have thought it would be counter-productive to appeal to the apostolic authority because he was writing letters when the Judaizers were making such a disturbance among the churches he established.[16] Despite the decision at the Jerusalem Council as described in Galatians 2:7–9, the circumcision party continued their campaign. The decree was a good compromise for Paul and Jewish believers at the time of the apostolic council. However, the decree did not contain the specific decision on the real issue for which the council was originally called. The decision whether or not the Gentile believers should be circumcised was not clearly spelled out in the decree.[17] This seems to have become a real problem later on.

The decree was thus open to interpretation from both sides for their advantage. Paul must have pointed out that it did not require that the Gentile believers should keep the law and be circumcised. The Judaizers, however, could have asserted that the Jerusalem Council did not expressly rule out the requirement of circumcision for the Gentile believers. Thus there was no point for Paul to build his argument on the basis of that decree. We contend that it is likely that this is why he does not mention or use it. Paul's silence

---

[15] Bruce, 'St Luke's Portrait', 184; *idem*, *Acts: Greek*, 50 n. 17.
[16] Bruce, 'St Luke's Portrait', 184.
[17] *Pace* Wilson, *Our Father Abraham*, 50, who asserts that the council gave a clear and definite answer to the issue that was raised. However, see Manson, as in Williams, *Acts*, 29: 'The decrees are the answer to the questions raised in Gal.ii.14; they are not, and cannot be, the answer to the issue raised in Acts xv.1'.

about the decree does not mean that it was drawn up later or at the second conference where Paul was not present,[18] or that he was unaware of it or refused to accept it.[19] A. Loisy inferred that it would not have been possible for Paul, who insists so strongly on his independence from the Jerusalem authority, to accept the decree, the embodiment of apostolic ruling.[20] However, Paul shows he has a good relationship with the Jerusalem leaders (Gal 1:18–19; 2:1–2, 7–9). Especially during the early days of his ministry, Paul maintained close links with the apostles. Thus, there is no reason why we should assume that he had rejected the apostolic decree. At the same time Paul's silence does not necessarily suggest that the decree was Luke's invention.

While the Paul of Acts uses his Roman citizenship to appeal not to be flogged (Acts 16:37–38; 22:23–29), the Paul of the letters does not say whether he has Roman citizenship or not. The fact that he says he had been flogged severely could be taken to suggest that he did not possess such citizenship (2 Cor 6:4–5; 11:23–25).[21] M.E. Thrall offers three possibilities on this issue: (1) Paul did not have Roman citizenship, and so Luke was incorrect; (2) he had such citizenship but the circumstances prevented him from exercising the right of appeal; (3) he had it but chose not to use his legal right.[22] Paul does not explain the circumstances which led to his flogging. According to Luke, Paul's arrests were the result of huge public protests against him (Acts 16:19–23; 19:28–34; 21:30–36). In Acts 16 the Lucan Paul had already been arrested, beaten up and flogged and it was only later that he appealed, using his Roman citizenship. So it is in the case of Acts 21 where Paul had already been beaten. Here, it seems possible that Paul had Roman citizenship,[23] but he could not possibly appeal in the midst of such hostility from an angry mob. Or perhaps he deliberately did not claim it, either to avoid suspicion from his converts who might not appreciate the fact that he was a Roman citizen, or because he did not want to get involved in a lengthy legal process that would prevent him from getting on with his missionary work.[24]

At the trial before Felix, Paul's accusers were powerful individuals, politically, religiously and materially. It would normally be very difficult for

---

[18] *Pace* Wilson, *Gentiles*, 186; Conzelmann, *Acts*, 119; Lüdemann, *Paul*, 72–4.

[19] Longenecker, *Paul, Apostle of Liberty*, 258.

[20] Loisy in Lake, 'Apostolic Council of Jerusalem', 211.

[21] Cf. *pace* Pervo, *Mystery*, 130, 148, for asserting that Paul's Roman citizenship is made up as a literary device.

[22] Thrall, *2 Corinthians 8–13*, 740–42.

[23] Thrall, *2 Corinthians 8–13*, 740–42; Lentz, *Luke's Portrait*, 59–60. Neither of them excludes the possibility of Paul's possession of Roman citizenship. See Riesner, *Paul's Early Period*, 147–56: 'the apostle preferred to portray for his churches his suffering in Christ rather than some privileges of status.'

[24] Thrall, *2 Corinthians 8–13*, 742.

someone like Paul to defend himself against their accusations. The Roman governors obviously showed favour towards the Jewish religious authorities (Acts 24:27; 25:9, 25). However, the fact that Paul did not lose the case seems to suggest that it was due to his only advantage, his Roman citizenship.[25] Furthermore, it was due to his citizenship that he was able to appeal to Caesar and have his appeal accepted (Acts 25:10–12, 21, 25; 26:32; 28:19). That members of the Jewish community were granted Roman citizenship by being seduced to Antony's side may provide a historical context for how Paul's father got Roman citizenship.[26] However, it is also to be noted that both Paul and Luke write that Paul had been beaten and flogged, despite his status as a Roman citizen (2 Cor 11:23–25; Acts 16:22–23).

One cannot build an argument from silence. The silences are there on both sides, from Paul and from Luke, but the two accounts do not directly contradict each other, and therefore the silence of one party on a particular issue should not serve to discredit the other. 'All historical writing, after all, demands a selection and creative shaping of materials'.[27] The fact that Luke selected and shaped his material a certain way does not mean that stories were invented.

The Description of Paul's Jewishness

Luke has often been criticized for mispresenting Paul as a law-observing Jew, especially in the case of initiating the circumcision of Timothy, having his hair cut off because of a vow he had taken, and joining the purification rites of Jewish believers at the Jerusalem temple by paying their expenses (Acts 16:1–3; 18:18; 21:24–26). Luke portrays Paul, on his arrival in new towns and cities, as entering into the synagogues first, 'as his custom was', to preach the gospel to the mainly Jewish congregations, even during his mission among the Gentiles (Acts 13:5, 14; 14:1; 17:1–3, 10, 17; 18:4, 19; 19:8; 28:17; cf. 9:20). The Lucan Paul is consistent in this practice from his first missionary trip to the last one at Rome. The real Paul is perceived differently: he presents himself as a preacher of the law-free gospel, and was fully aware of his mission call to the Gentiles,[28] and if Paul went to the synagogues, he did so to speak to the Gentile God-fearers.[29]

---

[25] So plausibly, Rapske, *Book of Acts*, 158–9.
[26] Murphy-O'Connor, *Paul*, 39–41.
[27] Johnson, *Acts*, 7.
[28] Marshall, *Luke: Historian and Theologian*, 184: '[This discrepancy] is one of the burning questions of contemporary research into Acts, and it is often argued that here in particular Luke has mispresented the situation by idealization or downright misinterpretation of what happened.'
[29] E.g. Kim, *Origin*, 60–66.

However, we need to notice that while Luke describes Paul visiting the synagogues first, he also makes it clear that Paul was called for a mission to the Gentiles (Acts 9:15; 22:21; 26:17, 20, 23). It is also to be noted that when the Lucan Paul makes his missionary reports, he singles out his mission to the *Gentiles* (Acts 14:27; 15:3, 12; 21:19). Likewise, while the real Paul is so conscious of his calling to the Gentiles, he also expresses his fundamental concern for the salvation of his people (Rom 9:1–5; 10:1; 11:14).

Often interpreters do not fully take into account the contexts of Paul's writing, and so they misunderstand Paul. One needs to realize that the reason why the Galatians were so quickly persuaded by the Judaizers is because Paul had not prepared them with the law-free gospel, as presented in the letter, while he was there planting their churches.[30] One should note a shift in the emphasis in his message of justification by faith. During his missionary work in Galatia, he preached the message of justification by faith *in the death and resurrection of Christ*. However, later in the letter he stresses the gospel of justification by faith *apart from the law*. In Paul's *missionary* preaching, the notion of 'apart from the law' had hardly been stressed, certainly not as strongly as in Galatians,[31] and we need to remember that Luke is covering Paul's *missionary* days. Thus F.C. Baur is incorrect to discredit Luke for his silence in Acts on the Galatian conflict and the Antioch incident.[32]

Furthermore, it is significant to note that Paul positively comments on the law as good, spiritual and holy (Rom 7:12, 13, 14, 16). For Paul, the law is one of the prerogatives for Jews (Rom 9:4); it is the law of God (Rom 7:22). Circumcision is still a high privilege and advantage for a Jew (Rom 2:25; 3:1). Paul would not find it difficult to circumcise Timothy the 'Jew'. He would not tell the Jews 'not to circumcise their children, or live according to [their] customs' (Acts 21:21), and 'Paul would conduct himself [in the purification rite] as a practicing Jew' (Acts 21:26).[33] 'There is not a shred of evidence in the Pauline epistles that Paul ever taught Jewish Christians to forsake the Law of Moses.'[34] Paul rebukes the Galatians for 'observing special days and months and seasons and years' (Gal 4:10–11), but when writing to the Romans he accepts those Christians who consider one day more sacred than another (Rom 14:5–6; cf. Acts 16:8; 20:16). The interpreters need to

---

[30] So rightly, Ramsay, *St Paul the Traveller*, 183: 'all [Galatians] were ready to accept the belief that, as the Jews were always the first in Paul's own plans, and as Christianity came from the Jews, therefore it was right to imitate the Jews.'

[31] See above, pp. 74–76; see also Chae, *Paul*, 302-7 for a fuller argument.

[32] Baur, *Paul*, 1:7, 10: 'Any writer who is purposely silent upon so many points, and thereby places the facts of his narrative in a different light, cannot certainly be considered as just and conscientious'.

[33] Bruce, *Acts: Greek*, 57.

[34] Gasque, *History*, 288.

discern the context within which Paul is presenting his argument and teaching. As argued in the earlier chapters, Luke's account of Paul's *missionary* preaching to convert his audience cannot be compared with the apostle's later *theological* presentation to the converted in the context of defending the legitimacy of the salvation of the Gentiles obtained by faith alone.

With regard to the law and circumcision, they also need to consider Paul's audience and his purpose for the particular arguments. Our understanding may offer a solution to J. Weiss's dilemma: 'In the epistles we find two trains of thought about the law, one radical and in opposition, and one up to a certain point conservative and favorable. It is only with the greatest difficulty that they can be harmonized with one another, indeed they cannot be altogether accommodated to each other'.[35]

The priority of the Jews is also maintained in Acts. The Lucan Paul often declares, 'We had to speak the word of God to you first. Since you reject it and do not consider yourselves worthy of eternal life, we now turn to the Gentiles' (Acts 13:46; 18:6; 28:28; cf. 22:17–21). The chronological priority of the Jews for salvation is a biblical theme for both Jesus and Paul.[36] Although Paul establishes the equality of Jew and Gentile, still, for him, the gospel is 'first for the Jew' (Rom 1:16). So it is natural for him to preach the gospel to the Jews first and also to the Gentiles, as Luke reports in Acts. He clearly says that the Jews are the original olive tree on which the Gentile wild olive shoots are to be grafted (Rom 11:17–24). Paul expresses his genuine concern for his people; he has an agonizing and yearning spirit for his people to believe in Jesus Christ (Rom 9:1–3; 10:1; 11:14). It was natural for him to approach the Jews whenever possible to explain and prove from the Scriptures that the crucified Jesus is the awaited Messiah.[37] Paul clearly expresses his mission strategy towards the Jews as well as the Gentiles:

> Though I am free and belong to no man, I make myself a slave to everyone, to win as many as possible. To the Jews I became like a Jew, to win the Jews. To those under the law I became like one under the law (though I myself am not under the law), so as to win those under the law. To those not having the law I became like one not having the law (though I am not free from God's law but am under Christ's law), so as to win those not having the law. To the weak I became weak, to win the weak. I have become all things to all men so that by all possible means I might save some. I do all this for the sake of the gospel, that I may share in its blessings (1 Cor 9:19–23).

---

[35] Weiss, *Earliest Christianity*, 1:228.
[36] John 4:22; Matt 10:5–6; 15:21–28; Mark 7:24–30; Rom 1:16; 3:1–2; 9:4–5; 15:8–9.
[37] We disagree with Bruce, 'St Luke's Portrait', 186, who asserts that Paul entered synagogues to find the group of God-fearers who could be 'a bridgehead for the gospel in the Gentile population of a new city to which he came'. Paul seems to show genuine desire to preach the arrival of the awaited Messiah to the Jews.

As strongly as he wants to reach the Gentiles with the gospel, so does he desire to save the Jews! Paul does not express a lesser degree of desire to reach the Jews than to reach the Gentiles. The interpreters of Paul need to note that he has written letters to the *Gentile*-majority churches which were often under attack from false teaching. This is why Paul stresses his apostleship to the Gentiles in order to affirm the legitimacy of the salvation of the Gentiles, which was obtained by faith alone, apart from keeping the Jewish law. We may imagine that if he had written letters to the Jewish-majority churches, the content and argument would have been rather different; we might have got something similar to what is written in Romans.[38]

Furthermore, one must understand that the agreement reached at the Jerusalem Council, as described in Galatians 2:7–9, is not about demarcation of ethnic groups or even geographical boundaries.[39] If that was the case, Peter breaks the agreement by his presence and fellowship at the Antioch church, and also by writing letters to 'God's elect, strangers in the world, scattered throughout Pontus, Galatia, Cappadocia, Asia and Bithynia' (1 Pet 1:1; 2 Pet 1:1).[40] This would be even more so, if Peter ministered 'in Corinth and had a pernicious effect there'.[41] Eusebius asserted that Peter was writing to the Jews,[42] but the statement, 'Once you were not a people, but now you are the people of God; once you had not received mercy, but now you have received mercy' (1 Pet 2:10), suggests that Peter includes the Gentile believers as well.

The legend tells us that Peter had some time of activity in Rome until his death there, though we have no information about his ministry in that city or the length of his stay. The fact that the Judaizers also travelled to Antioch, Galatia, Corinth and Philippi, and attempted to influence the Gentile believers, indicates that there was no strict demarcation for the apostles about geographical or ethnic boundaries. Furthermore, Paul's Jewishness has become more recognized in recent years.[43] A new understanding of Paul will enhance the position of upholding the reliability of Luke's portrait of Paul in Acts.

---

[38] It is not easy to reconstruct the ethnic composition of the Christian community in Rome. However, it is notable that Paul presents his argument to establish the equality of Jew and Gentile here. The numerous citations from the Old Testament show that Paul attempts to persuade the Jews in favour of the recognition of such equality. At the same time, he mentions some positive comments on the law and even circumcision. See Chae, *Paul, passim*.

[39] *Pace* Schmithals, *Paul and James*, 46–61, who asserts that Paul gave up the mission to the Jews after the council meeting; more plausibly Marshall, *Luke: Historian and Theologian*, 185: Gal 2:1–10 is about 'a roughly territorial division'.

[40] The argument on the authorship of 1 Peter and 2 Peter is beyond our scope in this volume.

[41] Lietzmann as quoted in Hengel and Schwemer, *Paul Between Damascus and Antioch*, 328 n. 63.

[42] Eusebius, *Ecclesiastical History*, xxv.

[43] Gager, *Reinventing Paul, passim*.

Taking all these points into account, we can conclude that Luke is not misrepresenting Paul with regard to his Jewishness. This is especially so when he reports on Paul's practice of going to the Jews first and not strongly stressing salvation 'apart from the law' during his initial missionary work. I.H. Marshall is of the opinion that 'at the point at which he was writing, this [law/circumcision] problem was not Luke's concern'.[44] However, it seems more plausible to perceive that Luke's presentation of this issue is not as serious as what Paul writes in Galatians, because he is describing events as they happened, rather than because 'the Judaizing problem had disappeared', as E.J. Goodspeed infers.[45] Rather, M. Hengel seems right at this point: 'at an earlier stage the circumcision of non-Jews was only a matter of indifference for him [Paul].'[46] For Paul, it became an *issue* only later when some members of the circumcision party insisted that the Gentile believers must be circumcised and keep the Mosaic law (Gal 2:4; Acts 15:1, 5), and extended their campaign to wider regions where Paul had planted churches.

Luke must have known of Paul's strife with his opponents who demanded that the Gentile believers observe the Jewish law and practise circumcision. However, he does not write about how such struggles progressed to set a context in which both the Antioch incident and the Galatian conflict could happen. Luke describes only the earliest stage of the conflict and the resolution of the issue. Chronologically, the demand to keep the law was first made after Paul and Barnabas returned from their missionary journey in Galatia. Since it was not an issue while they were in Galatia the first time, Paul and Barnabas did not see the need to express their 'apart from the law' position during their missionary work there. They did not need to do so since the Gentile believers had no reason to keep the Jewish law, and also there was no occasion to prompt any focus on it. Thus Luke seems to have accurately conveyed how the issue in the earliest stage was less intense than what we read from the letters.

The Number of Paul's Visits to Jerusalem

Luke reports that, up to the time of the Jerusalem Council, Paul visited Jerusalem on three occasions: the 'acquaintance visit' (Acts 9:26–30), the 'famine visit' (Acts 11:27–30) and the 'council visit' (Acts 15:1–34). However, the Paul of the letters mentions only two visits: the acquaintance visit (Gal 1:18–19) and the council visit (Gal 2:1–10). C.S.C. Williams asserts that this

---

[44] Marshall, *Luke: Historian and Theologian*, 186.
[45] Goodspeed, *Paul*, 236.
[46] Hengel and Schwemer, *Paul Between Damascus and Antioch*, 149.

discrepancy is the weightiest reason to deny the credibility of Luke's portrayal of Paul.[47] C.J. Hemer also notes that this issue is 'the heart of the historical question . . . It is commonly regarded as a decisive condemnation of Luke'.[48] This topic requires a detailed study, but we offer only a brief survey to resolve this discrepancy.

Despite F.C. Baur's advice that any attempt to reconcile Paul's visit to Jerusalem mentioned in Galatians 1 – 2 with Luke's narrative is 'useless trouble',[49] such an endeavour is important. There is no dispute in identifying and correlating the visit of Galatians 1 with that of Acts 9. The view that Paul's description of the Jerusalem Council in Galatians 2:1–10 is consistent with the meeting Luke writes about in Acts 15:1–34 has enjoyed almost universal consensus.[50] According to this majority position, Paul did not know about the famine visit. However, this explanation seems too simplistic and unconvincing.[51] We need to note that Paul talks about something that appears to be related to the famine visit. Towards the end of his summary of the Jerusalem conference, Paul writes: 'All they asked was that we should continue to remember the poor [in Jerusalem], the very thing I was eager to do' (Gal 2:10). The fact that the apostles asked Paul to remember the poor suggests that Paul may have previously 'remembered the poor in Jerusalem', probably from Antioch.[52] The present active subjunctive verb *mnēmoneuōmen* connotes an action to be continued. Paul's choice of this verb, 'continue to remember', together with the verb *espoudasa* (I *was eager* to do) in the aorist tense, alludes that he may have previously remembered *their* poor (*tōn ptōchōn*).[53]

Others identify the visit of Acts 9 with that of Galatians 1, and the visit of Acts 11 with that of Galatians 2, and contend that Galatians was written before the Jerusalem Council in Acts 15.[54] However, this view seems unconvincing as well, as Galatians contains some critical issues. For example, the

---

[47] Williams, *Acts*, 24; so also Marshall, *Luke: Historian and Theologian*, 75, singles out Acts 15 as 'the principal problem' raised to disprove Luke's account of the Jerusalem Council. See Williams, *Acts*, 24–9, for a brief but helpful summary of the theories that have been offered to understand the number of visits Paul made to Jerusalem; for a briefer one, see also Wenham and Walton, *Exploring the New Testament*, 287–8.

[48] Hemer, *Book of Acts*, 247.

[49] Baur, *Paul*, 1:109–10.

[50] Most notably, Lightfoot, *Galatians*, 123–4.

[51] *Pace* Streeter's suggestion, as in Williams, *Acts*, 26, that Barnabas went to Jerusalem not with Paul, but with someone else.

[52] So also Goodspeed, *Paul*, 35.

[53] Zerwick and Grosvenor, *Grammatical Analysis*, 567; so also Pervo, *Dating Acts*, 79; Hall, 'St. Paul', 310.

[54] Notably, Hemer, *Book of Acts*, 247–51. Also Marshall, *Luke: Historian and Theologian*, 75; cf. Achtemeier, *Quest*, who unconvincingly identifies Gal 2:1–10 with Acts 11:1–18.

occasion of the visit to Jerusalem recorded in Galatians 2:4–5 fits better with that of Acts 15:1–2 than with the famine visit in Acts 11. The fact that Peter and some Jewish believers were eating with the Gentile believers seems to suggest that the Antioch incident took place *after* the Jerusalem Council, which opened a way for table fellowship for the Jewish and Gentile believers. Furthermore, it seems most unlikely that the Jerusalem Council of Acts 15 was called after the Antioch incident and the Galatian conflict. It is equally unlikely that Peter and Barnabas would vigorously uphold the policy of 'no circumcision' after the Antioch incident.

Here we offer an alternative explanation: that Paul may refer to the famine visit in Galatians 2:1–3 and to the Jerusalem Council in Galatians 2:4–10.[55] T.W. Manson is one of the very few scholars who plausibly note the significant break between Galatians 2:3 and 2:4–5, and this may suggest different occasions of Paul's visits to Jerusalem. He contends that Galatians 2:3 belongs to the time of the conference and Galatians 2:4–5 belongs to another later time. He then says that in Galatians 2:6–10 Paul continues to describe the conference.[56] Such an allocation may seem unconvincing. However, his contention, that the significant break between Galatians 2:3 and 2:4 may denote different occasions of Paul's visits to Jerusalem, is plausible.

Here we summarize the main points of our contention: (1) the description that Paul did not yield even for an hour (Gal 2:4) conveys the same sense of urgency and promptness that is quite similarly expressed in Acts 15:1–2;[57] (2) the occasion and the issues raised in Galatians 2:4–10 are very similar to those Luke describes in Acts 15:3–34;[58] (3) although Luke is silent about Titus, he may have gone to Jerusalem as Paul mentions, probably for the famine visit. Luke does not mention Titus in Acts at all.[59] However, does Paul imply that Titus has anything to do with the relief fund? In this connection it is interesting to see that Paul highly commends Titus as he had initiated the collection in Corinth: 'So we urged Titus, since *he had earlier made a beginning*, to bring also to completion this act of grace on your part' (2 Cor 8:6).

P.E. Hughes argues that this statement refers to 'a beginning which Titus had previously made at Corinth in organizing the collection [for the Jerusalem believers, as mentioned in 1 Cor 16:1–4]'.[60] However, we find that the

---

[55] See Chae, 'Paul, the Law and the Mission to the Gentiles'.

[56] Manson, *Studies*, 175–6; see also Lake, 'Apostolic Council of Jerusalem', 196–9, for the textual difficulties of Gal 2:4–5 and the possible interpretations.

[57] So correctly, Hahn, *Mission*, 78.

[58] *Pace* Johnson, *Acts*, 6.

[59] Certainly Titus is an important co-worker for Paul, and Paul often mentions his name. Some suggested that Luke's silence about him is due to his modesty as Titus might be his own brother or a relative; see Ramsay, *St Paul the Traveller*, 390.

[60] Hughes, *2 Corinthians*, 293–4.

pluperfect *proenērxato* refers to an earlier occasion (i.e. the collection in Antioch: Acts 11:29) than the one mentioned in 1 Corinthians 16:1–4. In Galatians 2:1–3 Paul possibly alludes to the occasion when Barnabas, Titus and he went to Jerusalem with the relief fund. Paul questions why the Judaizers suddenly now insist on circumcision for the Gentile believers, while Titus was not compelled to be circumcised although he was known as a Gentile believer when he went to Jerusalem with the famine fund. Paul mentions two visits to Jerusalem (Gal 1:18; 2:1–3) as well as alluding to another (Gal 2:4–10), while Luke records three visits by Paul (Acts 9:26; 11:27–30; 15:1–2).[61] Although we have attempted to explain the discrepancy as to the number of Paul's visits to Jerusalem between his conversion and the Jerusalem Council, we cannot know for sure. This is simply because, as D. Guthrie rightly puts it, 'It requires us to suppose that Paul is stating *all* the occasions when he visited Jerusalem',[62] and there is no evidence that Paul mentions *all* of them.

Paul's Relationship with Jerusalem

According to Paul, he went up to Jerusalem three years after his conversion in order 'to get acquainted with Peter and stayed with him fifteen days', and during that time he met James as well (Gal 1:17–19). 'Fourteen years later' he visited Jerusalem again, this time with Barnabas and Titus (Gal 2:1). During this visit he presented the gospel he was preaching among the Gentiles [in Antioch] to some leading apostles, and he did this privately for fear that he was running or had run his race in vain (Gal 2:2). In the early years Paul appears to have sought fellowship and affirmation from the Jerusalem leaders, and to desire to secure their acceptance of the gospel he was preaching to the Gentiles. Paul understood, from the fact that Titus was not compelled to be circumcised,[63] that the apostles did not make the circumcision of Gentile believers a mandatory issue, and also that they had no objection to Paul's preaching to the Gentiles without demanding circumcision. Furthermore,

---

[61] For some, Acts 11 and 15 do not correspond to Galatians 2, and they totally reject the credibility of Acts. Sahlin in Williams, *Acts*, 28, is of the opinion that the accounts in Acts 11 and 15 are Luke's fraudulent mistake to put Paul's name in Acts 11. This is too harsh a judgement in the light of the high level of compatibility we have shown above.

[62] Guthrie, *New Testament Introduction*, 356, his emphasis.

[63] Some scholars contend that Paul opposed the demand that Titus should be circumcised (e.g. Windisch in Guthrie, *New Testament Introduction*, 357). But this is not what Paul is saying; he says that the Jerusalem apostles did not demand Titus's circumcision even though they knew that he was a Gentile. Haenchen, *Acts*, 610, seems right to suggest that the Gentile believers who brought the collection to Jerusalem (Acts 20:4) were not required to be circumcised.

Paul secured their recognition and agreement for his mission to the Gentiles (Gal 2:4–9). We can see that by the time of the Jerusalem conference, Paul regarded himself as under the jurisdiction and leadership of the Jerusalem apostles.[64]

Luke describes a similar relationship in the early days of Paul. 'When he [Paul] came to Jerusalem, he tried to join the disciples' (Acts 9:26). In Antioch the Lucan Paul worked 'under' Barnabas who had been sent by the apostles (Acts 11:26; 13:1). When 'some men came down from Judea to Antioch' and insisted that the Gentile believers should keep the Jewish law in order to be fully saved, Paul and Barnabas brought this issue to the apostles in Jerusalem to give their judgement (Acts 15:1–4). Luke reports that the apostles endorsed Paul's position, and did not demand that the Gentile believers should accept circumcision.[65]

The description of the Jerusalem Council

Both Paul and Luke describe the occasion of the Jerusalem conference in a similar way. Both of them say that it was prompted by 'some false brothers [from Jerusalem who] had infiltrated our ranks to spy on the freedom we have in Christ Jesus and to make us slaves' (Gal 2:4). Luke describes the same incident: 'Some men came down from Judea to Antioch and were teaching the brothers: "Unless you are circumcised, according to the custom taught by Moses, you cannot be saved"' (Acts 15:1–3a). Paul writes that 'we [Paul and Barnabas] did not give in to them for a moment' (Gal 2:5). Luke reports a similar reaction: 'This brought Paul and Barnabas into sharp dispute and debate with them [the Judaizers]' (Acts 15:2).

At the council meeting, Peter supports Paul's position with a passionate speech based on his experience with the salvation of Cornelius and his household. '[God] made no distinction between us and them, for he purified their hearts by faith. Now then, why do you try to test God by putting on the necks of the disciples a yoke that neither we nor our fathers have been able to bear? No! We believe it is through the grace of our Lord Jesus that we are saved, just as they are' (Acts 15:9–11). Here Peter proposes not to put a yoke on the Gentile believers, because it is through grace that Jesus saves Jews as well as them. Peter's proposal was most fitting and supportive for Paul's argument. This is probably why Paul writes that the apostles gave him 'the right hand

---

[64] *Pace* Segal, *Paul*, 4: 'Luke purposely eliminates the disorganization, disunity, and rancor of early Christianity', and that 'Luke entirely abandons historical accuracy.'

[65] *Pace* Conzelmann, *Acts*, 44; his assertion that any unity that can be seen during the time of the apostles is because 'Luke has radically reworked the material in order to avoid the impression of an internal crisis' is groundless.

of fellowship' (Gal 2:7–9). Here Peter already knew that there was no distinction in the salvation of Jews and Gentiles, and that it is by the faith of the believers and by the grace of the Lord Jesus. The phrase, 'just as he did to us' (v. 8), indicates the equal terms for salvation for Jews and Gentiles. So, he declares, 'He made no distinction between us and them, for he purified their hearts by faith', and so 'it is through the grace of our Lord Jesus that we are saved, just as they are' (Acts 15:9; 11).

This is identical with Paul's theological position which is repeatedly expressed in Romans, especially. '[The gospel] is the power of God for the salvation of everyone who believes: for the Jew first and also equally for the Gentile' (Rom 1:16: my translation[66]); 'For God does not show favouritism [between Jew and Gentile]' (Rom 2:11); 'There is no difference between Jew and Gentile' (Rom 3:22; 10:12; Gal 3:28; Col 3:11). This suggests that Luke correctly grasped the theological positions of both Paul and Peter.

However, by the time Paul was writing the letters to the Galatians and the Corinthians, the situation had changed with the increase of the Christian zealots who grew to many thousands in the Jerusalem church (Acts 21:20). Despite the decision at the Jerusalem conference not to impose circumcision on the Gentile believers, the Judaizers continued their campaign in the churches Paul had planted. They were, directly or indirectly, supported by the Christian zealots in Jerusalem. What Paul is writing in the letters with regard to the law and the Jerusalem leadership seems closely related to this later situation. We need to note that the accounts of the Jerusalem Council by Paul (Gal 2:1–10) and Luke (Acts 15) are presented in different modes. Paul tells the story in an argumentative way while Luke describes the event as a narrator.[67]

Thus, Luke portrays no schism between the Jerusalem apostles and Paul. Paul's issue was rather with the Judaizers based in Jerusalem. Through the determined visit of Acts 21, he hoped to resolve their disturbance to the preaching of a consistent gospel with the understanding and help of the apostles. By bringing the collection to Jerusalem (which was a commitment on Paul's part: Gal 2:10), Paul seems to symbolically ask the apostles to keep the commitment on their part, namely, not to demand the circumcision of Gentile believers. Haenchen plausibly notes that the Gentile delegates who accompanied Paul were not asked to be circumcised;[68] rather the original Jerusalem decree was reaffirmed (Acts 21:25).

Paul protests, 'As for those who seemed to be important – whatever they were makes no difference to me; God does not judge by external appearance – those men added nothing to my message' (Gal 2:6). His insistence seems to be based on the common gospel. The present tense in 'whether . . . I or they, this is what we preach' (*houtōs kēryssomen*: 1 Cor 15:11) indicates that

---

[66] See Chae, *Paul*, 46–51, for the argument for this translation.
[67] So correctly, Marguerat, 'Paul After Paul', 72.
[68] Haenchen, *Acts*, 610.

Paul and other apostles still preached the same gospel that the Corinthians believed (cf. 1 Cor 1:23).[69] Paul indicates that he and the Jerusalem apostles have been continuously, repeatedly and customarily preaching even at the time of his writing 1 Corinthians (1 Cor 15:1–4, 11).[70] 'He also admits that he derived his knowledge of Christianity from others (1 Cor 15:3)'.[71] Hengel is also right to argue that 'such a basic statement as I Cor 15.11, which modern "theologies of the New Testament" like to suppress, presupposes real "agreement"'.[72] So he asserts that 'Gal 1.12 should not lead us to imagine him, even to begin with, as a theological solipsist'.[73]

Moreover, Paul shows his respect and recognition by singling out Peter's name before mentioning the Twelve to whom the risen Christ appeared. Then he lists himself as the last with a comment that he is 'the least of the apostles' (1 Cor 15:9). Paul indicates that he sought to secure the endorsement of the apostles for his mission among the Gentiles (Gal 2:2). He testifies that the Jerusalem apostles recognized God's grace given to him, and so agreed with him that he should concentrate on the mission to the Gentiles, just as Peter would go to the Jews. Despite his tone at the time of writing Galatians, Paul does not allude to any tension between the pillar apostles and himself *at the time of the council*. Rather he presents their relations as an amicable agreement.[74] One needs to keep in mind that Paul's protest has been made in the course of defending the legitimacy of the salvation of the Gentiles, especially after the Galatian churches had been severely disturbed by the Judaizers, who most probably insisted on their authority under the apostles in Jerusalem.

We can detect a similar change in Paul's tone in his letters to the Corinthians. He was conscious that he was the least of the apostles and did not deserve to be called an apostle, because he had persecuted the church (1 Cor 15:9). But later he asserts, 'I do not think I am in the least inferior to those "super-apostles"' (2 Cor 11:5). This claim is not, however, made to undermine the Jerusalem apostles, nor to express his enmity towards them. This statement is made in order to defend his apostleship from the attack of the self-claiming false teachers from Jerusalem, for the sake of his converts in Corinth (2 Cor 11:13–15).

Luke is often criticized for making no account of the real Paul's strong

---

[69] So also Fee, *First Corinthians*, 736; *pace* Park, *Either Jew or Gentile*, 37: the gospel of the circumcision and the gospel of the uncircumcision: 'These two gospels represented two different soteriologies as well as two different mission fields.'

[70] Holzner, *Paul*, 159; Nock, *Early Gentile Christianity*, 29; Munck, *Paul*, 81–6; Hahn, *Mission*, 82 n. 1.

[71] Hanson, *Acts*, 25.

[72] Hengel and Schwemer, *Paul Between Damascus and Antioch*, 44.

[73] Hengel and Schwemer, *Paul Between Damascus and Antioch*, 45, similarly 94, 147.

[74] Achtemeier, *Quest*, 23–4.

insistence on his apostleship, except insignificantly in passing (Acts 14:4, 14).[75] However, Luke does not question Paul's apostleship because he knew that an important criterion for an apostle was to have been a witness of the resurrection of Jesus (Acts 1:22), and Luke presents Paul as the most proactive witness of the resurrection of Jesus. Furthermore, the fact that Luke allots three-quarters of his second volume to describing the life and ministry of Paul is clear evidence that he regarded him to be highly significant in the apostolic ministry in earliest Christianity.

Nevertheless, it is true that Luke does not stress Paul's apostleship. This may indicate that Luke reflects the truth that during his missionary work, the scope which Luke covers, Paul did not assert his apostleship. The fact that Paul insists on his apostleship so strongly in the letter to the Corinthians (1 Cor 9:1–18) indicates that he did not emphasize it during his missionary work there. Rather he presented his weaknesses to manifest Christ's power (1 Cor 1:27–29; 2 Cor 12:9–10; 13:4). Paul puts himself and Barnabas on an equal level with James and Peter, but he says both Barnabas and Paul worked for their living without asserting the apostolic right of support (1 Cor 9:5–6). He thought of himself as 'the least of the apostles', who does 'not even deserve to be called an apostle' (1 Cor 15:9). This shows that Paul did not assert his apostleship in the early years. He stresses it only at a later stage when the authenticity of his apostolic ministry has been undermined by false teachers. From this point of view, what Luke portrays seems rather close to the level of Paul's insistence on apostleship during the church-planting stage.

The relationship during the Antioch incident

This was also the case during the so-called Antioch incident. Paul's rebuke of Peter was occasioned some years after the Jerusalem conference (Gal 2:11–14). By this time Peter's leadership was much reduced even in Jerusalem. James became the leader and Peter 'was afraid of those who belonged to the circumcision group' who 'came from James' (Gal 2:12). When the 'certain men from James' came, Peter withdrew himself from eating with the Gentile believers. His action affected other Jewish believers and even Barnabas. Realizing the critical ramifications of their hypocrisy, Paul immediately and publicly rebuked Peter. Paul's reaction was neither a personal confrontation nor a political power struggle. His foremost intention was to safeguard the truth of the law-free gospel for the Gentiles. It is most probable that Paul criticized Peter on the basis of the decision agreed at the Jerusalem conference, which had decisively been influenced by Peter's own experience with Cornelius (Acts 10 – 11).

However, the Judaizers extended their campaign even to Galatia, and quickly persuaded the hearts of the Gentile believers there (Gal 1:6). This

---

[75] *Pace* Pervo, *Mystery*, 31, 148.

incident set the occasion and the tone of the letter to the Galatians. By this time Paul expresses his frustration towards the leading apostles: 'those who seemed to be important . . . added nothing to my message' (Gal 2:6). Despite the intensity of the expression, he talks about the common gospel (1 Cor 15:11), and the difference in its application to the respective ethnic groups. It must also be noted that Paul describes James, Peter and John as 'pillars' of the church (Gal 2:9). With this honourable title Paul recognizes them as 'occupying [the] leading spiritual offices' in the early church.[76] Moreover, he still uses the fact that the 'pillar apostles' endorsed his law-free gospel and his mission to the Gentiles to counter-attack the claims of the Judaizers. Luke is silent on the crises with the Judaizers in the churches in Antioch, Galatia, Corinth and Philippi, and it seems more so because he focuses on the initial stage of the expansion of the gospel in different cities (Acts 16 – 21) than because he attempts to cover up their disunity.

The Judaizers came from Jerusalem to Antioch and Galatia, and they were readily accepted by the Gentile believers (Gal 2:11, 12; cf. Gal 1:7; Acts 11:22–24; 15:2). They might have considered themselves as 'branches of the Jerusalem church' (see Acts 9:31).[77] This fact indicates that the Gentile believers did not notice at first any disunity between Paul and the people from Jerusalem. It also suggests that Paul did not prepare them negatively with regard to the church in Jerusalem. Paul's emphasis on the collection for Jerusalem (cf. 1 Cor 16:1) might have given the impression to the Gentile believers in Galatia that they were to appreciate and respect the believers in and from Jerusalem.

After the Jerusalem conference, Paul was committed to collecting the offering from the Gentile churches for the church in Jerusalem (Gal 2:10; 1 Cor 16:1–4). It was more than a relief fund. He was convinced that it was the duty of the Gentile churches to express their gratitude by sending material blessings to the church in Jerusalem for their sharing spiritual blessings with the Gentile churches (Rom 15:25–27; 2 Cor 8:14). The churches in Macedonia made a sacrificial donation for the believers in Jerusalem (2 Cor 8:1–5). The Corinthians also collected offerings as Paul instructed (1 Cor 16:2; 2 Cor 8:10).

Furthermore, Paul dedicates two chapters in order to explain the reasons for the collection and encourage the Corinthians to give generously towards the poor in Jerusalem (2 Cor 8 – 9). Paul calls the believers in Jerusalem 'God's people' (1 Cor 16:1; 2 Cor 9:12) or 'saints' (Rom 15:25–26, 31; 2 Cor 9:1), and so does the Lucan Paul in Acts 26:10. Paul also asks the church

---

[76] Kraft, 'στῦλος', *Exegetical Dictionary*, 3:281; Rienecker and Rogers, *Linguistic Key*, 505: 'The metaphor was used by the Jews in speaking of the great teachers of the law.'

[77] Bruce, 'St Luke's Portrait', 183.

in Rome to pray that the collection would be accepted by the leaders in Jerusalem (Rom 15:31). All these show that Paul had a genuine desire to maintain unity with the leaders and believers in Jerusalem.

The 'divisions' in the church in Corinth (some following Paul and some following Peter) do not necessarily mean that Paul and Peter were divided (1 Cor 1:12). Rather, Paul refutes them by saying that they should not be divided just as Christ is not divided and Peter and Paul are not divided. Paul regards himself and Peter as co-workers who are fulfilling the tasks assigned to them by planting the seed and watering it (1 Cor 3:4–5). Furthermore, the fact that some Corinthians wanted to follow Peter (whom they had not met in person)[78] may suggest that Paul had presented him to the Corinthians as an important leader-apostle.

Luke also briefly reports this visit to Jerusalem with the collection towards the end of Paul's third missionary campaign (Acts 24:17). Both Paul and Luke are in agreement that Paul feared for his life as he was on his way to Jerusalem, and yet he was determined to visit the city (Rom 15:31; Acts 21:1–17). Luke then explains what happened to Paul in Jerusalem at the hands of the unbelieving Jews as Paul had feared (Rom 15:31; Acts 21:27ff.).

At this point it is interesting to note what Peter says about Paul. According to 2 Peter 3:14–16,[79] Peter knows that Paul has written letter(s) to the recipients of his own letters, and there is no hint at all that he was unhappy about Paul writing to the churches under his leadership or influence. Peter recognizes Paul as having received wisdom in writing letters. He also acknowledges that Paul's letters 'contain some things that are hard to understand' (2 Pet 3:16). With this remark he means that Paul has written something profoundly solid and deep. What Peter says is that what he writes about regarding the Parousia is much the same as what Paul has written to them already (cf. 1 Thess 1:9–10; Acts 3:19–21).[80] It is to be noted that even long after the Antioch incident, Peter calls Paul, 'our dear brother Paul' (2 Pet 3:15).[81] We have already seen that Paul regarded Peter as the first of the 'pillar' apostles, and so he took the initiative to go to Jerusalem to get acquainted with him. He also singles out Peter's name from the Twelve as the first one to whom the risen Lord had appeared. The two men seem to have recognized and

---

[78] Cf. Hengel and Schwemer, *Paul Between Damascus and Antioch*, 16: Peter himself or his representatives may have visited Corinth.

[79] See Bauckham, *Jude, 2 Peter*, 138–51, 158–62; Reicke, *James, Peter and Jude*, 143–7; Green, *2 Peter*, 13–35, for critical discussions on the authorship of 2 Peter.

[80] Holzner, *Paul*, 159, who notes that both Paul and Peter display much the same doctrine in their letters.

[81] Under the strong influence of the Tübingen School, this expression is held as a decisive piece of evidence to deny Petrine authorship of 2 Peter; see Green, *2 Peter*, 13–35; Bauckham, *Jude, 2 Peter*, 158–62.

valued the ministries of each other.[82]

Furthermore, there are considerable parallels between Paul's teaching and Peter's, on such themes as judgement by works,[83] brotherly love,[84] doing good works,[85] living a godly life[86] and the election of believers.[87] B. Reicke is thus right to note, 'As to its theological character First Peter reminds us to an astonishing degree of Paul. Not only is the line of thought characteristic of Gentile Christianity, but a considerable number of phrases correspond to similar expressions in the Pauline epistles; long lists of parallels to the whole Pauline corpus can be produced.'[88] Both Paul and Peter not only preached the common gospel but also taught believers similar lessons to live as the followers of Christ.

The exchange of co-workers

We also note that Peter and Paul interchanged some of their co-workers. According to Luke, the apostles and the early believers were meeting at the house that belonged to John Mark's mother (Acts 12:12). John Mark probably became a believer under Peter's ministry ('my son Mark': 1 Pet 5:13). John Mark followed his cousin Barnabas when he returned to Antioch after delivering the relief fund to Jerusalem (Acts 12:25). Then he joined Paul and Barnabas on a missionary journey, though he prematurely left them and returned home (Acts 13:13). So when Paul and Barnabas were planning to go on the second tour, Barnabas wanted to take him along, but Paul did not. The dispute between them was so sharp that they parted from each other. John Mark continued his missionary service with Barnabas, though we do not hear much about their mission from Acts. Paul later instructs Timothy to bring John Mark to him, saying, 'because he is helpful to me in my ministry' (2 Tim 4:11). So we find Mark being with Paul a second time, under his special favour (Col 4:11), and later he is with Paul in prison in Rome (Phlm 24). We also see Peter mention Mark's name at the end of his letter, as sending greetings to the recipients of Peter's letter. He refers to him as 'my son Mark' (1

---

[82] The contention that Peter's favourable comments about Paul are an attempt to play down the tension and disunity between them is groundless speculation: *pace* Achtemeier, *Quest*, 63.

[83] E.g. Rom 2:6; 1 Cor 3:12–13; 2 Cor 5:10; 1 Pet 1:17; cf. Matt 16:27.

[84] E.g. 1 Cor 13:1–7; Gal 5:13; Col 3:12–14; 1 Thess 4:9; 1 Pet 1:22; 3:8; 4:8–10; cf. 1 John 2:10; 3:16–18; 4:7–11, 20–21.

[85] E.g. Eph 2:10; Col 1:10; Titus 2:14; 3:8; 1 Pet 2:12, 15; 3:11; cf. Matt 5:16.

[86] E.g. Rom 13:12–14; 1 Cor 3:16–17; 6:9–10, 18–20; Gal 5:19–21; 1 Thess 4:2–3, 7–8; 1 Pet 1:14–16; 2:11–12; 4:3–4; 2 Pet 3:11–12.

[87] E.g. Rom 9:25–26; 1 Cor 1:26–29; Eph 1:4; 1 Pet 2:9–10.

[88] Reicke, *Epistles*, 70. See Marshall, *1 Peter*, 21–5, for a brief survey of the discussion on the authorship and readership of 1 Peter, where Marshall takes it as authentic by the apostle Peter.

Pet 5:13). Mark was with Peter first in Jerusalem, then joined Paul's ministry. Later on he is a part of the Petrine mission.

Silas is another good example. He was one of the prophets in the Jerusalem church, and was sent by the apostles to deliver the Jerusalem decree to the Gentile churches. He then joined Paul for his second missionary journey, and he is added as the co-sender of the letters to the Thessalonians (1 Thess 1:1; 2 Thess 1:1). Together with Paul and Timothy, he preached Jesus as the Son of God and Christ (2 Cor 1:19). His name does not appear in Acts during the period of Paul's third missionary journey. However, we see him with Peter, who mentions him as 'a faithful brother'. This suggests that Silas has joined in the Petrine mission as his helper and writing secretary. He carries Peter's letter to the recipients scattered abroad (1 Pet 5:12). It is not easy to exactly reconstruct the movements of the co-workers, but one thing that is clear is that Peter and Paul shared some of them with each other. Furthermore, the fact that Paul's closest missionary colleagues, Barnabas and Silas, are from Jerusalem implies that Paul's ministry among the Gentiles has been endorsed or supported by the Jerusalem apostles.

The leadership transition in the Jerusalem church

Both Paul and Luke present many similar descriptions with regard to Paul's relationship with the leadership and the church in Jerusalem. Despite the tension in Acts 15 and 21, Luke paints a relationship that is still workable and mutually respectful between Paul and the Jerusalem apostles. That Paul was 'effectively an excommunicant from his own movement' is far from the truth and cannot be supported.[89] Paul's opponents are not really the apostles in Jerusalem, but Judaizers who impose the law of Moses and circumcision on the Gentile believers as among the conditions for salvation. 'If the main opposition to Paul came, not from the "pillars" in Jerusalem, as Paul calls them, but from quite different groups, then Acts has not seriously mispresented Paul's position.'[90]

Paul's visit to meet the apostles as described in Acts 21 suggests that Paul had a hope that they would understand him, support him once again in securing the law-free gospel for the Gentile believers, and stop the activities of the Judaizers. It is important to consider that despite the rhetorical element in Paul's presentation to the churches, for example, in Galatia and Corinth, Paul desires to maintain a good relationship with Jerusalem as particularly shown in the collection and delivery of the donations. The relationship between Peter and Paul during the Antioch incident seems to be the exception rather than

---

[89] *Pace* Chilton, *Rabbi Paul*, 170.

[90] Hanson, *Acts*, 26: though his wording still suggests that Acts has mispresented Paul's position in some measure; *pace* Baur, *Paul*, 1:7: 'Peter, the head of the Judaizers'.

the norm, and even then, the strain was not personal, but theological.

The fact that Luke correctly describes the leadership transition in the Jerusalem church can serve us further as evidence that his description of Paul's relations with the authorities in the Jerusalem church is reliable. As already discussed, Paul lists Peter first and separately from the disciples to whom the risen Christ appeared: 'he appeared to Peter, and then to the Twelve. After that, he appeared to more than five hundred of the brothers at the same time, most of whom are still living, though some have fallen asleep. Then he appeared to James, then to all the apostles' (1 Cor 15:5–7). Then he writes that he went to Jerusalem 'to get acquainted with Peter and stayed with him fifteen days. I saw none of the apostles – only James, the Lord's brother' (Gal 1:18–19). Up to this point Paul indicates that Peter was the leader in the Christian community in Jerusalem. However, as he describes the apostolic council, Paul mentions James as the leader by listing his name first among the three pillar apostles (Gal 2:9). He also describes the visitors from Jerusalem to Antioch as 'certain men ... from James' (Gal 2:12), indicating James as the leader in the Jerusalem community.

Luke reflects the same change in his writing. Peter is presented as the obvious leader in the new Christian community in Jerusalem in choosing Matthias, addressing and preaching to the crowd, defending Christian faith, disciplining sin, inspecting the ministry in Samaria and leading Gentiles to the Lord (Acts 1 – 12). After being miraculously rescued from prison, however, 'he left for another place' (Acts 12:17).[91] Then we see Peter in Jerusalem at the apostolic council, though it is not clear when he returned to the city, and how long he was away. However, James speaks as the leader at the council by summarizing and concluding the meeting with the decree (Acts 15:13–21). Later Luke reports James as the leader among the apostles in Jerusalem by writing that 'Paul ... went to see James' with the collection after returning from his third missionary journey (Acts 21:18).

Luke reports that, on this occasion, James suggested to Paul that he could remove negative rumours that were spreading about him if Paul were to pay for others to take part in a purification rite: 'Then everybody will know there is no truth in these reports about you' (Acts 21:22–24). He also writes that earlier, at the Jerusalem conference, James had supported Paul's position: 'It is my judgment, therefore, that we should not make it difficult for the Gentiles who are turning to God' (Acts 15:13–19). Luke presents James and Paul as having a good relationship. Paul himself speaks well of James in his letters as a pillar apostle, the leader of the church in Jerusalem and the Lord's brother (1 Cor 15:7; Gal 1:19; 2:9, 12).

Although James does not mention Paul in his letter, he writes a number

---

[91] Here Luke seems to provide us with the background of the leadership transition, not only with Peter's departure but also with his words, 'Tell *James* and the brothers about this [i.e. his departure]'.

of things similar to Paul's own teaching. James lists the nine items of wisdom that come from heaven and these are very similar to Paul's list of the nine elements of the fruit of the Spirit (James 3:17–18; Gal 5:22–23). Both James and Paul give strong warnings not to judge fellow believers in Christ (James 4:11–12; Rom 14:1, 4, 10, 13). Both insist that 'whoever keeps the whole law and yet stumbles at just one point is guilty of breaking all of it' (James 2:10; Gal 3:10). James stresses doing good works to those who have already been saved by faith alone (James 2:1), and this is abundantly clear from his vocative, 'my [beloved] brothers', which is repeated fifteen times in his letter. Paul also stresses the importance of doing good works after being saved (2 Cor 8:21; Eph 2:10; 2 Tim 3:17; Titus 2:14; 3:1, 8, 14), even though his primary focus is to defend the legitimacy of the salvation of the Gentiles obtained by faith. Despite differences in the emphasis of their writings, they preach the common gospel (1 Cor 15:11) and they seem to have been in good relationship as Luke portrays in Acts.

Conclusion

We have paid special attention to the major discrepancies between Paul's letters and Luke's Acts. First, we looked at the topics that Luke does not mention but which Paul does, and vice versa. Luke does not write about Paul's sojourn to Arabia and his ministry of sending letters to the churches. Luke scarcely mentions the collection for the poor in Jerusalem, while Paul puts much emphasis on it. Equally Paul is silent about the Jerusalem decree. However, we found that the silence from each author does not contradict the other, and therefore the topics which form this silence cannot be used to discredit Luke's reliability.

A special mention needs to be made of the work of R.I. Pervo. He has compiled no fewer than 89 or 90 cases where, he contends, Luke uses vocabulary from Paul's letters, and also 20 parallels on itineraries and 11 thematic correspondences between Acts and Galatians. He then concludes that 'Luke had access to a collection of Pauline epistles'.[92] His study further strengthens the case that Luke's account of Paul is credible.

The second area of discrepancy we looked at was the description of Paul's Jewishness. Luke has often been criticized for mispresenting Paul as a law-observing Jew as well as preaching to the Jews first in their synagogues, while the historical Paul insists on his apostleship to the Gentiles.[93] However,

---

[92] Pervo, *Dating Acts*, 144; 139–43, who also presents 'the hypothesis that Luke worked (or spent a good deal of time) in Ephesus' where Paul's letters were collected and kept (Pervo, *Making of Paul*, 151).

[93] Pervo, *Mystery*, 30–31.

in recent years Paul's Jewishness has been more recognized from his letters. We showed that some earlier scholars have misread and misinterpreted Paul, and so have unduly discredited Luke's portrait of Paul in Acts. When we compare Luke's account of Paul with the early years of the historical Paul, Luke's portrayal is rather close to the real Paul.

Third, the discrepancy in the number of Paul's visits to Jerusalem has received weighty criticism. Following the contention of D. Guthrie, we have pointed out that such critique presupposes that both Paul and Luke mention *all* of the visits. Furthermore, we proposed an alternative interpretation, namely, that the famine visit made by Paul is to be identified with Galatians 2:1–3, and the council visit with Galatians 2:4–10. On that basis, both Paul and Luke mention three of Paul's visits to Jerusalem between his 'conversion' and the council visit.

Finally, it is often contended that there is a huge discrepancy in the two accounts of Paul and Luke in regard to Paul's relationship with Jerusalem. Our study has shown that Luke's description of Paul's relation with the Jerusalem apostles is not different from Paul's own description on this issue. The level of discrepancy is often exaggerated through the misunderstanding of Paul's letters. Since F.C. Baur of the Tübingen School, scholars have unduly highlighted the schism and disunity between Peter and Paul, and this has frequently led to extreme interpretations. It is often due to an inaccurate interpretation of Paul and his theology that they insist on this incompatibility,[94] and so they unfairly blame Luke for covering up their division and enmity. They often arrive at their conclusion too soon, without adequately examining a wide range of material.[95] J. Munck is correct to deny that there was any serious conflict between Jewish believers and Paul in their theology, in general, and their view of the missionary task to Jews and Gentiles. He also plausibly argues that such opposition is only a displaced reconstruction of the Tübingen School's ideas.[96] The new Tübingen scholar M. Hengel has rightly pointed out: 'Scholarship still suffers to the present day from this bias [of the Tübingen School], which wrongly limits the possibilities of our knowledge.'[97]

R.P.C. Hanson is right to warn us not to 'view the conflict provided for us in Galatians [as] a letter of violent protest, written quickly, in a moment of intense anger and disgust'.[98] Simply because Paul is emotional in presenting his message to the Galatians, it should not of itself be used as a pretext to question the quality or reliability of Paul's message. Peter and Paul were not divided nor in strife. Rather, they respected each other, more especially on

---

[94] So rightly, Riesner, *Paul's Early Period*, 30; Keener, *Acts*, 1:232.
[95] Notably, Haenchen, *Acts*, 114–15.
[96] Munck, *Paul*, 81–6; affirmatively referred to by Hahn, *Mission*, 82 n. 1.
[97] Hengel and Schwemer, *Paul Between Damascus and Antioch*, 20–21.
[98] So rightly, Hanson, *Acts*, 25.

The Historical Paul in Acts

Paul's side. '[T]he difference between his [Paul's] teaching and that of the community at Jerusalem was one of emphasis rather than of substance.'[99] As we have seen above, Luke's presentation of the relationship between Paul and Jerusalem is rather close to the reality, as neither Peter nor Paul suggests any serious schism between them.

So what S.E. Porter aptly expressed sums up our conclusion well:

> I am not convinced that there is as great a separation between the Paul of Acts and the Paul of the letters as many have posited. At the least, the arguments that have often been marshalled to establish the differences between the two, when critically scrutinized, do not seem compelling. Whatever differences there are seem to be fully explicable in terms of Acts and the letters being written by two different authors.[100]

---

[99] So correctly, Nock, *Early Gentile Christianity*, 29.
[100] Porter, *Paul in Acts*, 6–7.

4

The 'We-Passages' and Luke's Portrayal of Paul

There are three 'we-passages' in Acts: 16:10–17; 20:5 – 21:18;[1] 27:1 – 28:16.[2] In those sections Luke uses the pronoun 'we', suggesting that he was present at the scenes, travelling together with Paul. Paul also affirms that Luke was his travelling companion: 'Our dear friend Luke, the doctor, and Demas send greetings' (Col 4:14); 'Epaphras, my fellow-prisoner in Christ Jesus, sends you greetings. And so do Mark, Aristarchus, Demas and Luke, my fellow-workers' (Phlm 23–24); 'for Demas, because he loved this world, has deserted me and has gone to Thessalonica. Crescens has gone to Galatia, and Titus to Dalmatia. Only Luke is with me' (2 Tim 4:10–11).[3] This may show that Luke is an eyewitness to the things recorded in these we-passages, and possibly in the wider sections.

This certainly has huge implications in discerning the reliability of what Luke has written in these passages of Acts or even in the book as a whole. It opens up the possibility that Luke collected much of his material from the apostle Paul himself. As a travelling companion, he must have heard Paul's

---

[1] Some scholars divide this passage into two sections: 20:5–15; 21:1–18. However, even if this is justified, there can be no issue at all in putting the two passages together, since the author obviously must have stayed on with Paul when he was giving a speech to the elders of the Ephesian church. Some texts start the we-passage from Acts 11:28: see Hengel and Schwemer, *Paul Between Damascus and Antioch*, 439 n. 1052.

[2] Porter, *Paul in Acts*, 27–41, esp. 34, argues for a theory of five 'we-passages', by dividing 27:1–29 and 28:1–16. Porter, *Paul in Acts*, 11, 39–41, 47, repeatedly asserts that the five we-passages had been written by another author as one document, but Luke divided it into five passages to meet his literary device; see pp. 10–66 for a thorough treatment of form-critical discussion on the 'we-passages' in Acts.

[3] 'Our dear friend Luke, the doctor' is most probably a Gentile, from the fact that he is listed separately from the Jewish companions (Col 4:10–14); *pace* Williams, *Acts*, 22–3: 'Luke was a Greek-speaking Jew.'

stories, for example, about his pre-Christian life, his Damascus experience, missionary journeys, the trials before the Roman governors, and so on. Hence Lucan scholarship has paid enormous attention to these sections. The we-passages have been one of the most discussed portions in Lucan scholarship since the eighteenth century, and the debate still goes on.[4]

At least three perceptions are offered with regard to these we-passages. The first is that the author uses the first-person pronoun not to indicate his own involvement, but rather as a literary device in order to give his story credibility and vitality, or to enhance the reader's experience.[5] However, if that is the case, one may wonder why he uses them only in a few passages, mainly when he describes his travels, especially by ship.[6] He could have used them more during some crucial incidents, for example, the riot in Ephesus or the farewell speech to the Ephesian elders or Paul's meeting with the Jerusalem apostles or even in one of the trial scenes of Paul.

The second understanding of the we-passages is that Luke was not an eyewitness but he uses his sources' experiences as his own.[7] However, Luke does not use the first-person plural when utilizing many of the materials from other sources he had available to write Acts.[8] It is also to be noted that Luke did not use the first-person plural in his Gospel when employing the sources of other eyewitnesses. He does not use first-person pronouns in Acts 1 – 15 to express his source's experience, on whose material he totally depended.

Furthermore, in Luke 1:3 and Acts 1:1 the author does not use the first-person singular or plural in order to indicate the sources of the eyewitnesses; rather, he indicates his own involvement. W.G. Kümmel points out that Luke says in Luke 1:1–4 that he was not an eyewitness.[9] It is true in the case of the Gospel of Luke; he had to depend totally on the sources of other eyewitnesses to write the entire Gospel. But it is different for Acts. Paul himself testifies

---

[4] Campbell, *'We' Passages*, has recently written a short but profound book, solely focusing on the 'we-passages' of Acts. A number of reviews show the interest in this subject. See also his later article, 'Narrator', 385–407; Cadbury, '"We" and "I" Passages', 128–32; Sheeley, 'Getting into the Act(s)', 203–20; Wedderburn, 'We-Passages in Acts', 78–98; Adams, 'Relationships', 125–42; Porter, *Paul in Acts*; Phillips, 'Paul as a Role Model', 49–63; Keener, 'First-Person Claims', 9–23; and there is a lively discussion on the online blogs as well. A notable exception is Lentz, *Luke's Portrait*, who offers no treatment of the 'we-passages', and Porter, *Paul in Acts*, 11 n. 3, finds this 'quite surprising'.

[5] Dibelius, 'Style Criticism', 7–8; Kümmel, *Introduction*, 184–5; Conzelmann, *Acts*, xxxix–xl, 215; Robbins, 'We-Passages in Acts', 5–18. For a critique of Robbins, see Hemer, 'First Person Narrative', 79–109, also in his *Book of Acts*, 317–19.

[6] Every we-passage starts with a description of a sailing (Acts 16:9–10; 20:5–6; 21:1; 27:1).

[7] Kümmel, *Introduction*, 184–5; more recently, Porter, *Paul in Acts*, 39–41.

[8] So rightly, Bock, *Acts*, 14.

[9] Kümmel, *Introduction*, 174.

that Luke is his fellow worker and travelling companion. It would be natural for Luke to include some of the stories and incidents which he collected himself. However, he minimizes his self-reference, and gives priority to the main figures, such as Paul and Silas, and to the main events and subject matter.

The third position is that Luke writes those we-passages from his own experience as an eyewitness. Luke, as Paul's travelling companion, includes himself as a part of the stories which he is writing.[10] He presents himself as one who knows much about the apostle and his movements. Thus he gives the impression that what he has written in Acts, especially in the we-passages, is highly reliable and accurate.[11] So, J.D.G. Dunn is right to say, 'They [the we-passages] certainly provide *prima facie* evidence that the author was personally present during the sequence described'.[12] Moreover, as H.J. Cadbury stresses, Luke's remark in the preface of the Gospel of Luke is also applicable to Acts.[13] C.J. Hemer draws our attention to L.C.A. Alexander's study, which finds close parallels between Luke's preface in Luke 1:1–4 and the words of the Greek medical writer Galen. This research helps identify the author of Luke-Acts as Luke the physician.[14]

We will now turn to examine the we-passages, but we will only pay attention to the first two. This is because our immediate purpose for this study is to discern Luke's credibility in his portrayal of Paul by comparing the accounts of Luke and Paul, and Acts 27:1 – 28:16 has little to compare with the material in the letters.

The 'we' in Acts 16:10–17

Luke records that 'after Paul had seen the vision [of a Macedonian], *we* got ready at once to leave for Macedonia, concluding that God had called *us* to

---

[10] Ramsay, *Church in the Roman Empire*, 6–8; Hanson, *Acts*, 23; Bruce, *Acts: Greek*, 41; Munck, *Acts*, xiii; Hengel, *Acts and the History*, 66; Marshall, *Acts*, 39; Hemer, *Book of Acts*, 321; Thornton, *Zeuge*, 141, 272–80. Dunn, *Beginning*, 64–8. For the debate whether or not Luke includes himself in the we-passages, see Campbell, 'Narrator', 389, 407, who concludes that Luke does not include himself in the we-passages just as other authors of ancient historiographies did not. However, see Keener, 'First-Person Claims', 9–24, who, in a dialogue with Campbell, has strongly argued for Luke's inclusion and participation in the narratives. See also Fitzmyer, *Acts*, 51, for the list of the modern scholars who recognize the authorship of Acts by Luke.

[11] Keener, 'First-Person Claims', 9–24; Carson and Moo, *Introduction*, 293; Witherington, *Acts*, 480–86; Bock, *Acts*, 13–14; Fitzmyer, *Acts*, 103, 580.

[12] Dunn, *Beginning*, 75.

[13] As in Hemer, *Book of Acts*, 327.

[14] Hemer, *Book of Acts*, 322–3.

preach the gospel to them' (Acts 16:10). This is the first usage of 'we', and then Luke continues to use it until Acts 16:17, which describes how he and Paul, among others, encountered a demon-possessed slave girl in Philippi. However, this does not mean that Luke left the scene just before Paul cast out the demon, and therefore saw nothing more. The demon-possessed 'girl followed Paul and the rest of *us*', and Paul cast the demon out of her. It is most probable, then, that the author witnessed the whole incident till Paul and Silas were arrested and put into prison. Then he uses the pronoun 'them': '[The owners of the girl] brought *them* [Paul and Silas] before the magistrates' (Acts 16:20). Then the story carries on until Acts 16:40 with the pronouns 'they/them/their' because he is writing about the episode with Paul and Silas. So, even if the author was there in the city he would not write 'we', because he was writing about Paul and Silas who were arrested, imprisoned and released.

Luke continues to use the pronoun 'they', indicating Paul and Silas, from Acts 17:1. These two leaders of Paul's second missionary campaign are the main figures in this section of Acts 16:19 – 17:13. It is to be noted that even though Timothy joined the team in Acts 16:1–3, he is not included in the 'they' in Acts 16:4: 'As *they* travelled from town to town, *they* delivered the decisions reached by the apostles and elders in Jerusalem'. The pronoun 'they' here refers to Paul and Silas as those specially chosen for the role of delivering the Jerusalem decree (Acts 15:27, 32, 40). At Acts 17:14, Paul is sent to the coast and Silas and Timothy stay at Berea. At this stage the author is most probably still with Paul.

After Paul arrives at Athens he becomes the single main literary figure from Acts 17:16 till the end of the episode in Athens. Here Luke uses 'he' referring to Paul and 'they' referring to the Athenians. Paul remains as the single literary figure from the arrival in Corinth till the end of the second missionary journey (Acts 18:1–22). Luke writes, 'Then he [Paul] set sail from Ephesus. When he landed at Caesarea, he went up and greeted the church and then went down to Antioch' (Acts 18:21–22). Through this report Luke did not mean that only Paul set sail and returned. He is writing with the eyes of a reporter, paying attention to the main literary figure.[15] Since the author, who is indicated by the we-passage, was travelling with Paul, it is likely that he too visited Athens and Corinth, and returned to Antioch with him.

Luke uses 'we' in Acts 16:10, but scholars have debated when and where Luke first joined Paul's missionary team. F.F. Bruce infers a possibility that Luke may have joined the team as a ship's doctor from Troas.[16] But the fact

---

[15] An accompanying reporter would never write the headline 'The Queen, Her Officials and I Return Home', but simply 'The Queen Returns Home', even though he returned together with the Queen on her official plane from a particular state visit.

[16] Bruce, *Acts: Greek*, 308; Barnes, *Notes*, 275. See Haenchen, *Acts*, 490–91, for various discussions on whether Luke rejoined the team at Troas or not.

that he writes, 'God had called *us*', indicates that Luke is not a new convert from Troas, but rather was already a member of Paul's team.[17] It seems probable that he is from Antioch,[18] and joined Paul and Silas when they set out for the second missionary campaign together with Timothy. Even if Timothy was there with Paul, Luke did not include him in the pronoun 'they', but refers only to Paul and Silas.[19] However, he uses 'we' at Acts 16:10 and this is probably because he intends to stress the fact that *the whole team* agreed that in the vision, God compelled them to go on to Macedonia. He then uses 'we' for a little while, but soon turns back to 'they' referring to the main characters, namely, Paul and Silas.

The 'we' in Acts 20:5 – 21:18

Luke resumes the 'we-passage' from Acts 20:5. How could he be in Macedonia? E.H. Trenchard is of the opinion that Luke has just rejoined Paul after a long separation from him.[20] Some scholars infer likewise because they see the first we-passage end at Acts 16:17 (while 'we' were in Philippi), and then the second 'we' section start at Acts 20:5 (where 'we' sailed from Philippi).[21] However, this seems unlikely. The text does not seem to suggest that. If that were the case, it could mean that Luke stayed a long time in Philippi, from the beginning of the second missionary journey till near the end of the third campaign. Paul's letter to the Philippian church does not suggest that Luke is their familiar member.

Paul travels from Ephesus to Greece, and then to Macedonia. He was accompanied by seven men from different provinces where Paul had planted churches. Sopater and Aristarchus came from Macedonia, Gaius and Timothy from Galatia, and Tychicus and Trophimus from Asia. At this point Luke writes that these regional representatives went ahead and waited for '*us*' at Troas. '*We*' (Paul, Silas and Luke at least) sailed from Philippi to Troas to join the others (Acts 20:5–6). Then 'we' met all together at Assos and arrived at Miletus (Acts 20:15). At this point the 'we' section ends. However, the absence of 'we' does not necessarily mean that the author left the team at that

---

[17] So rightly, Arrington, *Acts*, 585; Williams, *Acts*, 193.

[18] Eusebius, *Ecclesiastical History* 3.4.6; Arrington, *Acts*, xxxii: according to the Anti-Marcionite Prologue to Luke's Gospel, Luke was a Greek from Syrian Antioch.

[19] Luke seems to leave out junior members from the list of the team. Luke does not mention John Mark's name in Acts 13:4, but just writes, 'the two of them', when it is obvious that Mark set off with them (Acts 13:13; 15:37–38). Can this be the reason why Titus is not mentioned in Acts?

[20] Trenchard, 'Acts', 1373.

[21] Ramsay, *St Paul the Traveller*, 201.

point.²² The fact that the 'we-passage' resumes right after Paul's speech and farewell, that is, at Acts 21:1, makes it clear that Luke was with Paul during the time when the apostle was meeting and addressing the elders of the Ephesian church (Acts 20:17–38). Luke seems to use 'they' and 'he' in order to focus on Paul's speech to the elders. However, there is little doubt that Luke was there and heard Paul's farewell speech himself.²³

Luke records 'our' trip from Miletus to Jerusalem via Tyre, Ptolemais and Caesarea, just to mention a few places. There seems to be at least ten people in the group during this voyage. Luke witnesses to the appeals by different people urging Paul not to go to Jerusalem. He saw and heard Paul's determination to visit Jerusalem. The day after their arrival at Jerusalem, 'Paul and *the rest of us* went to see James, and all the elders were present' (Acts 21:18). This is the end of the we-passage in this particular section. However, the disappearance of the 'we' at Acts 21:18 does not suggest that the author left the team at that point.

By ceasing the usage of 'we', the author simply plans to shed more light on Paul and his conversation with the apostles in Jerusalem. Luke makes it clear that he arrived at Jerusalem together with Paul and the regional delegates, and then as he writes, 'Paul and *the rest of us* went to see James' (Acts 21:17). This means that he was there when Paul met James, and so heard their conversation as an observer. Thus it is also highly likely that he and other Gentile delegates witnessed Paul's participation in the purification rite at the temple as well as his subsequent arrest and his defence before the angry Jewish crowd. It seems unlikely, though, that Luke was able to hear (and see) Paul's trial in the Sanhedrin as part of a court audience, due to the hostility of the Jewish leaders.

If Luke was in Jerusalem, we can safely assume that he travelled to Caesarea when or after Paul had been taken there. Thus it seems probable that he was allowed to visit Paul as the governor Felix gave Paul 'some freedom and permit[ted] his friends to take care of his needs' (Acts 24:23). Thus he would be able to collect first-hand information from Paul himself. Furthermore, Luke could probably attend Paul's trial before Felix and Festus. H.W. Tajra explains the judicial procedures in the Roman provincial governor's courts:

> In *extra ordinem* cases, judicial procedure was usually as follows: A) The case was heard by the governor in person (personal *cognitio*). He was normally seated on the tribunal (*in sede tribunalis*) and was seated by his *consilium* or council of advisors. A *notarius* was responsible for writing up the minutes of the proceedings. The trial itself (although not the preliminary hearings) was usually open to the public.²⁴

---

²² Guthrie, *New Testament Introduction*, 367 n. 2.
²³ Bruce, *Speeches*, 26.
²⁴ Tajra, *Trial*, 115. Here Tajra follows Urch, 'Procedure', 93.

Then he adds: 'Paul's appearances before the Governors Felix and Festus are very good examples of the workings of *extra ordinem* procedure in the provincial court of an imperial province'.[25] Since 'the trial ... was *usually open to the public*', it is highly probable that Luke and Paul's supporters were present at his trial.[26] The hearing before King Agrippa is a different case. Without the presentation of the case from an accuser or prosecutor, it was not strictly a trial but an official gathering to hear Paul's defence, and no verdict was to be given here.[27] The distinguished guests from military and civil services were at the hearing before King Agrippa, and their presence excludes the possibility of Luke or Paul's friends being there.

Although Luke does not confirm whether he was present in Caesarea or not, he seems to imply that he remained with Paul from Acts 21:18 till Acts 27:1.[28] Luke does not say anything about any supporters either from Jerusalem or from Caesarea. But his silence does not necessarily imply that Paul was alone through his trials and custody. The fact that the high priest came with a group of supporters (Acts 24:1) may suggest that the defendant could bring some of his supporters too. There were friends who, with Felix's permission, took care of Paul's needs (Acts 24:23). B.M. Rapske contends that Paul was 'in a lightened military custody', with 'a fairly generous degree of access [for his helpers]'.[29] Philip, one of the Seven who lived in Caesarea, may have visited Paul in prison (Acts 6:5–6; 21:8–9). It is also highly probable that his travelling companions and the Caesarean believers were visiting the apostle at the most crucial time of suffering. 'The Caesarean church's history with Gentile ministry, its Gentile inclinations and makeup, and its kinship in ministry with Paul actually argue persuasively for a firm embrace rather than abandonment.'[30] This suggests that Paul had ongoing influence in the Caesarean Christian community, and that they were visiting him in prison.

Later, from a prison in Rome, Paul writes to Timothy. After mentioning that all of his co-workers are scattered for various reasons, Paul adds, 'Only

---

[25] Tajra, *Trial*, 115.

[26] Paul's remark, 'At my first defence, no one came to my support, but everyone deserted me' (2 Tim 4:16), seems to refer to his trial in Rome rather than in Caesarea.

[27] BAGD, *Greek-English Lexicon*, 33.

[28] Keener, *Acts*, 1:4. Aristarchus seems to be another person who was with Paul from the time of his arrival at Jerusalem till he left Caesarea for Rome (Acts 20:4; 27:2).

[29] Rapske, *Book of Acts*, 151, 168, 172; Rapske, 'Helpers', 19. After a thorough comparative study of Paul's custody as Luke describes it in Acts under the Roman custodial system and procedures, Rapske, *Book of Acts*, 429, concludes, 'He [the Lucan Paul] is thus a historically credible figure'.

[30] Rapske, *Book of Acts*, 434.

Luke is with me' (2 Tim 4:10–11). This shows the character of Luke. Probably he felt responsible for looking after Paul's health. Luke seems to be the last person to leave Paul, especially when he was in chains.[31] Paul was not only a Roman citizen who had appealed to Caesar but also a high-profile prisoner.[32] To that extent, he would have been treated with care,[33] and so even the governors might have valued Luke's medical expertise and service to the prisoner. F.F. Bruce is right to say that 'it would be safe to think of him [Luke] as spending much of his time in or around Caesarea (where Paul was kept in custody).'[34] It seems probable that during these years Luke collected material on the life and teaching of Jesus for his Gospel.

Another we-passage starts at Acts 27:1, which indicates that Luke sailed from Caesarea together with Paul soon after the hearing before Agrippa. Aristarchus, who came to Jerusalem together with Paul and other delegates of the Gentile churches, gets on board the ship as well to sail for Rome (Acts 20:4; 27:1). This suggests that they have already been in Caesarea for some time, for they would not have joined Paul just the day before to sail to Rome with him. If Luke was there for the whole or most of the period of Paul's custody in Caesarea, he could have experienced some events as an eyewitness, or he could have collected fresh first-hand information from the apostle himself, such as details of the hearing before King Agrippa.

J. Munck plausibly contends that the 'we' section should be considered as extending from 20:1 to 28:31, the end of Acts, even if the 'we-passages' appear in 20:5–15; 21:1–18; and 27:1 – 28:16, because it is obvious that Luke is present even if he does not mention 'we' all the way through.[35] There is no reason, then, why we should not infer that he was with Paul from Acts 16:18 to 20:1,[36] and even from Paul's departure from Antioch for the second missionary journey. If our reconstruction is right, the author of Acts has been with Paul during most of his ministry and activity from the beginning of his second missionary tour to his time in Rome. Thus most of the material concerning Paul's ministry in Acts is the source that the author himself witnessed, or collected from Paul himself, or his friends.[37] So the level of the

---

[31] Rapske, *Book of Acts*, 436: '[Luke] stood alongside him [Paul] [as a] best friend who sticks closer than a brother'.

[32] Rapske, *Book of Acts*, 151–72.

[33] Rapske, *Book of Acts*, 168, is of the opinion that Felix must have wanted to preserve Paul's health 'to his own political and monetary advantage'.

[34] Bruce, *Acts: Greek*, 476; *pace* Hengel, *Between Jesus and Paul*, 127, for implying that Luke did not stay in Caesarea during Paul's imprisonment there.

[35] Munck, *Acts*, xliii.

[36] At this point, Munck implausibly does not apply the same logic to Acts 16:18 – 20:1 by saying, 'he [Luke] stayed several years in Philippi [until Paul returns to the city]' (*Acts*, xliii).

[37] See Pervo, *Dating Acts*, 347–58, for a useful survey of the scholarship on the sources of Acts.

credibility of Luke's portrayal of Paul goes up much higher than has usually been assumed.

The 'We-Passages' and Paul's Ministry in the Corresponding Regions

We now turn our attention to the material in Acts that is closely connected with the 'we-passages', and compare them with what Paul writes in his letters to the corresponding regions. This study should enable us to discern further the level of the accuracy of Luke's material in Acts.

If Luke was from Antioch and joined Paul's second missionary journey, he travelled with Paul through the regions of Galatia, Philippi, Thessalonica, Berea, Athens, Corinth and Ephesus, and then during the third campaign he visited Ephesus, Macedonia, Greece and Miletus, and returned to Jerusalem. Among these, Macedonia (Philippi, Thessalonica and Berea), Greece (Corinth and Athens) and Asia (Ephesus) are important areas for our purpose, because Paul has written letters to the churches in these regions. Galatia is not relevant at this point because Luke was not with Paul during the first journey when he ministered in the province of Galatia. Although Luke accompanied Paul during his revisit to Galatia on the way to the areas of the third campaign, it was a rather brief visit.

Corinth

Luke mentions some new names as he records Paul's ministry in Corinth: Priscilla and Aquila as a couple, Crispus, Sosthenes and Apollos. It is not a coincidence that all these names appear in Paul's letters to the Corinthians. Paul sends the greetings of Aquila and Priscilla from the province of Asia (i.e. Ephesus) to the Corinthians (1 Cor 16:19). This demonstrates two things: the Corinthians know Aquila and Priscilla, and the pair are in Ephesus when Paul is writing 1 Corinthians. Luke explains the background: it was in Corinth that Paul met this couple, staying at their house and working together as tentmakers (Acts 18:1–3). Luke further explains how the couple came to Ephesus: 'Paul stayed on in Corinth for some time. Then he left the brothers and sailed for Syria, accompanied by Priscilla and Aquila . . . They arrived at Ephesus, where Paul left Priscilla and Aquila' (Acts 18:18–19).

To the Romans, Paul says Priscilla and Aquila are 'my fellow-workers in Christ Jesus. They risked their lives for me. Not only I but all the churches of the Gentiles are grateful to them. Greet also the church that meets at their house' (Rom 16:3–5). They are now in Rome, but Paul says that all the Gentile churches owed them for their service, by which he probably means at least two Gentile churches, in Corinth and Ephesus. Luke explains that the couple came from Rome (Acts 18:2), and most probably they had been expelled from Rome due to the edict of Claudius in AD 49.

Paul also mentions Crispus as one of the few people he baptized (1 Cor 1:14), and Luke explains the background: he was a synagogue ruler who, together with his entire family, believed in Jesus after listening to Paul's preaching (Acts 18:8). Sosthenes is listed as the co-sender of the first letter to the Corinthians (1 Cor 1:1), and Luke tells us that he was beaten up by his fellow Jews even though he was a synagogue ruler, because he had become a follower of the Way (Acts 18:17).

Paul mentions Apollos a number of times in his first letter to the Corinthians, especially when he explains that the Corinthians should not be divided by following prominent leaders (1 Cor 1:12; 3:4–6, 22). Paul presents him as a fellow worker whom he holds in esteem (1 Cor 4:6; 16:12). Luke also presents Apollos as one of the effective preachers who strengthened the church in Corinth. Luke provides us with the information about his connection with the Corinthian church. Apollos, a fervent preacher of the gospel, first met Priscilla and Aquila in Ephesus, who helped him to present 'the way of God more adequately'. Then he arrived at Corinth with a letter of commendation from the church in Ephesus, and served as a fine preacher and leader (Acts 18:24–28; 19:1).

Thessalonica

Luke writes briefly about Paul's time in Thessalonica. Both Paul and Luke are in agreement that Paul arrived at Thessalonica from Philippi, and especially because of the suffering they had faced in Philippi. There was also strong opposition in Thessalonica. Paul writes: 'We had previously suffered and been insulted in Philippi, as you know, but with the help of our God we dared to tell *you* this gospel in spite of strong opposition.' Then he adds, 'Surely you remember, brothers, our toil and hardship' (1 Thess 2:2, 9). The episode seems like what Luke describes in Acts. The Jews started a riot to oppose Paul and his team, intruded into Jason's house and severely insulted him before the public, and incited the crowd and the city officials, throwing them into turmoil. Furthermore, they chased Paul even to Berea, and agitated the crowd there, stirring them up against Paul. With the words, 'You suffered from your own countrymen', Paul most probably refers to the sufferings of 'Jason and some other brothers' (1 Thess 2:14; cf. Acts 17:5–13).

Paul tells the Thessalonians that he and his companions 'were torn away from you' at Thessalonica (1 Thess 2:17), and Luke also describes how 'As soon as it was night, the brothers sent Paul and Silas away to Berea' (Acts 17:10). The unexpected, hurried and reluctant departure from Thessalonica is obvious in both accounts. Paul sends Timothy to Thessalonica to strengthen and encourage the believers in faith so that they might be steadfast despite persecution and hardship (1 Thess 3:1–6). Paul says that he stayed in

Athens and sent Silas and Timothy to Thessalonica. Luke also notes the separation of Paul from Silas and Timothy around this time. Luke further writes that Paul was escorted to Athens, and was waiting for Silas and Timothy there (Acts 17:15–16). Then they returned to Paul in Corinth from Macedonia (Acts 18:5), and if Paul writes 1 Thessalonians from Corinth, both Paul and Luke are in agreement as to the movements of Silas and Timothy.

Philippi

Paul writes to exhort the Philippians to 'stand firm in one spirit . . . without being frightened in any way by those who oppose you.' Then Paul reminds them of his own suffering during his missionary work there: 'you are going through *the same struggle you saw I had*, and now hear that I still have' (Phil 1:27–30). He says the same thing to the Thessalonians: 'We had previously suffered and been insulted in Philippi, as you know' (1 Thess 2:2). Luke also records the suffering, opposition and imprisonment which Paul experienced when he preached the gospel in Philippi (Acts 16:16–40), and Paul seems to refer to such incidents in writing to the Philippians and Thessalonians.

As he plans to send Timothy to Philippi, Paul commends him: '*You know that Timothy has proved himself*, because . . . he has served with me in the work of the gospel' (Phil 2:22). This comment proves that Timothy was with Paul, working together for the gospel (Acts 16:1–3). Luke also writes that Timothy was in Paul's team while he preached the gospel in Philippi and later in Thessalonica and Berea (Acts 17:14).

Paul also reminds the Philippians to follow his example and to 'live according to the pattern we gave you . . . as I have often told you before and now I say again even with tears' (Phil 3:17–18). Paul seems to refer to his previous teaching when he visited them after he had been released from prison and before he left the city. Luke briefly writes in Acts 16:40: 'After Paul and Silas came out of the prison, they went to Lydia's house, where they met with the brothers and encouraged them. Then they left.' Paul was concerned about their spiritual growth and godly living: 'Whatever you have learned or received or heard from me, or seen in me – put it into practice' (Phil 4:9). Luke also depicts Paul as a leader who revisits his new converts to encourage and strengthen them to 'conduct [themselves] in a manner worthy of the gospel of Christ' (Acts 14:21–25; 16:40; 18:23; Phil 1:27).

Paul also reminds the Philippians that in the early days of their acquaintance with the gospel, they supplied his needs when he left the city (Phil 4:15). Luke writes that Lydia and her family most readily offered Paul and the team generous hospitality right after they accepted the gospel. It is probably in such generous spirit that the Philippians may have given material support when Paul left Macedonia and again later (Phil 4:10, 15, 18; Acts 16:15).

Ephesus

Towards the end of his third missionary campaign, Paul was determined to visit Jerusalem. He repeatedly expressed his desire to visit Rome on his way to Spain. He even says that 'there is no more place for me to work in these [eastern] regions, and since I have been longing for many years to see you, I plan to do so when I go to Spain' (Rom 15:23–24; so earlier, Rom 1:11–15). But in the very next verse he abruptly declares, 'Now, however, I am on my way to Jerusalem' (Rom 15:25). And he eventually arrives in Jerusalem.

Luke writes the same outline but with more explanation. He writes when and where Paul changed his mind to visit Jerusalem first. After having seen huge results from the ministry in Ephesus, Luke reports that Paul decided to go to Jerusalem: 'After I have been there . . . I must visit Rome also' (Acts 19:21). Luke must have known of the change in Paul's plan to visit Rome,[38] because he was, most probably, with Paul during those days.

Luke records that Tychicus is from the province of Asia (i.e. Ephesus), and he is with Paul (Acts 20:4). Then we see Paul sending his letter to the Ephesians through Tychicus as he returns to Ephesus (Eph 6:21). Later Paul sends him to Colossae together with Onesimus and the letter to the Colossians (Col 4:7). In his letter to the Ephesians Paul presents deeply profound doctrinal and practical teachings, much deeper than in any other letters of his (with the exception of Romans). Paul tells the Corinthians that he could feed them only 'milk, not solid food, for [they] were not ready for it' (1 Cor 3:2). But in the case of the Ephesians Paul feeds them with solid food in the letter, since he regards them as mature in Christ. This is most probably because Paul taught them in the Tyrannus hall for more than two years, and also gave their elders intensive teaching at Miletus (Acts 19:9; 20:17–35), and he taught them further by writing a letter to them earlier (Eph 3:3).[39] So Paul reminds them: 'Surely you heard of him [Christ] and were taught in him in accordance with the truth that is in Jesus. You were taught . . .' (Eph 4:21–22).

Conclusion

We have found many corresponding pieces of information between what Paul writes in the letters concerning his missionary days and what Luke describes about Paul's work in those regions with the 'we-passages'. Although some seem to be minor details, such correspondences are remarkable. This result gives us further assurance that Luke was travelling with Paul in those regions, and so he accurately presents his information in describing Paul and

---

[38] For the reason for this change, see Chae, 'Paul's Apostolic Self-Awareness', 116–37.

[39] We do not know about this letter.

his mission in Corinth, Thessalonica, Philippi and Ephesus. Our study has also shown that Luke spent substantially extended periods with Paul – probably from the start of the second missionary journey till Paul's time in Rome. Luke was with Paul much longer than the periods covered by the we-passages. The implication is important. It means that Luke heard Paul's stories directly from him, heard him preaching to Jewish and Gentile audiences, and saw their different responses. More significantly, it means that Luke knew the apostle intimately, and he would have collected much of the source of his accounts on Paul from the apostle himself. The sections of Acts 6:8 – 8:3; 9:1–30; 11:19–30 and 12:25 – 28:31 contain stories and speeches that are related to Paul. They occupy over 60 per cent of the verses in Acts. It is almost certain that Luke obtained those materials (verbally) from Paul himself.

Earlier, in Chapter 2, we established that there is a strong compatibility between the real Paul and the Lucan Paul in their missionary preaching in Corinth and Thessalonica.[40] Likewise, the agreement between the Paul of the letters and the Paul of Acts is at a very high level, especially in the we-passages, as well as in other detailed descriptions of Paul's ministry in the above-mentioned regions. Often Paul's material verifies what Luke writes in Acts, and vice versa. This shows that Luke uses highly reliable sources.

There are two more points to be mentioned with regard to the we-passages and Luke's sources. The first is related to Acts 21 – 28. Scholars wonder why Luke writes this large portion, which is not about Paul's evangelistic campaign but about Paul's trial and defence. Some argue that Luke wrote Acts for primarily apologetic purposes to support Paul's trial. However, that does not seem convincing as the twenty earlier chapters are not directly related to Paul's defence case. Acts as a whole would have been written for the Christian community rather than for Roman officials.

It seems more probable that Luke writes this long section of Acts 21 – 28 because he has his own first-hand source material and his own experience in writing these chapters. He may have thought that he could include, in this section, many more pieces of valuable information about Paul, such as his Jewish and Hellenistic background, his conversion/call testimony, Jewish opposition to his mission to the Gentiles, his itinerary to get to Rome, and his ministry in Rome. Without these chapters, our understanding of Paul would be somewhat limited. As we have shown above, Luke travelled with Paul, or he was near the apostle, during the period described in Acts 21 – 28. Luke seems to highlight this section because he could write it with confidence as he himself was a travelling companion and an eyewitness of what he saw and experienced or heard from Paul himself.

Second, there is a general consensus among scholars that Luke used Mark as his source in writing his Gospel. There we see Luke rewriting Mark's material, expressing the content in his own words. Like any author he writes by

---

[40] See above, pp. 72–78.

selecting and editing his source and tradition. This does not degrade his reliability as an author. Rather, both the Gospel of Matthew and the Gospel of Mark testify that the Gospel of Luke has been written carefully by an author who has collected material through his thorough investigation, and has applied careful editing. Luke's chronological presentation of Jesus' life is known as the most thorough of all the Gospels. So, there is no question about the reliability of Luke's Gospel.

Among the authors of the Gospels, Luke had no acquaintance with Jesus. What, then, made him so committed to collecting the materials and writing his Gospel? It seems probable that he was intrigued by the Jesus about whom Paul was preaching; Paul's absolute love and loyalty to Jesus and his message must have compelled Luke to know more about Jesus, his life and teaching, and to make him known by writing an accurate and full account of Jesus' life. With his Gospel, Luke proved himself to be a reliable author by demonstrating his thoroughness in collecting materials from other reliable sources, and in presenting them in an orderly manner. Thus there is no reason why we should believe that his characteristics as an author would be different when he writes his second volume.[41] Just as he did for the first volume, he must have 'carefully investigated everything from the beginning' and written 'an orderly account' in his second book to the same recipient, Theophilus (Luke 1:1–4; Acts 1:1).

---

[41] *Pace* Dibelius, 'Style Criticism', 4–11, who asserts that Luke employed a free-style method in writing Acts, unlike the method he had employed for his Gospel.

5

Luke's Portrayal of Paul's Life and Ministry

In this chapter we shall attempt to investigate the credibility of Luke's account of Paul in Acts by examining the thesis of John Knox. Knox's conclusion and methodology are briefly commented on in the Introduction to this volume. However, his precise methodology is worth mentioning here: 'a fact only suggested by Paul in the letters has a status which even the most unequivocal statement of Acts, if not otherwise supported, cannot confer. We may, with proper caution, use Acts to supplement the autobiographical data of the letters, but never to correct them.'[1] Knox has maintained his thesis all along, and he clearly summed up his position in 1983:

> There is nothing new in my proposal that Paul's own letters were a better source for Paul than Acts could be; I suppose that no one could deny so obvious a fact. Any novelty my proposal could claim lay in my conception of the dimension of the superiority. I argued . . . (a) that the merest hint in the letters is to be deemed worth more than the most explicit statement of Acts; (b) that a statement in Acts about Paul is to be regarded as incredible if it conflicts directly with the letters (as many statements do) and is to be seriously questioned even if a conflict is only suggested; and (c) that statements about Paul in Acts are to be accepted with confidence only if such statements are fully and explicitly confirmed in the letters. In a word, it was argued that we can rely only on the letters for completely assured biographical information.[2]

---

[1] Knox, *Chapters*, 32. Followers of Knox include Lüdemann, *Paul* and Jewett, *Dating Paul's Life*; prior to Knox, Lake, 'Apostolic Council of Jerusalem', 198–9; McNeile, *St Paul*, x, have already contended: 'Where *Acts* and epistles agree, our confidence can be complete; where they differ, the latter must be allowed full weight, while the former is used with the recognition that it is a secondary authority.' McNeile does not list F.C. Baur in his bibliography. However, it would be incredible if he had made this statement independently of Baur. More recent advocates of the Knox principle include Murphy-O'Connor, *Paul*, vi and *passim*; Roetzel, *Paul*, 4, 10–11.

[2] Knox, 'Chapters', 342.

Although Knox accepts that Luke 'had some excellent primitive sources [and that] he used these sources carefully and faithfully',[3] he asserts that Luke arranged the order of his materials, and also freely composed very large parts of the speeches for Paul in order to make them suit the purpose of his book. So, in practice, Knox hardly accepts Luke's account of Paul's life and ministry. Rather, he insists on reconstructing the life and ministry of the apostle on the basis of data solely provided by the letters.[4] When he examines Luke's account of Paul it is primarily in order for him to identify Luke's special interest, which he claims was different from that of Paul, as shown in the letters.

Knox highlights three particular areas where Luke's purpose has coloured his description of Paul's life and ministry. Luke's first tendency is to emphasize the role of Jerusalem in the beginnings of the church. Knox argues that Luke endeavours to establish that 'Christianity is the continuance of authentic Judaism as the true Israel'. Second, Luke portrays Paul as acknowledging the authority of the church in Jerusalem, and as working under its direction, and Luke depicts a situation where, despite some problems occurring from time to time, the Jewish and Gentile churches remained united and harmonious under the leadership of the Jerusalem apostles. Third, Luke's presentation of material is politically shaped by his conception that Paul's religion is Judaism in a real sense, and therefore Paul had done nothing wrong to deserve severe punishment.

Certainly one should accept that 'Paul's letters [are] a better source for Paul than Acts could be', and Knox expects this to be taken for granted as 'no one could deny so obvious a fact'. However, if this assumption is to stand, certain prerequisites must be established first: that both Paul and Luke are writing on the same or similar subjects, covering the same or similar scope with the same or similar purpose. However, as we have shown earlier, in the Introduction, Paul's letters and Acts are quite different in nature and scope.[5] Having this basic understanding in mind, in this chapter we shall compare the accounts of Paul and Luke on several details of Paul's life and ministry. This will include Paul's Jewish background, his early Christian years, his missionary journeys, his co-workers and the persecution he suffered. The wide-ranging aspect of our comparative study will enable us to determine the extent of the reliability of Luke's portrayal of Paul's life and ministry. Although we may not argue point by point against Knox, our investigation will offer an alternative to Knox's methodology and conclusion.

---

[3] Knox, *Chapters*, 10–11.

[4] Murphy-O'Connor, 'Pauline Missions', 90–91, has attempted this approach, but earlier Weiss, *Earliest Christianity*, 1:148, warned: 'It has been a minor self-deception of Criticism to believe itself capable of drawing a picture of Paul solely from his letters.'

[5] See above, pp. 6–8.

Paul's Early Life

Paul's Jewish background

Paul did not intend to write an autobiography in his letters, partly because he had already told his converts about his life during his missionary work: 'you have heard of my previous way of life in Judaism' (Gal 1:13). Nevertheless, we can collect some information from his letters about his pre-Christian life. He was a Jew, a Benjamite and a Pharisee (Rom 11:1; Phil 3:5), who was thoroughly trained in the Jewish law, and was extremely zealous for Jewish traditions even more than his contemporaries (Gal 1:14). Driven by this zeal, he may conceivably have become a Judaic missionary to the Gentiles before his conversion (Gal 5:11). The Lucan Paul also says that he was a Jew and a Pharisee, who lived according to the strictest sect of Judaism (Acts 22:3–4; 23:6; 26:4–5).

Paul writes that he 'intensely . . . persecuted the church of God and tried to destroy it' (Gal 1:13), and this is what Luke describes in Acts: 'Saul began to destroy the church. Going from house to house, he dragged off men and women and put them in prison' (Acts 8:3). Luke's description of the intensity of Paul's persecuting activities seems correct in the light of the language Paul himself uses in Galatians. That Paul intensely persecuted the church is repeatedly mentioned both in the letters and in Acts.[6] Some scholars have asserted that Luke indicates that Paul persecuted the church in Jerusalem while Paul does not indicate it. Their assertion is based on Galatians 1:22: 'I was not personally known to the churches of Judea'.[7] However, one must note that Paul continues to write that the church in Judea heard the report: 'The man who formerly persecuted *us* is now preaching the faith he once tried to destroy' (Gal 1:23). Here the pronoun 'us' refers to the believers in Judea. Furthermore, it is most unlikely that he would have neglected the main Christian centre when he tried to destroy the church of God (Gal 1:23).

A.J. Hultgren argues that the phrase, 'I was not personally known', means that Paul 'simply did not "show his face" in the churches of Judea as an apostle'. He continues to argue that in the broader context of Galatians 1:18–24, Paul says that after his brief visit with Peter and James, he went directly to the region of Syria and Cilicia. Therefore, no one except Peter and James could personally know him. Hultgren is right to conclude that 'there is essential agreement between Acts and Galatians that [Paul] did persecute the

---

[6] 1 Cor 15:9; Gal 1:13, 23; Phil 3:5–6; 1 Tim 1:13; Acts 7:54 – 8:3; 9:1–2, 13–14, 21; 22:3–5, 19; 26:9–11.

[7] E.g. Bultmann, 'Paul', 113; Haenchen, *Acts*, 297–8; Bornkamm, *Paul*, 15; Guignebert in H. G. Wood, 'Conversion', 277. On the other hand, those who affirm Paul's persecution in Jerusalem/Judea include Dodd, *Meaning*, 23; Dibelius, *Studies*, 46–7; Klausner, *From Jesus to Paul*, 318; Wood, 'Conversion', 277; Kim, *Origin*, 49.

church in Judea first'.[8] The verb (*portheō*) occurs nowhere else in the New Testament, except once in Acts and twice in Galatians (Gal 1:13, 23; Acts 9:21), and it is significant to note that this very rare verb is used by both Paul and Luke in their description of the intensity of Paul's hostility towards the church.[9] It is also significant to see both Paul and Luke use the same phrase, *zēlōtēs huparchōn*, 'being a zealot', to describe Paul (Gal 1:14; Acts 22:3).

The Lucan Paul adds that he was born in Tarsus and brought up in Jerusalem, receiving education under Gamaliel (Acts 21:39; 22:3; cf. 9:11; 11:25; 23:34; 26:4). Paul does not mention Gamaliel in his letters, and so J. Knox disregards Luke's reference to Gamaliel. However, R. Riesner seems right to argue that the way Paul uses the Old Testament to support his arguments indirectly suggests his training under Gamaliel.[10] He was fluent in Aramaic (Acts 21:40; 22:2; 26:14) and in Greek (Acts 21:37). J. Knox accepts only two rather insignificant accounts from Acts as reliable: that Paul's Jewish name was Saul, and that he was born in Tarsus of Cilicia. But there is no information in the letters either to affirm or deny these two accounts. However, it is likely that Paul's father gave him the name after the most prominent figure in his tribe, King Saul.[11]

Overall, Luke's report seems credible because it explains why Paul was so familiar with Greek language and culture, and also with the Hebrew Scriptures. It explains his career in Jerusalem, how he could travel the Roman world so freely, and why he could appeal to the emperor for a trial. Paul's great command of Greek indicates that he is certainly a Hellenistic Jew of the Diaspora, and one cannot rule out the possibility that he was from Tarsus.[12] Paul says that he returned to Jerusalem after fourteen years (after his conversion) (Gal 2:1), but he does not give us information on where he had been in those ten years or so. Luke writes that he had been to Tarsus for about ten years (Acts 9:30; 11:25). Paul's silence on Tarsus does not necessarily negate Luke's information; rather it may explain and fill the gap of about ten years in his itinerary.

Conversion/call and early Christian years

Paul writes that at the peak of his persecuting activities, God revealed his Son

---

[8] Hultgren, 'Paul's Persecutions', 105–7.

[9] Haenchen, *Acts*, 297–8, does not seem correct in asserting that Luke dramatically portrays Paul's persecution in order to maximize his transformation.

[10] Riesner, *Paul's Early Period*, 154; Murphy-O'Connor, *Paul*, 59, also accepts Paul being a disciple of Gamaliel; Neusner, *Rabbinic Traditions*, 15, 294–5, does not see a family link between Hillel and Gamaliel.

[11] The Lucan Paul mentions 'Saul son of Kish, of the tribe of Benjamin' (Acts 13:21); see Hengel, *Pre-Christian Paul*, 8–10, for some useful points on Paul's name.

[12] Paul's origin in Tarsus is questioned by Burchard, *dreizehnte Zeuge*, 34–5 n. 42, but defended by Hengel, *Pre-Christian Paul*, 1: it is 'barely doubted'.

in him unexpectedly and dramatically, and that during this event he received the gospel by revelation from Jesus Christ (Rom 1:1, 5; Gal 1:12–16; cf. 1 Tim 1:12; 1 Cor 9:1; 15:8). Luke also reports that Christ appeared to Paul while he was 'still breathing out murderous threats against the Lord's disciples' (Acts 9:1). Both Paul and Luke use the same word, *ōphthēn*, to describe how the Lord *appeared* to Paul with a purpose (1 Cor 15:8; Acts 26:16). Both of them also agree that Paul saw the Lord and heard a voice (1 Cor 9:1, 17; 15:8; Acts 9:17; 22:14). Paul says that he received a commission to preach the gospel to the Gentiles (Gal 1:15–16). Luke writes that Paul was appointed beforehand (*proecheirisato* in Acts 22:14; 26:17), and this verb has the same connotation which Paul conveys in Galatians 1:15: God 'set me apart from birth and called me by his grace'. Paul's phrase, 'when God . . . was pleased' (Gal 1:15), denotes God's free decision, and this is also shown as God's election in Acts 9:15; 22:14; 26:16–17. Paul talks about the unconditional nature of God's free initiatives. Likewise, all of Luke's three accounts make it clear that the Christophany was a completely unexpected and undeserved act of God with the motif of election,[13] especially to commission Paul to preach the gospel to the Gentiles (Acts 9:15; 22:15; 26:16–18).[14]

What Luke writes about the immediate response of Christians after Paul's conversion is also in agreement with what Paul says (Acts 9:21; Gal 1:23–24). Luke provides vivid details of the Christophany event, including the location and the nature of the revelation. However, it is often noted that Luke says that Paul was called for Jews and Gentiles, while Paul insists that he was called for Gentiles. What one needs to take into account is that Paul talks about his calling to the Gentiles in the course of defending his ministry among the Gentiles, and also of writing to the Gentile churches. But in Romans, where Paul directs his argument more towards the Jews, he expresses his fundamental concern for his people and his ministry among them (Rom 9:1–5; 10:1; 11:14). The account of the Christophany is given three times not to expose the nature of fiction or contradiction, but to affirm the importance of the event.

Luke writes about the involvement of Ananias immediately after the Damascus event in Paul's experience of receiving sight and baptism, and thus for many scholars this record is proof that Luke's account is not reliable in the light of what Paul says to the Galatians (Gal 1:1, 12, 16). However, Hengel is right to argue that Paul would not baptize others if he himself were not baptized, and that 'historically, Paul's baptism can hardly have taken

---

[13] Hengel and Schwemer, *Paul Between Damascus and Antioch*, 41.
[14] After a comprehensive examination, Hengel and Schwemer, *Paul Between Damascus and Antioch*, 35–50, esp. 49–50, conclude that all three variant accounts of Paul's experience of Christophany near Damascus, and also baptism by Ananias and his preaching in Damascus, are historical.

place anywhere but in Damascus'.[15] Hengel also insists that Paul's assertion, 'I did not consult any man' (Gal 1:16b), is primarily connected to the Jerusalem apostles ('nor did I go up to Jerusalem': 1:17a), not to Ananias.[16] God arranged for someone to welcome Paul to the Christian community in Damascus as well as to baptize him by giving him instruction and by receiving a commitment from him, and there is no reason to deny that Ananias carried out such roles. In receiving baptism from him, Paul called on the name of the Lord and made a commitment to him (cf. Acts 22:16; Rom 10:13). For such a role God provided Ananias as his human agent.[17] All was done by divine initiative, not by the church authorities. Therefore, Paul's insistence is valid: he is 'an apostle – sent not from men nor by man, but by Jesus Christ and God the Father,' and he declares, 'I did not receive it [the gospel] from any man, nor was I taught it; rather, I received it by revelation from Jesus Christ' (Gal 1:1, 12).

We must note, however, that Paul's declaration is made in order to refute the claim that he is inferior to the apostles in Jerusalem (cf. 2 Cor 11:5; 12:11). He did not receive the gospel and his commission from any human being (presumably including Ananias), but neither does Luke say that Paul received it from Ananias. Luke makes it very clear that Ananias was only the human agent of the heavenly Commissioner. By quoting what Jesus says to Ananias, and the subsequent story (Acts 9:10–19), Luke explains how Paul the persecutor was introduced to the Christian community in Damascus and was received by them. Luke presents Ananias as the mediator between Paul and the church rather than between Paul and Christ.[18]

S.G. Wilson seems right to interpret Luke's approach as one of gradually reducing the role of Ananias from Acts chapter 9 compared to his role in chapters 22 and 26. He finds that this is the main reason why accounts of Paul's call vary.[19] During his defence before King Agrippa, the Lucan Paul explains his conversion and call experience without mentioning Ananias' involvement (Acts 26:12–23). The real Paul was in a similar situation of defending himself when he was writing the letter to the Galatians. We cannot discredit Luke on the basis of his mention of Ananias in Acts 9 and 22 when Paul is silent about him in the letters.

According to Luke the Christophany took place near Damascus (Acts 9:1–19; 22:6; 26:12, 20). Although Paul does not specify Damascus as the place of his conversion, the implication is obvious. He says that he went to

---

[15] Hengel and Schwemer, *Paul Between Damascus and Antioch*, 43–4.
[16] Hengel and Schwemer, *Paul Between Damascus and Antioch*, 43–4.
[17] Hengel and Schwemer, *Paul Between Damascus and Antioch*, 46 n. 211, following Barrett, *Acts*, ICC, 1:444.
[18] Cf. Dunn, *Baptism*, 73–8; Hengel, *Earliest Christianity*, 84.
[19] Wilson, *Gentiles*, 162.

Arabia soon after[20] the revelation of Christ to him, and then he returned to Damascus (Gal 1:16–17). The fact that he *returned to* Damascus indicates that he had left for Arabia from Damascus as a new person. Luke is silent about Paul's three-year sojourn in Arabia. Paul tells the Corinthians that he escaped arrest by being lowered in a basket from a window in the city wall of Damascus, and the background of this incident is described in Acts in more detail (2 Cor 11:32–33; Acts 9:23–25). Both accounts show that Paul was associated with Damascus because he had been converted near the city, and he had joined the Christian community there.

Again, in both sources Paul went to Jerusalem from Damascus where he tried to get to know the apostles (Gal 1:18; Acts 9:26). Paul says that he spent some time with Peter and James, while Luke says that Paul 'stayed with the [apostles]' (Gal 1:18–19; Acts 9:26–28). Luke provides more detail: that it was through the mediation of Barnabas that the apostles accepted Paul who before had severely persecuted the church. There is no reason to disregard Luke's report because it is fully understandable why the apostles were afraid of Paul. They may not have been sure of the genuineness of his conversion. This could be the reason why Paul had a private meeting with Peter and James (Gal 1:18–20). Or they might have wanted to keep his visit a secret to protect him from his former Jewish zealot colleagues, who would regard him a traitor, and thus he was someone at risk as a target for revenge.[21] These considerations may form the background of Paul's low-profile visit to the Holy City: why Paul met only Peter and James, stayed for only fifteen days, and did not come to Jerusalem for the next ten years or so. According to Luke it was Paul, however, who exposed himself to the Hellenistic Jews by debating in the name of Jesus. Both accounts agree that Paul's next move was from Jerusalem to Syria and Cilicia (Gal 1:21; Acts 9:30). Luke reports in more detail that, due to the Jewish plot to kill him, Paul moved to Tarsus via Caesarea.

Then Paul writes that 'fourteen years later' he went up again to Jerusalem, together with Barnabas and Titus (Gal 2:1–3). Paul does not tell us from where he went to Jerusalem, or where he met Barnabas, or when and how he left Cilicia. Luke fills in the gap; he explains that Barnabas went to Tarsus to invite Paul to work with him in the church in Antioch (Acts 11:25–26). It is most likely, then, that Paul worked together with Barnabas in Antioch, from where they went up to Jerusalem. Later Paul says that he went to Jerusalem 'in response to a revelation' and that he presented the gospel that he preached among the Gentiles (Gal 2:2–3), but he does not tell us where he went to from

---

[20] The Greek, *all' apēlthon eis Arabian*, does not indicate that he went to Arabia immediately after his conversion as the NIV rendering shows, but that he did not immediately go up to Jerusalem to see the apostles.

[21] Hengel and Schwemer, *Paul Between Damascus and Antioch*, 134, following Lietzmann.

Jerusalem. For Luke, Paul's second visit to Jerusalem was to deliver the relief fund from the Antioch church in response to Agabus' prophecy, and then he returned to Antioch (Acts 11:27–30; 12:25). This appears to be a major difference between the accounts of Paul and Luke. We have suggested above that Galatians 2:1–3 most probably refers to Acts 11:27–30, and Galatians 2:4–10 to Acts 15.[22] If we are right, even if both accounts are presented with different purposes and emphases, they do not contradict each other.

Paul the Missionary Apostle

Paul's missionary journeys

Paul is fully conscious that he was 'set apart' to proclaim the gospel (Rom 1:1; cf. 1 Tim 1:12), and even says that he was set apart from birth (Gal 1:15). Luke also uses the same root-word, *aphorizō*, to say that Paul was 'set apart' for the work God had prepared for them (Acts 13:2). It was for the proclamation of the gospel to both Gentiles and Jews as a missionary that God called him. Luke provides us not only with the background and occasion of Paul's missionary beginning but also his missionary career which extends for a few decades. It is not easy to reconstruct Paul's missionary journeys solely from his letters, for he says little about them in the letters. However, we may start the investigation from Romans. Paul is going to Jerusalem with the collection from the Gentile churches in Galatia, Macedonia and Achaia (Rom 15:25–32; 1 Cor 16:1; 2 Cor 8:1–15). By this time his work in the east has been regarded as completed, and so he was eager to go to Rome and Spain (Rom 15:23–24, 32). Thus Romans was written after the churches in Galatia, Asia, Macedonia and Achaia were established. They include the churches in Galatia, in Thessalonica, in Philippi, in Corinth and in Ephesus, to all of which Paul sent letters. The different destinations of Paul's letters provide clear evidence that he had planted those churches through his itinerant missionary campaigns.[23]

The first missionary journey

To the Galatians Paul writes with reference to the event of the Jerusalem conference: 'We did not give in to them for a moment, so that the truth of the gospel might remain with *you*' (Gal 2:5). The pronoun 'you' refers to the Christians in Galatia. This clearly shows that Paul carried out the missionary work in Galatia *before* the Jerusalem conference. Furthermore, the Jerusalem apostles gave Paul and Barnabas the right hand of fellowship, recognizing

---

[22] See above, pp. 89–92.
[23] *Pace* Knox, *Chapters*, 25: 'the letters of Paul reveal not the slightest awareness on his part that he is engaged in great journeys.'

that God had given Paul the apostleship to the Gentiles (Gal 2:7–9). This indicates that Barnabas worked with Paul among the Gentiles before the Jerusalem conference. Moreover, the fact that Paul was in Antioch together with Barnabas at the time of the Antioch incident suggests that Antioch was probably the return base for their missionary work, as Luke writes (Gal 2:13; Acts 14:26–27; 15:30, 35).

Luke's account fits into this skeleton framework. Paul's missionary journey described in Acts 13 – 14 precedes the Jerusalem conference reported in Acts 15. He also writes that the first tour started from Antioch and ended there; and it was from Antioch that Paul and Barnabas went to Jerusalem for a conference (Acts 13:1–5; 15:1–2, 34–35; Gal 2:4–10). The areas where the churches had been planted, as mentioned in Acts 13 – 14, belong to the province of Galatia, to which Paul's letter was sent.[24] At the conference in Jerusalem he defended the practice of uncircumcision, so that the truth of the gospel he had preached to the Galatians might remain with them (Gal 2:5).

The second missionary journey

Luke records that Paul left for the second journey together with Silas. Starting from Antioch, he travelled through the provinces of Syria, Cilicia, Phrygia and Galatia, including Derbe and Lystra (Acts 15:40 – 16:6). Having been kept from preaching the word of God in Asia and Bithynia, Paul arrived at Troas. From there he went over to Philippi of Macedonia after seeing the vision of a Macedonian (Acts 16:6–10). Only at this point does Paul begin to talk about his campaign: 'I went to Troas . . . and went on to Macedonia' (2 Cor 2:12–13), and so in effect he confirms Luke's account. Furthermore, he indicates that he had visited Philippi before he went to Thessalonica (1 Thess 2:2). Paul's order of travel through the cities (Troas → Macedonia [Philippi] → Thessalonica) fits that of Luke: Troas → Philippi → Thessalonica → Berea → Athens → Corinth (Acts 16:11; 17:1, 10, 15; 18:1). Paul's references to the movements of Silas and Timothy from Asia Minor to Macedonia and Achaia (1 Thess 2:2; 3:1) largely fit with what Luke writes in Acts 16:12 – 20:2.

Luke continues to write about how Paul preached the gospel in Berea, Athens, Corinth and Ephesus, and returned to Antioch via Caesarea and Jerusalem (Acts 17:10, 16; 18:1, 21, 22). Paul says very little about what he did during this period. However, he tells the Thessalonians that he sent Timothy to them from Athens to strengthen and encourage them, and then he anxiously waited for Timothy's return (1 Thess 3:1–2). According to Luke, Paul was brought to Athens where he anxiously waited for Silas and Timothy, whom he had left in Macedonia (Acts 17:15–16). Later they joined Paul in

---

[24] It is to be noted that Galatians is the only letter of Paul addressed to the *churches* (in plural) (Gal 1:2).

The Historical Paul in Acts

Corinth from Macedonia (Acts 18:5). Though only Paul mentions Timothy's name, his account is very similar to that of Luke. Luke's record that Paul worked in Corinth during the second missionary journey can also be substantiated from Paul's remark: 'Now I am ready to visit you for the *third* time' (2 Cor 12:14). Paul's second visit had been planned as indicated in 1 Corinthians 16:5: 'After I go through Macedonia, I will come to you'. By the time he was writing the 'second' letter to the Corinthians he had already been there a second time (2 Cor 13:2).[25] The fact that he writes the first letter to them clearly indicates that he had made an earlier visit, and there is no reason why we should reject Luke's account of it in Acts 18.

The third missionary journey

Luke reports that Paul 'spent some time in Antioch' after the second journey (see Acts 18:23). It seems probable that the Antioch incident took place during this time (Gal 2:11–13).[26] Luke reports that Paul started his third missionary journey, including the return visits to Galatia and Phrygia, and then arrived at Ephesus. Paul writes to the Corinthians about his time in Ephesus: 'I will stay on at Ephesus until Pentecost, because a great door for effective work has opened to me, and there are many who oppose me' (1 Cor 16:8–9). Luke also describes the openness and opposition at Ephesus (Acts 19).

To the Corinthians Paul indicates that he would come to them after going through Macedonia. He even plans to spend the winter in Corinth, and eventually go to Rome (1 Cor 16:1–6). But before going to Rome he plans to go first to Jerusalem (Rom 15:23–25). According to Luke, Paul had the same plan: 'Paul decided to go to Jerusalem, passing through Macedonia and Achaia. "After I have been there," he said, "I must visit Rome also"' (Acts 19:21; cf. 20:16; 21:1–19).[27]

Paul was in Ephesus when he wrote the first letter to the Corinthians (1 Cor 16:9, 19), and he was planning to make a return visit to them, after going through Macedonia (1 Cor 16:5). He planned to visit the Corinthians on his way to Macedonia and come back to them from Macedonia, and then to travel from Corinth to Jerusalem (2 Cor 1:16). But later he explains why he had to reluctantly cancel his plan to visit Corinth (2 Cor 1:23). Luke seems to know of this change of plan: Paul travelled through Macedonia, and finally arrived in Greece, where he stayed for three months. Though he planned to return to

---

[25] Luke does not say anything about Paul's second visit to Corinth. Probably Luke wanted to focus on Paul's evangelistic work in Corinth, and to omit to mention this painful visit as it was outside the scope of his writing.

[26] See above, pp. 96–99, for our reasoning.

[27] Luke does not say anything about Paul's plan to visit Spain (Rom 15:24, 28). This is either because the plan came to Paul only by the time he wrote Romans or, as Bruce, *Acts: Greek*, 51, infers, because Luke omits it as his literary goal is not beyond Rome.

Corinth and to sail for Syria, he decided to go back through Macedonia due to the Jewish plot against him. So Paul sent some of his companions to Troas, and then several days later he joined them in Troas via Philippi, and sailed to Jerusalem via Miletus (Acts 20:1–3, 17).

Paul was aware of the life-threatening danger waiting for him in Jerusalem, and so he asked the believers in Rome to pray for him to be rescued from the unbelievers in Jerusalem (Rom 15:31). Luke also reports that Paul was fully aware of such a threat, and many believers begged him not to go to Jerusalem, and yet he was determined to go (Acts 21:10–14). Both Paul and Luke say that Paul came to Jerusalem with the collection gathered from among the Gentile churches (Rom 15:25–27; Acts 24:17). Luke describes the details of Paul's arrest in Jerusalem, his defence in Jerusalem and Caesarea, and his voyage to Rome (Acts 21 – 28). Paul keeps silent on all these matters, most probably because these incidents happened after most of his major letters had been written.

Luke mentions that Paul travelled by ship eleven times, including one long voyage to Rome.[28] Sailing across the ocean in the first century must have been a challenge as the techniques of shipbuilding and navigation were not yet sufficiently developed. Paul's own testimony that he was shipwrecked three times (2 Cor 11:25) indicates that Luke's description of Paul's travel by ships is highly credible.

Paul the church planter

One of the most outstanding portraits of Paul that Luke paints in Acts is Paul as a church planter. The Paul of Acts is a passionate evangelist. He tirelessly preaches the gospel in the major cities in the regions of Galatia, Asia, Macedonia and Greece. He makes three missionary journeys to travel around these areas, constantly looking for new territories in which to preach the gospel, as well as revisiting the cities where he had preached previously (Acts 14:21–25; 15:41; 16:4–5). In so doing he faced much opposition and persecution, but no hardship could stop him from preaching the gospel. Towards the end of his third missionary journey, he declares, 'I consider my life worth nothing to me, if only I may finish the race and complete the task the Lord Jesus has given me – the task of testifying to the gospel of God's grace' (Acts 20:24).

However, the Paul of Acts is more than an effective evangelist; he is a church planter. He carries out his evangelistic campaign with a small group of his associates at each place. He then gathers up the converts and establishes local churches, strengthening the disciples and encouraging them to remain true to the faith (Acts 14:21–22; 13:43; 16:40; 20:1–2). Furthermore, he appoints elders as their leaders: 'Paul and Barnabas appointed elders for

---

[28] Acts 13:4–5, 13; 14:20–28; 15:38–40; 16:11–12; 17:14; 18:18–23; 20:1–2, 5–6, 13–14; 27:1 – 28:14.

them in each church and, with prayer and fasting, committed them to the Lord' (Acts 14:23). The farewell speech to the Ephesian elders is a good example and evidence of his appointment of the leaders in the churches he planted (Acts 20:16–38). The Lucan Paul reminds the elders that he started their church by his dedicated preaching of the gospel: 'You know that I have not hesitated to preach anything that would be helpful to you but have taught you publicly and from house to house. I have declared to both Jews and Greeks that they must turn to God in repentance and have faith in our Lord Jesus' (Acts 20:20–21).

The Paul of the letters is also a church planter. The churches he has written to, except those in Rome and Colossae, show clear evidence that he planted those churches in Corinth, Galatia, Ephesus, Philippi and Thessalonica.[29] Luke writes about Paul's missionary endeavour in all these regions. However, to the churches in Rome and Colossae Paul makes it clear that he has not planted these churches, but has heard about their faith, and so he expresses his desire to visit them one day (Rom 1:11–13; 15:23–24; Col 1:4, 7–9). It is not a coincidence that Luke does not report any evangelistic work by Paul in these two cities as a free man conducting his own missionary activities.

The Paul of the letters is also a fervent evangelist. He is conscious of his calling as an evangelist, just like the Paul of Acts 20:24: 'Christ did not send me to baptise, but to preach the gospel' (1 Cor 1:17); 'Woe to me if I do not preach the gospel' (1 Cor 9:16; cf. 2 Cor 5:14–15). Paul makes it clear that the church in Corinth was planted through his preaching of the gospel: 'I want to remind you of the gospel I preached to you, which you received and on which you have taken your stand. By this gospel you are saved' (1 Cor 15:1–2). As he carries on his evangelistic preaching, he asks his churches to pray for him for more effective ministry (Eph 6:19–20; Col 4:3–4). After three missionary campaigns, Paul says, 'So from Jerusalem all the way round to Illyricum, I have fully proclaimed the gospel of Christ. It has always been my ambition to preach the gospel where Christ was not known' (Rom 15:19–20). The destinations of Paul's letters are obvious evidence of his evangelistic ministries in those regions, and Luke gives us information on how he planted the churches there. Both Paul and Luke clearly present the apostle as an evangelist and church planter.

It is also important to note, at this point, that both Paul and Luke emphasize Paul's work among the *Gentiles* in his missionary reports. Paul preached the gospel of Christ to the Jews as well as the Gentiles ('from *Jerusalem* to Illyricum'),[30] but he dares not boast of anything except what Christ has done

---

[29] That Paul does not write to the churches in Athens, Berea and Cyprus does not necessarily indicate that he did not preach the gospel there or plant churches in those cities.

[30] Cf. Riesner, *Paul's Early Period*, 241–4.

through him among the *Gentiles* (Rom 15:17–19; similarly 2 Cor 10:13–16). The Lucan Paul certainly preached to the Jews as well in Jerusalem and in the Gentile world during his first missionary journey (Acts 9:28–29; 13:5, 14, 26; 14:1). In his missionary reports, however, Paul stresses how God opened a door of faith to the *Gentiles* (Acts 14:27; 15:3, 12). The real Paul also was very conscious that his priestly duty was primarily to offer *Gentiles* to God by proclaiming the gospel to them (Rom 15:15–16).[31]

Paul the persecuted missionary

One of the characteristics of the Lucan Paul's missionary work is that he faced much opposition and persecution (Acts 14:5, 22; 16:19–40; 17:5–9, 13; 18:12–17; 20:1, 3; 21:4, 11–14, 27–36). The real Paul also speaks of such experience, and especially repeats his description of it to the Corinthians (1 Cor 4:9–13; 2 Cor 1:3–10; 4:8–12; 6:4–10; 11:23–27; 12:10). The comparison of their two accounts on persecution in *specific regions* may also contribute to judging the trustworthiness of Luke's writing on Paul's life and ministry.

Persecuted in the province of Asia

As Paul informs the Corinthians that he is planning to stay on in Ephesus until Pentecost, he adds that many people there oppose him (1 Cor 16:9). Later he also talks about his hardships in the same province of Asia: 'We were under great pressure, far beyond our ability to endure, so that we despaired even of life. Indeed, in our hearts we felt the sentence of death' (2 Cor 1:8–10).

According to Luke, Paul spoke boldly in the synagogue in Ephesus for three months, arguing persuasively about the kingdom of God. But some Jews publicly maligned his preaching, and so he left the synagogue. The Lucan Paul reminds the Ephesian elders of the fact that in Ephesus '[he] was severely tested by the plots of the Jews' (Acts 20:19). So he took the disciples to the hall of Tyrannus, and taught them there for two years. As a result, 'all the Jews and Greeks in the province of Asia heard the word of the Lord', accompanied by miracles (Acts 19:8–11). Luke concludes, 'In this way the word of the Lord spread widely and grew in power' (Acts 19:20). Most probably this is what the real Paul is talking about: 'But I will stay on at Ephesus until Pentecost, because a great door for effective work has opened to me, and there are many who oppose me' (1 Cor 16:8–9).

The opposition came from the Gentiles as well. Luke reports that the Gentile opponents were asserting, 'This fellow Paul has convinced and led astray

---

[31] See Chae, *Paul*, 21–32, for details.

large numbers of people here in Ephesus and in practically the whole province of Asia' (Acts 19:26). 'There arose a great disturbance about the Way' in Ephesus. The whole city was in an uproar, and the people arrested Paul's companions. The crowd shouted in unison for two hours (Acts 19:23–34). Paul's testimony that God delivered him from 'a deadly peril' in Ephesus (2 Cor 1:8–10) seems to refer to such a threatening situation described in Acts.

Persecuted in the province of Macedonia

Paul tells the Thessalonians that he was insulted in Philippi (1 Thess 2:2), and Luke also reports that in Philippi Paul was publicly insulted by being stripped, beaten and severely flogged (Acts 16:22–23). Luke also writes that the Jews in Thessalonica formed a mob and started a riot against Paul and his converts (Acts 17:5–8, 13). They dragged Jason and some other brothers before the city authorities, and this indicates that their persecution was not merely directed against the missionaries but also against those who believed and followed their teaching. Being extremely zealous, the Jews agitated the Gentile crowd and stirred them up, claiming that Paul was defying Caesar's decrees, and so the crowd and city officials were thrown into turmoil. Due to such severe opposition, Paul and Silas were prematurely sent away by the believers to Berea (Acts 17:10), just as Paul says: the Jews 'drove us out [and kept] us from speaking to the Gentiles [and so] we were torn away from you' (1 Thess 2:15–17).

Paul confirms that there was severe persecution when he first preached the gospel in Thessalonica. He reminds the Thessalonians that 'with the help of our God we dared to tell you his gospel in spite of strong opposition' (1 Thess 2:2). His wording, 'in spite of severe suffering, you welcomed the message with joy', indicates that the believers also had gone through persecution because of their new faith in Christ (1 Thess 1:6). He also acknowledges that the Thessalonians had been enduring all the persecutions and trials (1 Thess 3:4; 2 Thess 1:5). In the context of persecution, Paul confirms to the Thessalonians, 'You suffered from your own countrymen' (1 Thess 2:14). Paul tells the Corinthians that the Macedonians have had 'the most severe trial' (2 Cor 8:2). Both Paul and Luke stress the fact that the believers in Thessalonica, as well as the missionaries, suffered extreme persecution.

Paul also reminds the Thessalonians of his earlier report that he suffered persecution and insult in Philippi (1 Thess 2:1–2). Writing to the Philippians, he acknowledges the sufferings they are going through, the same struggle they saw Paul himself had gone through in Philippi (Phil 1:29–30). Paul does not give the details of the persecution he experienced, because the Philippians know it and the Thessalonians have already heard from him (1 Thess 2:2: 'as you know').

Persecuted in the province of Achaia

As mentioned earlier in this section, Paul expresses his experience of suffering and opposition more frequently and openly to the Corinthians than to any other church (1 Cor 4:8–13; 2 Cor 1:8–11; 4:7–12; 6:1–10; 11:21b–29; 12:1–10):

> We are hard pressed on every side, but not crushed; perplexed, but not in despair; persecuted, but not abandoned; struck down, but not destroyed (2 Cor 4:8–9).

> Rather, as servants of God we commend ourselves in every way: in great endurance; in troubles, hardships and distresses; in beatings, imprisonments and riots; in hard work, sleepless nights and hunger (2 Cor 6:4–5).

> I have worked much harder, been in prison more frequently, been flogged more severely, and been exposed to death again and again. Five times I received from the Jews the forty lashes minus one. Three times I was beaten with rods, once I was stoned, three times I was shipwrecked, I spent a night and a day in the open sea, I have been constantly on the move. I have been in danger from rivers, in danger from bandits, in danger from my own countrymen, in danger from Gentiles; in danger in the city, in danger in the country, in danger at sea; and in danger from false brothers (2 Cor 11:23–26).

Here Paul may mention his hardship in general and comprehensive terms, or more specifically, the persecution he experienced in other places, such as in Asia (1 Cor 16:9; 2 Cor 1:8–10) and Macedonia (2 Cor 8:2). However, the present verbs and the phrase 'to this very hour' in 1 Corinthians 4:11–13 indicate that Paul has been brutally treated, cursed, persecuted, slandered and regarded as scum and the refuse of the world throughout his missionary career thus far, including the suffering he had in Corinth as well as 'in Antioch, Iconium and Lystra' (cf. 2 Tim 3:11).

According to Luke, Paul suffered much from the Jews. They opposed him and became abusive. They made a united attack on Paul and brought him to court, and accused him of teaching people 'to worship God in ways contrary to the law' (Acts 18:6, 12). Furthermore, they became furious when their own synagogue rulers believed in Paul's message (Acts 18:8, 17). According to Luke, despite hardship Paul stayed in Corinth for a year and a half, and taught the Corinthians the word of God (Acts 18:11).[32] As we have just seen above, what Luke describes in detail about the persecution Paul and his converts suffered appears to be credible.

Furthermore, Luke depicts Paul as a suffering missionary. The Lucan Paul was told right at the beginning of his calling: 'But the Lord said to Ananias,

---

[32] Paul himself does not say much about his hardship in Corinth itself. Perhaps he did not need to mention it, for the Corinthians must have seen it.

"Go! This man is my chosen instrument to carry my name before the Gentiles and their kings and before the people of Israel. I will show him how much he must suffer for my name'" (Acts 9:15–16). He is not only persecuted but also imprisoned several times (Acts 16:23–40; 22:4; 23:18; 25:27; 26:20; 28:16–17). He suffered from his own people as well. He was considered a threat to the Jewish religious authorities. The real Paul also testifies that he has been put in prison more frequently than any of the other leaders (e.g. 2 Cor 6:4–10; 11:23–27; 2 Tim 1:8; 2:3, 9). The fact that Paul writes letters from prison(s) also makes it clear that he was arrested and imprisoned under Roman guards (Eph 3:1; 4:1; 6:20; Phil 1:7, 14, 17; 2 Tim 1:8, 16; 2:9; Phlm 1, 9), and Luke provides us with the stories of how he was arrested and how he came to be in prison in Rome (Acts 22 – 28).

Both Luke and the real Paul are also in agreement that Paul suffered persecution predominantly from the Jews: in Damascus (Acts 9:23–25), in Pisidian Antioch (13:50), in Iconium (14:5), in Lystra (14:19), in Philippi (16:22–24), in Thessalonica and Berea (17:5–9, 13), in Corinth (18:12–17), in Ephesus (19:23–41) and in Jerusalem (21:27–36; cf. 23:12, 15; 25:3). Paul himself testifies to the suffering he endured at the hands of the Jews (2 Cor 11:24, 26; 1 Thess 2:16). Further, Luke's portrayal of Jewish rejection of the gospel during Paul's missionary work, and of the Gentile welcome of it, is also what Paul writes in Romans 9 – 11 (9:27–33; 10:21; 11:1, 7–17, 28–32; 1 Thess 2:14–16).[33] Both the real Paul and the Lucan Paul describe the unbelief of the Jews using texts from the Old Testament (Rom 9:27–29; 10:21;[34] 11:7–10; Acts 13:40–41, 46–47; 28:26–27).

Paul's co-workers

Paul worked with a number of co-workers, and their names and activities are written in Paul's letters as well as in Luke's account. A comparative study of this particular topic may also shed some light on Luke's credibility in Acts.

Timothy and Silas

Paul worked with Timothy in Thessalonica, and later Paul sent him back there to strengthen the believers in their trials (1 Thess 3:2). Now Timothy has returned, and Paul writes the letter to the Thessalonians to encourage them and to answer the issues that have been raised via Timothy (1 Thess 3:6–7). Silas and Timothy are named as co-senders of the letters to the Thessalonians (1 Thess 1:1; 2 Thess 1:1).

Timothy also worked with Paul in Philippi, and he proved himself faithful among the Philippians. In the letter to them, Paul indicates his plan to send

---

[33] See Chae, *Paul*, 215–88, for a fuller treatment.
[34] See Chae, *Paul*, 234–50, for Paul's use of the Scriptures to affirm the unbelief of the Jews.

Timothy to Philippi to see how they are doing (Phil 2:19–23). Again Timothy is named as the co-sender of the letter (Phil 1:1). Luke does not mention Timothy in his description of Paul's work at Philippi, but he certainly alludes to his involvement by mentioning that Paul took him on his second missionary journey (Acts 16:1–3). Luke also says that Paul sent Timothy to Macedonia, and he may have included the visit to Philippi, 'the leading city of that district of Macedonia' (Acts 16:12; 19:22).

The church in Corinth was founded through the preaching of Paul, Silas and Timothy (2 Cor 1:19). The fact that Timothy is mentioned, without any introduction, as the co-sender of the letters to Corinth, Thessalonica and Philippi further suggests that he worked with Paul in these regions. After some initial missionary work, Paul sent Timothy back to Corinth (1 Cor 4:17; 16:10). He was again with Paul in Corinth when Paul wrote the letter to the Romans (Rom 16:21). Luke also writes that Silas and Timothy were with Paul in Corinth (Acts 18:5).

It is interesting to note that Luke's order of their names, 'Silas and Timothy', is always the same as Paul's (2 Cor 1:1, 19; 1 Thess 1:1; 2 Thess 1:1; Acts 17:14, 15; 18:5), and this indicates that Luke correctly reflects Paul's perception of the importance of their positions as his helpers.[35] Both Paul and Luke show that Timothy travelled with Paul towards the end of the third missionary campaign (Rom 16:21; 1 Cor 4:17; 16:10; Acts 19:22; 20:4).

Barnabas

Paul indicates that he and Barnabas worked together in Antioch (Gal 2:11–21) and during his (first) missionary journey among the Gentiles as self-supporting missionaries (1 Cor 9:6), and this is confirmed by Acts (11:25–30; 13:1 – 15:35). Both of them visited Jerusalem together (Gal 2:1–9; either Acts 11:27–30, or 15:1–35, or both). They went to Jerusalem to attend the conference, and there they were recognized by the Jerusalem apostles because of their mission to the Gentiles (Gal 2:4–10; Acts 15:25–36).

They started the missionary tour as a team (Gal 2:1–10), but Paul does not mention Barnabas when he talks about his journey across Asia Minor into Greece. Rather, he writes that he preached the gospel to the Corinthians with Silas and Timothy (2 Cor 1:19). What is written in Acts 15:36–41 seems to provide us with an explanation for their separation before the beginning of the second missionary journey. They had the same theology and practice with regard to the Gentiles until Peter was 'in the wrong' (Gal 2:11–14). This may show that their separation was not theological but due to differences in personal opinions, such as the quarrel over John Mark which Luke describes (Acts 15:36–41). Luke writes that Paul didn't want to take John Mark on the

---

[35] Silas was already a prophet in the Jerusalem church before he joined Paul for missionary work (Acts 15:32), and Paul was also a prophet (Acts 13:1).

second missionary journey, and this account seems credible when Paul says later that he needed John Mark; and in fact later they were together again in ministry (2 Tim 4:11; Col 4:10; Phlm 24).

Priscilla and Aquila

The records about Priscilla and Aquila in both Paul's letters and Acts also support each other. Paul passes on their greetings to the church in Corinth (1 Cor 16:19). This confirms that they worked with Paul in Corinth as Luke reports. What Luke writes explains the background to their greetings from Ephesus. According to Luke, Paul left Corinth with Priscilla and Aquila for Syria. On the way they arrived at Ephesus. Paul stayed there briefly, preaching in the synagogue. He then left for Syrian Antioch, while Priscilla and Aquila stayed in Ephesus (Acts 18:18–19). Now, during his third missionary campaign Paul has returned to the church in Ephesus, meeting at their house. Paul is writing to the Corinthians from Ephesus, and Paul adds their greetings to the Corinthians (1 Cor 16:8, 19).

In his letter to the Romans, Paul sends greetings to Priscilla and Aquila, who were pastoring a house church in Rome. Paul says that they are his fellow workers who risked their lives for him. He adds, 'all the churches of the Gentiles are grateful to them' (Rom 16:3–4). Most probably Paul had in mind the churches in Corinth and Ephesus in particular. Luke provides us with vital information to connect Corinth and Rome: they first came to Corinth because of the edict of Claudius, which expelled all Jews from Rome (Acts 18:2). Now they are back in Rome after Nero waived Claudius' edict (Rom 16:3–4; cf. 2 Tim 4:19). Again, it is noteworthy that both Paul and Luke often use the same order of the names, 'Priscilla and Aquila' (Rom 16:3; 2 Tim 4:19; Acts 18:18, 19, 26; cf. 1 Cor 16:19), uniquely putting the wife's name first, while Paul puts the husband's name first in the case of Andronicus and Junias (Rom 16:7).

Crispus and Sosthenes

Luke writes that Crispus was the synagogue ruler in Corinth who became a believer, and he and his entire family were baptized. Paul names this Crispus as one of the few whom he baptized in Corinth (1 Cor 1:14). Luke writes, 'many of the Corinthians who heard him [i.e. Crispus] believed and were baptised [presumably by Crispus]' (Acts 18:8). According to Luke, Sosthenes was also one of the synagogue rulers in Corinth who became a believer, and he is now mentioned in the first letter to the Corinthians as the co-sender (1 Cor 1:1; Acts 18:17).

With the notable exception of Titus, most of Paul's co-workers in Acts are found in Paul's letters: Mark,[36] Aristarchus,[37] Tychicus,[38] Sopater/Sosipater[39] and Trophimus[40]. It is clear that Luke was well aware of Paul's inner-circle colleagues. Luke also appears to know much of Paul's interactions with the major apostles, namely Peter, James and John (Acts 15:7, 13; 21:18; 1 Cor 1:12; 3:12; 9:5; 15:5, 7; Gal 1:18–19; 2:7–14).

Paul's characteristics

We now turn to compare the descriptions of some of the characteristics of Paul in the letters and in Acts. This study will enable us to consider the compatibility between these two sources regarding the reported lifestyle and/or personality of the apostle.

Hard work

Paul often reminds us of his hard work. He tells the Thessalonians that he worked day and night in order not to be a burden to anyone while he preached the gospel to them (1 Thess 2:9; 2 Thess 3:7–8). Self-support was a matter of principle for Paul. Luke also portrays him putting the same principle into practice. He reports that Paul reminds the Ephesian elders, 'You yourselves know that these hands of mine have supplied my own needs and the needs of my companions. In everything I did, I showed you that by this kind of hard work we must help the weak, remembering the words the Lord Jesus himself said: "It is more blessed to give than to receive"' (Acts 20:33–35). Paul repeatedly talks to the Corinthians about his hard work among them. He says that he did not want to be a burden to his converts, and he did not work for his own profit (2 Cor 2:17; 11:9; 12:14–17). In effect, he says, 'Despite our right to be supported, Barnabas and I worked hard for our living in order not to be a burden to anyone, and so we work hard with our own hands' (see 1 Cor 4:12; 9:11–12; Acts 20:34).[41] But Paul does not need to specify what kind of work he did in Corinth, because his readers know about it. Luke informs *us* that he worked hard as a tentmaker together with Priscilla and Aquila (Acts 18:3).

Humility

Paul often talks about his humility in ministry, working in fear and trembling, often feeling, and seen to be, weak. He did not claim his rights, but humbled

---

[36] Acts 15:37–39; Col 4:10; Phlm 24; 2 Tim 4:11.
[37] Acts 19:29; 20:4; 27:2; Col 4:10; Phlm 24.
[38] Acts 20:4; Eph 6:21; Col 4:7; 2 Tim 4:12; Titus 3:12.
[39] Acts 20:4; Rom 16:21.
[40] Acts 20:4; 21:29; 2 Tim 4:30.
[41] Also 1 Cor 9:6, 11–12, 15–18; 2 Cor 2:17; 11:9; 12:14–18; 1 Thess 2:9; 2 Thess 2:6, 8; 3:8.

himself in service (1 Cor 2:3; 4:10; 9:22; 2 Cor 11:7, 29–30). He did not boast beyond proper limits, and confined his boasting to the field God assigned for him (2 Cor 10:13–18). When he boasts, he boasts only about his weakness and in fact delights in it (2 Cor 12:5, 9–11; 13:9). He struggled in tears for the welfare of the church (2 Cor 2:4; 11:28; Gal 4:19; Phil 3:18; Col 2:1). The fact that Paul insists on his apostleship in the letters to the Corinthians indicates that he did not exercise his apostolic authority during his missionary work in Corinth. Rather he worked for them like a nursing mother and a father in humility and love (cf. 1 Thess 2:7, 11). Paul also admonishes the Romans and the Ephesians to serve the Lord with complete humility (Rom 12:11; Eph 4:2). The Paul of the letters appears to be humble, boasting in weakness and agonizing over the issues facing the churches (2 Cor 7:5; 12:9–10). As the real Paul reminds the churches of his humility, so the Lucan Paul also reminds his churches that he had served the Lord with great humility and tears, especially for the sound establishment of the church (Acts 20:18–19, 31).[42]

Total commitment

Total commitment is another characteristic of Paul. He was totally committed to the Lord for the sake of the gospel. He testifies to his converts that for the sake of Christ he was willing to lose all the things that he had previously considered as profit. He was totally consecrated to the cause of the gospel. The value and purpose of his life is firmly set for the sake of Christ (Rom 14:8; 2 Cor 5:14–15; Gal 2:19–20; Phil 3:7–14). He is determined to finish the task given to him by God (2 Cor 4:1; 2 Tim 4:6–7). The Lucan Paul also reminds his converts of his determination to serve the Lord: 'I consider my life worth nothing to me, if only I may finish the race and complete the task the Lord Jesus has given me – the task of testifying to the gospel of God's grace' (Acts 20:24). Knowing the danger awaiting him in Jerusalem, he confirms: 'I am ready not only to be bound, but also to die in Jerusalem for the name of the Lord Jesus' (Acts 21:13). It is interesting to note that the Paul of Acts and the Paul of the letters use the same phrases, 'finish the race' and 'complete the task' (Acts 20:24; 2 Tim 4:7; Col 4:17; cf. Phil 3:13–14; 2 Tim 4:5).

Love for the churches

Both Paul and Luke write that Paul had love and concern for his converts and

---

[42] Luke often portrays Paul as a robust, triumphant missionary who never gives up in the face of hardship or persecution, and achieves good results as he advances confidently with the power of God. This is probably because he is describing Paul in his ministry as a bold, persistent missionary preacher, but Paul also talks about his vulnerability as he deals with a number of problematic issues in the churches.

the churches. This is expressed in his desire to visit them (again): 'For we wanted to come to you – certainly I, Paul, did, again and again'; 'Night and day we pray most earnestly that we may see you again and supply what is lacking in your faith' (1 Thess 2:18; 3:10; Col 1:3–14; 2:1, 5; cf. Rom 1:10–13). Paul expresses his desire to make a third visit to Corinth (2 Cor 12:14–18; 13:1–2). Luke describes Paul as a missionary who always wanted to visit his converts again. On their way back from the first missionary journey, Paul and Barnabas returned to the cities in which they had preached (Acts 13:43; 14:21b–25). It was the Lucan Paul who proposes to Barnabas, sometime after returning from the first missionary journey, to 'go back and visit the brothers in all the towns where we preached the word of the Lord and see how they are doing' (Acts 15:36). Even when he had to hurriedly leave Philippi, he went to Lydia's house to encourage the new believers (Acts 16:40). He visited the churches again 'throughout the region of Galatia and Phrygia, strengthening all the disciples' as he embarked on the third missionary campaign (Acts 18:23). Paul went to Ephesus again for an extended period of ministry, which resulted in much success (Acts 19:10; 1 Cor 16:8–9). When he had to leave the city after the uproar had ended, he met the disciples again not just to say goodbye but also to encourage them to stand firm in the faith (Acts 20:1–2).

A typical example is the Lucan Paul's meeting with the Ephesian elders. Since he couldn't visit them, he asked them to come to meet him in Miletus. There he gave a heartfelt farewell speech to them with words of encouragement and warnings by reminding them of his previous teaching and lifestyle (Acts 20:18–35).

Furthermore, when he himself could not visit his churches he sent his envoys. Paul often sent Tychicus on his behalf (Eph 6:21; Col 4:7; 2 Tim 4:12; Titus 3:12; Acts 20:4). Timothy too was chosen to go in his place to Corinth and Macedonia (1 Cor 4:17; 16:10; 1 Thess 3:1–6). Luke also writes that Paul left Timothy in Macedonia and that Timothy returned to Paul from there (Acts 17:13–15; 18:5). The purpose of his visit and that of his deputy in both Paul and Acts are the same: to strengthen the disciples and encourage them to remain true to the faith (1 Thess 3:10; Phil 1:8; Acts 13:43; 14:21b–25; 15:40; 16:5), or to give them warnings and to prepare them against any doctrinal attack by false teachers who would cause division (Rom 16:17–19; 1 Cor 16:13; 2 Cor 11:4, 13; Eph 4:14; 2 Tim 3:13; Titus 1:10; so also Acts 20:28–31).

Furthermore, almost all Paul's letters contain pastoral prayers in addition to his remarks that he constantly prays for his readers.[43] Luke also portrays Paul as sharing pastoral care and affection with his converts. He describes how Paul knelt down with all of the Ephesian elders and prayed for them.

---

[43] Rom 1:9–10; Eph 1:15–19; 3:14–21; Phil 1:3–4, 9–11; Col 1:9–14; 1 Thess 1:2; 3:11–13; 2 Thess 1:11–12; 3:3–5; 2 Tim 1:3; Phlm 4.

The elders all wept as they embraced him and kissed him (Acts 20:36–38). In this regard we can take Luke's portrayal of Paul as an affectionate and caring pastor as being compatible with the real Paul, who has deep concern for all the churches for their well-being, and who has a willingness to sacrifice himself for the sake of those who had been converted through his ministry (2 Cor 11:28; Phil 2:17).

Conclusion

We have attempted to compare the detailed descriptions of Paul's Jewish background, his early Christian years, his missionary journeys, his suffering, his co-workers and his characteristics in order to discern the reliability of Luke's accounts of Paul's life and ministry. Both the letters and Acts agree that Paul was a Pharisee, persecutor of the church, itinerant missionary, evangelist, church planter and pastor. Both accounts portray how Paul defended the gospel for the sake of the Gentiles, and so secured his mission to the Gentiles. Our study has shown that there are hardly any contradictory descriptions between the letters and Acts. Despite certain omissions in both accounts, and one or two controversial points, they do not contradict each other, but rather their differences are largely explicable. Furthermore, the degree of correspondence is overwhelming, and many details – though some may not seem significant – affirm that Luke's report on Paul's life and ministry is highly reliable.[44]

In the light of our examination above, we conclude that both Paul and Luke provide us with very impressive parallel and highly compatible accounts.[45] Despite the different nature and scope of the two accounts, they show overwhelming correspondence. They present many similar descriptions with regard to Paul's relationship with the leadership and the church in Jerusalem. It is important to consider not only the rhetorical element in Paul's presentation in Galatians, for example, but also the subsequent developments in Paul's relationship with Jerusalem, and to reconstruct the relationship accordingly.

It is not plausible, therefore, to deny the reliability of Luke's account by underestimating such a vast volume of correspondence between the two accounts, and then by highlighting the 'differences' largely due to silence on

---

[44] In this respect, it is interesting to note that Luke says nothing about Paul's work in Colossae, and Paul makes it clear that he did not plant the church in Colossae, but only heard about them (Col 1:9).

[45] Bruce, 'St Luke's Portrait', 186, has arrived at the same conclusion. However, we have attempted here to provide many more points of comparison.

certain topics on Paul's part in the letters.[46] Again we must remember that most of Paul's letters to the churches represent only the second part of his teaching; the first part was given orally during his missionary work in those cities. We must also remember that Luke is covering Paul's initial *missionary* work to convert his audience, and that Paul is concerned with *pastoral* issues for the converted, without repeating much of what he taught earlier. Despite these elements, the compatibility of the two accounts is much more justifiable than modern sceptical scholarship has allowed. The degree of their correspondence is sufficient for us to contend that Luke's portrayal of the apostle Paul is highly reliable.[47] This also means, in turn, that Luke's accounts can fill in such gaps as exist in the letters. For example, Acts 10 – 11 provides an explanation of how Peter 'used to eat with . . . Gentiles' in the first place (Gal 2:12). Luke's accounts also bear witness that Paul's accounts are truly credible despite their rhetorical and retrospective element, as often the testimony of a witness carries more weight than that of the person concerned.[48]

---

[46] Arguing against Haenchen's contention, Porter, *Paul in Acts*, 189–99, arrives at the same conclusion as ours: 'Differences between the two accounts seem easily to fall within the realm of the kinds of differences one would expect from two different authors writing in two different literary genres (narrative and epistle), even when writing about the same subject' (p. 199).

[47] So also Witherington, *Acts*, 430–38.

[48] So correctly, Gager, 'Some Notes', 699; Watson, *Paul*, 53–6; Taylor, *Paul*, 62; Betz, *Galatians*, 81; Räisänen, *Paul and the Law*, 232.

Conclusions

It is now time to draw conclusions from the evidence so far presented. We have sought to investigate the credibility of Luke's portrait of Paul from the internal material in Acts and his letters. Our study has exposed how the contention of sceptical scholars is often made on the basis of assumptions rather than of evidence. In the name of critical and academic study, there is a tendency to highlight the differences and separation between the Paul of Acts and the Paul of the letters. But many of these differences seem largely explicable when we apply objective and critical scrutiny.[1] We also found that much of the misunderstanding of the critics is derived from their misinterpretation of the purpose or context of Pauline texts. Furthermore, their conclusions are often coloured by the use of inadequate methodologies in comparing the accounts of Paul in Acts and in the letters at face value, without taking into account the different scope and nature of these two types of literary work.

Our study also highlighted the fact that there are many parallels and correspondences in Luke's portrayal of Paul in Acts that are remarkably compatible with the Paul of the letters. The compatibilities do not just cover the geographical and historical details, choice of vocabulary and sequence of events,[2] but also the portrayal of Paul's character and struggle with theological and ecclesiastical issues.[3] Luke's account of Paul is not contradictory to Paul's own account, although there are some topics on which it is silent or shows differences in emphasis. The parallels are too numerous to be taken as random coincidences, and the level of compatibility is too high to allow his account to be regarded as a fictitious product, especially when Luke does not

---

[1] So correctly, Porter, *Paul in Acts*, 6–7.

[2] For a geographical comparison, see Riesner, *Paul's Early Period*; Hengel, *Between Jesus and Paul*, 97–128, esp. p. 127; for a historical comparison, see Wenham, 'Acts and the Pauline Corpus', 215–58; Dunn, *Beginning*, 80–81; and for a literary comparison, Walton, *Leadership*.

[3] It is interesting to note that Pervo, *Mystery*, 146, who does not accept Luke's work as historical, nevertheless admits to his success in his portrayal of Paul: 'Luke's actual "sin" was not that he presented a revised Paul, but that his effort was so successful that to dislodge it from its privileged position is extremely difficult.'

show any knowledge of the existence of Paul's letters. He did not have Paul's writings from which he could copy certain details. Will a sceptical critic assert that Luke deliberately pretends to know nothing about Paul's writings in order to write *his own* theology, while he is borrowing details from the letters? No, they cannot do so in the light of numerous pieces of evidence produced in this work and by others in the past.

As we have shown in this volume, Luke's account of Paul is remarkably compatible with Paul's own account in many areas, despite the fact that the scope and nature of the two types of literary work are substantially different. Such compatibility seems even more remarkable as Luke did not write on the basis of the information in Paul's letters, but rather used sources related to what he himself had experienced or collected from the Christian communities.[4] We can safely conclude, therefore, that Luke's portrait of Paul is remarkably reliable and historical, and the Paul Luke is describing in Acts is the historical Paul whom we know from his letters.

This conclusion itself is not new. Even after the scepticism advocated by the Tübingen School, a stream of scholars have insisted on Luke's reliability in his portrait of the apostle.[5] F.F. Bruce has maintained, 'The Paul whose portrait Luke paints is the real Paul.'[6] I.H. Marshall also contended, 'The view that Paul's theology is inaccurately presented in Acts is a palpable exaggeration . . . It is unfair to suggest that he is a thoroughly tendentious and unreliable writer, freely rewriting the history of the early church in the interests of his own theology.'[7] More recently C.S. Keener has provided sets of very comprehensive lists of comparisons between Acts and Paul's letters, and has asserted that the parallels are overwhelmingly numerous, and the compatibility is too striking to be dismissed.[8] Our investigation has further substantiated the earlier conclusions. Here we present the summaries of each chapter, and we then assess our contribution to the scholarly field and highlight the implications of our study for New Testament studies in general and Pauline research in particular.

---

[4] Marguerat, 'Paul After Paul', 74–5; Butticaz, 'Salvation', 152.

[5] Most notably, Thornton, *Zeuge*, has convincingly demonstrated Luke as a credible historian. Earlier, Harnack, Ramsay, Munck, Campbell, Bruce, Marshall, Goulder, Hemer, Hengel, Gasque, and more recently Witherington, Walton and Keener. Cf. Porter, *Paul in Acts*, 170, who makes a cautious conclusion: 'It is not altogether clear that the Paul of Acts is the Paul of the letters'. However, he also states, 'but there is no conclusive argument in this area to show that he was not.'

[6] Bruce, *Acts: Greek*, 59; idem, 'Real Paul?', 282–305.

[7] Marshall, *Luke: Historian and Theologian*, 75.

[8] Keener, *Acts*, 1:237–50.

Summaries

Having noted these elements, we have carefully undertaken our investigation. In Chapter 1, we evaluated Philipp Vielhauer's thesis in four areas of his choice: natural theology, the law, Christology and eschatology. Most of the weaknesses of Vielhauer's thesis are derived from his methodology. He simply compares Luke's and Paul's accounts at face value without discerning the differences in scope and nature between the two. He does not attempt to compare the accounts of the real Paul and the Lucan Paul by adjusting for the differences in the scope of their writings. Nor does he consider the rhetorical contexts of Paul's argument in some letters. In most cases, his interpretation of Paul's theology is based on assumptions and thus arrives at incorrect conclusions. Vielhauer does not allow room for Paul to grow in his understanding of the gospel and certain theological issues by taking account of the different contexts between his missionary preaching and his later theological presentation. He also handles evidence unevenly; he highlights the differences between the two accounts but undervalues and ignores numerous important correspondences. His tendentiousness is obvious. Our study suggests that it is difficult for Vielhauer's thesis to be sustained.

In Chapter 2, we provided an alternative methodology with which we could legitimately compare Paul's account with Luke's at the same level and scope. We attempted to reconstruct Paul's *missionary* preaching from his *letters*. Though his letters do not contain his missionary messages, we were able to successfully rediscover their core messages by employing the reminder formula, by which Paul reminds his churches of his earlier preaching and teaching in person during his church-planting stage. Then we compared it with the Lucan Paul's *missionary* preaching in Acts. We found that all of the core elements in the real Paul's missionary preaching appear in the Lucan Paul's preaching, and they are compatible. We also found that both Paul's letters and Luke's Acts contain the same evangelistic topics, such as 'the kingdom of God', 'call to turn away from idols', 'call to repentance' and 'response to Paul's preaching', and their correspondences are remarkable.

Both accounts also present Paul as a confident preacher of the gospel and a Jewish apostle to the Gentiles. Even some phrases that describe Paul's style of preaching are identical. More significantly, we specifically compared Luke's accounts of Paul's missionary preaching in certain regions, such as Corinth, Thessalonica and Galatia, with what Paul writes to these churches. We found abundant similarities between the two accounts. In the Lucan Paul's speech to the Ephesian elders we also found numerous corresponding terms and concepts that Paul frequently uses in his letters. It is significant to find such correspondences between this one and only 'follow-up' speech in Acts and Paul's 'follow-up' letters. Our findings raise the level of the reliability of Luke's account of the apostle Paul.

Conclusions

In Chapter 3, we examined the discrepancies between Paul's and Luke's accounts that are often raised in the course of undermining Luke's credibility as a historian. The first area is related to several silences, topics where either Paul or Luke does not mention what the other author writes about. We have attempted to explain some possible reasons for the silences on each side. We cannot be certain, however, because we cannot build an argument from silence. What is important, nevertheless, is that the topics on which one is silent do not really contradict the compatibility between the two accounts, and therefore we should not allow the silence of one party to serve to discredit the other.

Luke's description of Paul's Jewishness is allegedly a more serious discrepancy. Luke is often criticized for mispresenting Paul as a law-observing Jew while he strongly advocates the law-free gospel, and also for presenting him going to the synagogues 'as his custom' during his missionary work, while the real Paul strongly asserts his apostleship to the Gentiles. More recent understanding of Paul's Jewishness helps to resolve the discrepancies. As contended above, we paid attention to the development and context of Paul's teaching on the law as the situations arose. Luke's portrayal of Paul as laying less stress on the 'apart from the law' element seems quite accurate because, at the period which Luke is describing, this issue may not have been as serious as the situation Paul writes about in Galatians. It became a serious issue after some years when the Judaizers began to disturb the Gentile churches. Rather, Luke seems to be accurate in showing that the issue in the earliest stage was less intense than we read from the letters.

Luke is also often blamed for his portrayal of Paul's good relationship with the authorities in the Jerusalem community. Here, critics should not compare the later Paul, who insists not only on his apostleship but also on his independence of any human authority over his apostleship (1 Cor 9:1–2; 2 Cor 11:5; Gal 1:1, 12; 2:6), with Luke's description as a whole. They need to find out whether the relationship was tense all the way through from the beginning, or whether it intensified and went sour somewhere along the way. They then need to discern which part Luke is writing about in particular episodes, and how to reconcile this with the fact that Paul himself acknowledges the authority of the Jerusalem apostles by seeking their judgement and endorsement (Gal 1:18; 2:1, 7–9; cf. Acts 15:3–4, 22–29). Paul writes that he and the Jerusalem apostles preach the common gospel (1 Cor 15:11). Until the very late days of his missionary career, Paul is totally committed to raising funds to support the saints in Jerusalem. Both Paul and Peter are sharing co-workers together. Luke's description of the leadership transition in Jerusalem from Peter to James is also compatible with Paul's indications. Putting all these elements together, we find that Luke has provided us with reliable and accurate information as a historian.

We have noted that scholars have unduly highlighted an alleged schism and disunity between Peter and Paul. Their contentions of incompatibility are often derived from their inaccurate interpretation of Paul and his theology. In many cases, the alleged contradictions do not really exist. With more careful and fair examination of the internal materials in Acts and the letters, we can conclude that many of the discrepancies are explicable from the wider context. As C.J. Hemer points out, 'the rejection of the evidence of Acts is arguably presuppositional itself'.[9]

However, when we say that the account of Paul in Acts is highly reliable, we do not mean it is absolutely accurate or infallible. It is impossible to compare Acts and Pauline letters with certainty on all points when the two writings were written independently to different readerships with different purposes. We cannot label Luke unreliable due to some omissions and topics that appear to be incompatible, especially when the correspondences are overwhelmingly numerous. Though we do not have all the answers, we are persuaded that Acts is substantially reliable. We must accept that Luke endeavoured to portray Paul's life and ministry as accurately and adequately as possible. Like ancient biographers and historians, Luke intended to communicate correct information with historical examples. 'Also, ancient biographers and historians used historical examples to communicate moral and other points. It was in fact novels that usually lacked other agendas.'[10] Luke's primary motivation in writing Acts was not to assert *his* theology. We must also accept that Luke did not intend to mislead his readers by misrepresenting Paul's apostolic ministry. The author did not intend, when writing Acts, to write a piece of fiction – nor did his readers expect him to do so.

In Chapter 4 we studied the 'we-passages'. They provide us with a crucial key in assessing the reliability of Acts as a whole, as well as information on Paul. The first we-passage starts at Acts 16:10, but it seems obvious that the narrator joined Paul earlier. If Luke is from Antioch, as is strongly supported by some ancient sources, it is possible, even probable, that he started to travel with Paul from the start of his second missionary journey. It is also most likely that Luke did not leave the team at the point of Acts 16:17 where the pronoun 'we' disappears (at least for the time being).

Luke takes on the pronoun 'we' again in Acts 20:5 – 21:18. It is unlikely that Luke stayed behind in Philippi until Paul's team returned to the city a few years later during his third missionary campaign. We have contended that Luke accompanied Paul till the end of the second journey, and joined Paul again for the third missionary journey from Antioch. It is obvious that Luke was with Paul at the meeting where the apostle gave his pastoral farewell speech to the Ephesian elders. Likewise, it is most likely that he was at the meeting where Paul met James and the elders of the Jerusalem church

---

[9] Hemer, *Book of Acts*, 19.

[10] I am grateful to Prof. Keener for sharing this view in personal correspondence (24 May 2016).

after returning from the third missionary campaign. Then we find Luke travelling by ship together with Paul to Rome from Caesarea, and arriving in Rome (Acts 27:1 – 28:16).

This account suggests two possibilities. First, Luke seems to be in Caesarea to support Paul during his imprisonment in that city. Second, he stayed on with Paul in Rome probably till his martyrdom. This reconstruction is highly likely. If this is the case, its implication is immense. It means that most of the material that extends from Acts 15:40 to the end of the book of Acts (28:31) is Luke's first-hand source which he himself witnessed, experienced or collected from Paul and his friends. Thus the level of Luke's credibility with respect to Paul as his travelling companion is extremely high. Even if we allow the least possibility, his credibility should still remain high. Because 'if he was with Paul for a few years, that's certainly enough for him to have learned about Paul's ministry in the other places'.[11]

Finally, in Chapter 5, we investigated the credibility of Luke's accounts of Paul's life and ministry, first, from looking at the data in his letters. There we found information that showed numerous correspondences with information in Acts in the areas of Paul's Jewish background, the Damascus road experience and his early Christian years, and his missionary journeys. We found that both Acts and the letters present the apostle as a passionate church-planter, and as a suffering and persecuted missionary. We identified the locations where he planted churches and where he experienced persecution, places that are also compatible in both accounts of Acts and of the letters. The descriptions of some of the characteristics of Paul in the two accounts also exhibit a high level of compatibility. Finally, the names and activities of Paul's co-workers correspond abundantly in the letters and in Acts. We conclude, therefore, that, in the light of such a vast volume of correspondences and parallels, we need to acknowledge that Luke's portrayal of Paul in the areas of his life and ministry is highly credible.

Contributions

Our unique contribution in support of the affirmative position, and thus in critique of the sceptics, derives from the methodology of comparison we have adopted. The collection of numerous and fresh parallels gleaned from this methodology is an added bonus. It is our contention that Luke's Acts and Paul's letters cannot be compared at face value, because they are different in nature, scope, audience and purpose. Therefore, we must expect a certain level of differences and omissions in both accounts.

Acts is the first church history, and it took some 200 years for another

---

[11] Keener, in the same correspondence.

'church history' to be written by Eusebius. However, Luke does not write a general history of the church, but focuses on the earliest Christian communities and their leaders. So, he highlights the ministries of Peter, Stephen and Paul especially. Nevertheless, he is not writing their biographies. Luke's intention is to write a history of the origin and expansion of earliest Christianity, and so he records the progress of the gospel from Jerusalem to Rome. By providing us with a narrow passageway between Jesus and Paul, Luke shows how the Great Commission has been carried out by the church as it undertakes the task of witnessing to the risen Jesus by the power of the Holy Spirit (Acts 1:8).

Luke puts emphasis on taking the gospel 'to the ends of the earth', and naturally he highlights Paul's missionary campaigns. Paul's conversion/call experience is added as it is the foundation for his missionary work. Luke primarily portrays Paul as a pioneering missionary in new cities, preaching the gospel and establishing churches with the new converts; Paul himself states that it was his ambition to pursue new territories of ministry (Rom 15:20–21). Luke also pays attention to the travels, responses and hardships experienced in the course of Paul's missionary endeavour. With the notable exception of Paul's farewell speech to the elders of the Ephesian church, Luke hardly ever draws our attention to Paul's pastoral ministries or even theological controversies. Moreover, Luke reports Paul's missionary preaching to both Jewish and Gentile audiences. However, Paul's letters were all sent to churches where Gentile membership was predominant. We do not have letters from Paul that were sent to a Jewish church, even though he certainly worked among the Jews as well (cf. Rom 9:3; 10:1; 11:13–14; 1 Cor 9:19–22).

Moreover, Paul's letters are all different; they are *ad hoc* correspondences, written to address certain theological or occasional issues raised by different churches. They are follow-up letters which assume a certain level of knowledge from his previous teaching in person (with the notable exception of Romans and Colossians). Therefore, Paul's missionary preaching to convert people is largely omitted from his letters. The content of his message was given verbally during his initial missionary work, and we can find much of this material in Acts.

As we pointed out, we need to note that the things Paul emphatically writes in the letters are, in most cases, topics which he did not teach (sufficiently) while he was with his churches during his missionary work. Paul's teaching on marriage (1 Cor 7), food sacrificed to idols (1 Cor 8 and 10), spiritual gifts (1 Cor 12 – 14), the resurrection of the dead (1 Cor 15; 1 Thess 4) and the collection (2 Cor 8 – 9) are some of these topics. Therefore, if one were to compare at face value what is written in these sections directly with the accounts in Acts, and attempt to assess the compatibility between the two, that methodology would not be fair and sound.

Conclusions

Paul's strong emphasis on 'justification by faith *apart from the law*', in his letter to the Galatians, also leads us to think that he did not stress it amply enough for them to be prepared to resist the demands of the Judaizers. What Paul preached in Galatia during his missionary work was 'justification by faith *in the death and resurrection of Jesus Christ*', and this is the scope which Luke is covering. Therefore, if one were to compare at face value what is in Galatians with Luke's report of Paul's missionary work in Galatia, that methodology would not be sound.

As noted earlier, Paul writes to churches to address their specific situations and issues, and thus his teachings are often presented with different contents and emphasis even if he deals with the same topics. For example, Paul appears to teach different eschatology in 2 Corinthians 4:16 – 5:10 and in 1 Thessalonians 4:13 – 5:11.[12] He presents Abraham in Galatians 3 and in Romans 4 with different emphases. The law in Galatians and Romans is presented rather differently on some points. Paul clearly expresses the negative side of the law as invalid for salvation (Gal 2:15–16; 3:2, 11, 23–25); the law contains a curse (Gal 3:13: 'the curse of the law'), and the law imprisons us (Gal 3:23). But in Romans he puts the law in a different light: the law and commandments are holy, righteous, good and spiritual (Rom 7:12, 13, 14, 16). To the Galatians Paul declares, 'If you let yourselves be circumcised, Christ will be of no value to you at all' (Gal 5:2–3); but to the Romans, 'What value is there in circumcision? Much in every way!' (Rom 3:1–2; 2:25). Again, Paul utterly denies any involvement of the Jerusalem apostles in receiving his call and the gospel (Gal 1:11–12). However, elsewhere he indicates their involvement as if he had received it from them ('what I received I passed on to you': 1 Cor 15:3), and so now both they and he preach the same common gospel (1 Cor 15:11).

Furthermore, Paul sometimes exhibits seeming incompatibilities within the *same* letter. For example, in Romans, he makes anti-law statements (Rom 3:20; 9:31) and pro-law statements (Rom 3:1, 31; 7:7, 12, 14, 16), and anti-Israel remarks (Rom 2:17–27; 11:28) and pro-Israel remarks (Rom 3:1; 9:4–5; 11:1, 26).[13] Sometimes he affirms the primacy of Jews (Rom 3:1; 9:4–5), but elsewhere he strongly asserts the equality of Jew and Gentile (Rom 1:16; 3:9–10, 22; 10:12–13).[14] There is nothing wrong in Paul saying such things, because he makes these remarks in different contexts, for different arguments and to different audiences.[15]

---

[12] Keener, *Acts*, 1:253.

[13] For comprehensive lists of such seemingly contradictory remarks in Paul, see Gager, *Reinventing Paul, passim*.

[14] See Chae, *Paul*, 289–90, and *passim*.

[15] *Pace* Räisänen, *Paul and the Law*, 264: 'Paul's thought on the law is full of difficulties and inconsistencies'; similarly, O'Neill, *Romans*, 16; O'Neill, *Recovery*, 8.

All we can say at this point is that, likewise, one should not expect Luke to make a replica of Paul's writings. Rather, differences may naturally be expected when two accomplished authors write, even on the same topic or incident.[16] This provides a way to understand Luke's three slightly different accounts of Paul's Christophany experience.[17] Despite considering all these, the extent of the parallels is still too extensive to deny Luke's credibility.[18] Furthermore, we must establish first the context so as to determine what out of Paul's teaching we are to apply in comparison with Luke's account. Often critics have blamed Luke when they could not find parallels with Paul's letters but only discrepancies. They may have compared wrong sets of accounts, or they may have misunderstood Paul and his theology.

Implications

Our findings have two implications. First, since both Paul and Luke give highly compatible accounts in those sections of Acts and of the letters which overlap one another by referring to the same events or people, this credibility should lead us to regard as reliable the accounts of non-overlapping sections as well. C.S. Keener's brave assertion below is not unacceptable. After exhaustive comparison of the accounts in Acts and the letters, he not only affirms the credibility of the accounts in Acts but also gives credibility to the material in Acts which could not be checked:

> Such Pauline correlation with Acts renders probable Luke's other information about Paul; his accuracy in these cases must represent a fair and unbiased sampling, since he could not have known what sources would remain extant. That is, we cannot attribute Luke's accuracy on these cases to coincidence or argue from silence that Luke was accurate on such a high proportion of points where we can check him, yet erred promiscuously wherever we cannot.[19]

Second, in the light of the high credibility of Luke's portrayal of Paul, which we have established in this book, more allowance needs to be given to the book of Acts in Pauline studies for our better understanding of the apostle and of his theology. Paul's letters, our primary source, do not provide us with

---

[16] So correctly, Porter, *Paul in Acts*, 60.
[17] So correctly, Klausner, *From Jesus to Paul*, 224–5.
[18] Keener, *Acts*, 1:229 n. 57: 'Differences of emphasis are not necessarily conflicts . . . though even conflicts do not disprove acquaintance.'
[19] Keener, *Acts*, 1:250.

Conclusions

sufficient or complete information to reconstruct his life, ministry and theology.[20] The book of Acts is indispensable in any attempt to reconstruct and to comprehend Paul's life and ministry as well as the development of earliest Christianity. We cannot afford to dispense with the material Luke provides in Acts, especially after discovering numerous correspondences with Paul's letters. Luke's account of Paul in Acts deserves more appreciation in Pauline studies than has usually been recognized.[21]

Paul's letters are often written with particular pastoral or theological purposes in mind. In achieving his immediate purposes, his teachings are sometimes rhetorical, one-sided, and even at times incompatible with his own writings to other churches. Luke's material can provide us with some relevant insights and keys for better understanding of the theological development in Paul's thought and in the earliest church.[22] Anyone in academic circles who uses Acts to understand the historical Paul is often labelled as uncritical and naive. In the light of what we have demonstrated in this study, we need to take courage, though carefully and critically, to use Luke's material to acquire a more adequate and accurate picture of the apostle.

---

[20] Jervell, *Unknown Paul*, 56–7, is right to acknowledge the value of Acts as a broader and balanced account on Paul's life and ministry, while Paul's letters are too occasional and rhetorical to give us a balanced portrait of him; and Keener, *Acts*, 1:233, affirmatively concurs with Jervell.

[21] Hengel and Schwemer, *Paul Between Damascus and Antioch*, ix: 'But we cannot give Paul a meaningful historical context without taking seriously the accounts which Luke has handed down to us'. Knox himself admitted in the revised edition, *Chapters*, 1987, 346–7, the difficulties of reconstructing Paul's life and ministry without the materials in Acts.

[22] Hengel, *Pre-Christian Paul*, xiii: Luke's account of Paul in Acts is 'a valuable addition to Paul's own accounts'.

Bibliography

Achtemeier, P.J. *The Quest for Unity in the New Testament* (Philadelphia: Fortress, 1987).

Adams, S.A. 'The Relationships of Paul and Luke: Luke, Paul's Letters, and the "We" Passages of Acts.' Pages 125–42 in *Paul and His Social Relations*, Pauline Studies 7 (ed. S.E. Porter and C.D. Land; Leiden: Brill, 2013).

Arrington, F.L. *The Acts of the Apostles: An Introduction and Commentary* (Peabody, MA: Hendrickson, 1988).

Ascough, R.S. 'Book Review of *Luke's Portrait of Paul*, by John Clayton Lentz Jr.'. *NovT* 36 (1994): 408–10.

Barnes, A. *Notes, Explanatory and Practical, on the Acts of the Apostles* (rev. S. Green; London: B.L. Green, 1851).

Barrett, C.K. *The Acts of the Apostles*, ICC (2 vols; Edinburgh: T&T Clark, 1994).

——. *From First Adam to Last: A Study in Pauline Theology* (London: A&C Black, 1962).

——. 'Paul's Address to the Ephesian Elders.' Pages 107–21 in *God's Christ and His People: Studies in Honour of Nils Alstrup Dahl* (ed. J. Jervell and W.A. Meeks; Oslo: Universitetsforlaget, 1977).

Bauckham, R.J. *Jude, 2 Peter*, WBC 50 (Waco, TX: Word, 1983).

Bauer, W., W.F. Arndt, F.W. Gingrich and F.W. Danker. *A Greek-English Lexicon of the New Testament and Other Early Christian Literature* (Chicago/London: University of Chicago Press, 2nd edn, 1979 [1957]).

Baur, F.C. *Paul, the Apostle of Jesus Christ: His Life and Work, His Epistles and His Teachings; A Contribution to a Critical History of Primitive Christianity* (2 vols; London: Williams & Norgate, 1873–5 [1845]. Reprinted in one volume (Peabody, MA: Hendrickson, 2003 [1845, 1876]).

Betz, H.D. *Galatians: A Commentary on Two Administrative Letters of the Apostle Paul* (Philadelphia: Fortress, 1979).

Bock, D.L. *Acts* (Grand Rapids: Baker Academic, 2007).

——. 'The Use of the Old Testament in Luke-Acts: Christology and Mission'. *SBL 1990 Seminar Papers* (Atlanta: Scholars Press, 1990), 494–511.

Bornkamm, G. *Paul* (trans. D.M.G. Stalker; London: Hodder & Stoughton, 1985 [1969]).

Bovon, F. 'The Law in Luke-Acts.' Pages 59–73 in *Studies in Early Christianity*,

WUNT 161 (Tübingen: Mohr Siebeck, 2003).

———. *Luke the Theologian: Fifty-five Years of Research (1950–2005)* (Waco, TX: Baylor University Press, 2nd edn, 2006).

Bowers, W.P. 'Studies in Paul's Understanding of His Mission' (PhD dissertation, University of Cambridge, 1976).

Bruce, F.F. *The Acts of the Apostles: The Greek Text with Introduction and Commentary* (Grand Rapids: Eerdmans; Leicester: Apollos, 3rd edn, 1990 [1951]).

———. *Commentary on the Book of the Acts: The English Text with Introduction, Exposition and Notes* (London and Edinburgh: Marshall, Morgan & Scott, 1977 [1954]).

———. *The Epistle to the Galatians. A Commentary on the Greek Text* (Exeter: Paternoster; Grand Rapids: Eerdmans, 1982).

———. 'Is the Paul of Acts the Real Paul?' *BJRL* 58 (1976): 282–305.

———. *Paul: Apostle of the Heart Set Free* (Grand Rapids: Eerdmans, 1977).

———. 'Paul in Acts and Letters.' Pages 679–92 in *Dictionary of Paul and His Letters* (ed. G.F. Hawthorne, R.P. Martin and D.G. Reid; Downers Grove, IL / Leicester: IVP, 1993).

———. *The Speeches in the Acts of the Apostles* (London: Tyndale, 1942).

———. 'St Luke's Portrait of St Paul.' Pages 181–91 in *Aksum–Thyateira: A Festschrift for Archbishop Methodios of Thyateira and Great Britain* (ed. George Dion Dragas and Methodios G. Phougias; London: Thyateira House, 1985).

Buckwalter, H.D. *The Character and Purpose of Luke's Christology*, SNTSMS 89 (Cambridge: Cambridge University Press, 1996).

Bultmann, R. *Kerygma and Myth: A Theological Debate* (ed. H.W. Bartsch; trans. R.H. Fuller; London: SPCK, 1972 [1961]).

———. 'Paul.' Pages 130–72 in *Existence and Faith: Shorter Writings of R. Bultmann* (ed. S. Ogden; London: Collins, 1964).

———. *Theology of the New Testament*, vol. 1 (trans. K. Grobel; London: SCM, 1952 [1948]).

Burchard, C. *Der dreizehnte Zeuge*, FRLANT 103 (Göttingen: Vandenhoeck & Ruprecht, 1970).

Burton, E.D.W. *A Critical and Exegetical Commentary on the Epistle to the Galatians*, ICC (Edinburgh: T&T Clark, 1921).

Bussmann, C. *Themen der paulinischen Missionspredigt auf dem Hintergrund der spätjüdisch-hellenistischen Missionsliteratur* (Frankfurt: Peter Lang, 1971).

Butticaz, S. '"Has God Rejected His People?" (Romans 11.1). The Salvation of Israel in Acts: Narrative Claim of a Pauline Legacy.' Pages 148–64 in *Paul and the Heritage of Israel: Paul's Claim upon Israel's Legacy in Luke and Acts in the Light of the Pauline Letters* (ed. D.P. Moessner, D. Marguerat, M.C. Parsons and M. Wolter; London / New York: T&T Clark, 2012).

Cadbury, H.J. 'The Speeches in Acts.' Pages 402–27 in *The Acts of the Apostles: Additional Notes to the Commentary*, vol. 5 of *The Beginnings of Christianity* (ed. F.J. Foakes-Jackson and K. Lake; London: Macmillan, 1933).

———. '"We" and "I" Passages in Luke-Acts'. *NTS* 3 (1957): 128–32.

Caird, G.B. *The Apostolic Age*, Duckworth Studies in Theology (London: Duckworth, 1975 [1955]).

Campbell, W.S. 'The Narrator as "He", "Me", and "We": Grammatical Person in Ancient Histories and in the Acts of the Apostles'. *JBL* 129 (2010): 385–407.

——. *The 'We' Passages in the Acts of the Apostles: The Narrator as Narrative Character*. SBLStBl 14 (Atlanta: Society of Biblical Literature, 2007).

Caragounis, C.C. 'L'universalisme moderne: Perspectives bibliques sur la révélation de Dieu'. *Hokhma* 45 (1990): 23–6.

Carson, D.A., and D.J. Moo. *An Introduction to the New Testament* (Grand Rapids: Zondervan, 2005).

Carter, C.W., and R. Earle. *The Acts of the Apostles* (London/Edinburgh: Oliphants, 1959).

Chae, D.J.-S. 'From Preaching the Gospel to Expounding Its Implications: Rediscovering Paul's Missionary Preaching and Its Development.' Unpublished paper presented at Paul Seminar, British New Testament Conference, Aberdeen (13 September 1996).

——. 'Paul'. Pages 275–9 in *Dictionary of Mission Theology* (ed. J. Corrie; Nottingham / Downers Grove, IL: IVP, 2007).

——. *Paul as Apostle to the Gentiles: His Apostolic Self-Awareness and its Influence on the Soteriological Argument in Romans*, PBTM (Carlisle: Paternoster, 1997).

——. 'Paul, the Law and the Mission to the Gentiles in the Earliest Church.' Unpublished paper presented at the KERF Research Seminar, Guildford (14–27 March 1997).

——. 'Paul's Apostolic Self-Awareness and the Occasion and Purpose of Romans.' Pages 116–37 in *Mission and Meaning: Essays Presented to Peter Cotterell* (ed. A. Billington, T. Lane and M. Turner; Carlisle: Paternoster, 1995).

Chase, F.H. *The Credibility of the Book of the Acts of the Apostles* (London: Macmillan, 1902).

Chilton, B. *Rabbi Paul: An Intellectual Biography* (New York: Doubleday, 2004).

Collins, R.F. 'The First Letter to the Thessalonians.' Pages 772–9 in *The New Jerome Biblical Commentary* (ed. R.E. Brown, J.A. Fitzmyer and R.E. Murphy; Englewood Cliffs, NJ: Prentice Hall, 1990 [1968]).

Conzelmann, H. *The Acts of the Apostles*, Hermeneia: A Critical and Historical Commentary on the Bible (trans. J. Limburg, A.T. Kraabel and D.H. Juel; Philadelphia: Fortress, 1987 [1963, 1972]).

——. 'The Address of Paul on the Areopagus'. Pages 217–30 in *Studies in Luke-Acts: Essays Presented in Honor of Paul Schubert* (ed. L.E. Keck and J.L. Martyn; London: SPCK, 1968 [1966]).

——. *An Outline of the Theology of the New Testament* (trans. J. Bowden; London: SCM, 1969 [1968]).

——. *The Theology of St. Luke* (trans. G. Buswell; New York: Harper & Row, 1960).

Bibliography

Crossan, J.D., and J. Reed. *In Search of Paul: How Jesus's Apostle Opposed Rome's Empire with God's Kingdom* (San Francisco: HarperSanFrancisco, 2004).
de Wette, W.M.L. *Kurze Erklärung der Apostelgeschichte* (rev. F. Overbeck; Leipzig, 1870).
Deissmann, A. *Paul: A Study in Social and Religious History* (trans. W.E. Wilson; New York: Harper & Brothers, repr. 1957 [1912, 1927]).
Dibelius, M. 'The Acts of the Apostles as an Historical Source' (1947). Pages 102–8 in *Studies in the Acts of the Apostles* (ed. H. Greeven; trans. M. Ling; London: SCM, 1956 [1951]).
——. 'Paul on the Areopagus' (1939). Pages 26–77 in *Studies in the Acts of the Apostles* (ed. H. Greeven; trans. M. Ling; London: SCM, 1956 [1951]).
——. *Studies in the Acts of the Apostles* (ed. H. Greeven; trans. M. Ling; London: SCM, 1956 [1951]).
——. 'Style Criticism in the Book of Acts' (1923). Pages 1–25 in *Studies in the Acts of the Apostles* (ed. H. Greeven; trans. M. Ling; London: SCM, 1956 [1951]).
Dodd, C.H. *The Apostolic Preaching and Its Developments* (London: Hodder & Stoughton, 1972 [1936]).
——. *Gospel and Law: The Relation of Faith and Ethics in Early Christianity* (Cambridge: Cambridge University Press, 1950).
——. *The Meaning of Paul for Today* (London: Collins/Fontana, 1958 [1920]).
Drane, J. *Introducing the New Testament* (San Francisco: Harper & Row, 1986).
Dunn, J.D.G. *Baptism in the Holy Spirit: A Re-examination of the New Testament Teaching on the Gift of the Spirit in Relation to Pentecostalism Today* (London: SCM, 1970).
——. *Beginning from Jerusalem*, vol. 2 of *Christianity in the Making* (Grand Rapids / Cambridge: Eerdmans, 2009).
——. *Romans*. WBC 38A–B (2 vols; Dallas: Word, 1988).
——. *Unity and Diversity in the New Testament: An Inquiry into the Character of Earliest Christianity* (London/Philadelphia: SCM/TPI, 2nd edn, 1990 [1977]).
Edwards, T.C. *A Commentary on the First Epistle to the Corinthians* (London: Hamilton, Adams & Co., 1885).
Elliott, N. *The Rhetoric of Romans: Argumentative Constraint and Strategy and Paul's Dialogue with Judaism*, JSNTSup 45 (Sheffield: JSOT Press, 1990).
Ellis, E.E. *The Gospel of Luke* (London: Nelson, 1966).
Enslin, M.C. *The Literature of the Christian Movement*, Part III of *Christian Beginnings* (New York: Harper, 1956 [1938]).
Eusebius. *Ecclesiastical History* (trans. C.F. Cruse; Grand Rapids: Baker, 1955).
Fee, G.D. *The First Epistle to the Corinthians*, NICNT (Grand Rapids: Eerdmans, 1987).
Fitzmyer, J.A. *The Acts of the Apostles*, AB (New York: Doubleday, 1997).
Flichy, O. 'The Paul of Luke: A Survey of Research.' Pages 18–34 in *Paul and the Heritage of Israel: Paul's Claim upon Israel's Legacy in Luke and Acts in the Light of the Pauline Letters* (ed. D.P. Moessner, D. Marguerat, M.C.

Parsons and M. Wolter; London / New York: T&T Clark, 2012).

Foakes-Jackson, F.J. *The Acts of the Apostles* (London: Hodder & Stoughton, 1931).

Gager, J. *Reinventing Paul* (Oxford: Oxford University Press, 2000).

——. 'Some Notes on Paul's Conversion'. *NTS* 27 (1981): 697–704.

Gärtner, B. *The Areopagus Speech and Natural Revelation* (Uppsala: Gleerup, 1955).

Gasque, W.W. *A History of the Criticism of the Acts of the Apostles* (Peabody, MA: Hendrickson, 1989 [1975]).

Gempf, C. 'Athens, Paul at.' Pages 51–4 in *Dictionary of Paul and His Letters* (ed. G.F. Hawthorne, R.P. Martin and D.G. Reid; Downers Grove, IL / Leicester: IVP, 1993).

Goodenough, E.R. 'The Perspective of Acts.' Pages 51–9 in *Studies in Luke-Acts: Essays Presented in Honor of Paul Schubert* (ed. L.E. Keck and J.L. Martyn; London: SPCK, 1968 [1966]).

Goodspeed, E.J. *Paul* (Philadelphia/Toronto: Winston Co., 1947).

Green, M. *2 Peter and Jude*, TNTC (Leicester: IVP, 1968).

Guthrie, D. *New Testament Introduction* (Leicester: IVP, 3rd edn, 1970 [1962, 1965]).

——. *New Testament Theology* (Leicester: IVP, 1981).

Haenchen, E. *The Acts of the Apostles* (Oxford: Basil Blackwell, 1971 [1956]).

Hahn, F. *Mission in the New Testament* (trans. F. Clark; London: SCM, 1965 [1963]).

Hall, D.R. 'St. Paul and Famine Relief: A Study in Galatians 2:10'. *ExpTim* 82 (1970–71): 309–11.

Hanson, R.P.C. *The Acts with Introduction and Commentary* (Oxford: Clarendon, 1967).

Harnack, A. *The Expansion of Christianity* (London: Williams & Norgate, 5th edn, 1958 [1904]).

Hawthorne, G.F., R.P. Martin and D.G. Reid, eds. *Dictionary of Paul and His Letters* (Downers Grove, IL / Leicester: IVP, 1993).

Hays, R.B. 'The Paulinism of Acts, Intertextually Reconsidered.' Pages 35–48 in *Paul and the Heritage of Israel: Paul's Claim upon Israel's Legacy in Luke and Acts in the Light of the Pauline Letters* (ed. D.P. Moessner, D. Marguerat, M.C. Parsons and M. Wolter; London / New York: T&T Clark, 2012).

Hemer, C.J. 'The Authorship and Sources of Acts.' Pages 308–64 in *The Book of Acts in the Setting of Hellenistic History*, WUNT 49 (ed. C.H. Gempf; Tübingen: Mohr Siebeck, 1989.

——. *The Book of Acts in the Setting of Hellenistic History*, WUNT 49 (ed. C.H. Gempf; Tübingen: Mohr Siebeck, 1989.

——. 'First Person Narrative in Acts 27–28'. *TynBul* 36 (1985): 79–109.

——. 'Speeches of Acts, I: The Ephesian Elders at Miletus'. *TynBul* 40 (1989): 77–85.

Hengel, M. *Acts and the History of Earliest Christianity* (trans. J. Bowden; London: SCM, 1979).

——. *Between Jesus and Paul: Studies in the Earliest History of Christianity*

Bibliography

(trans. J. Bowden; London: SCM; Philadelphia: Fortress, 1983).

———. *Earliest Christianity* (London: SCM, 1986 [1973, 1979]).

———. *Pre-Christian Paul* (trans. J. Bowden; London: SCM, 1991).

Hengel, M., and A.M. Schwemer. *Paul Between Damascus and Antioch: The Unknown Years* (trans. J. Bowden; London: SCM, 1997).

Holmberg, B. *Sociology and the New Testament: An Appraisal* (Minneapolis: Fortress, 1990).

Holzner, J. *Paul of Tarsus* (trans. F.C. Eckhoff; St Louis / London: Herder, 1946).

Hooker, M. 'Adam in Romans 1'. *NTS* 6 (1959–60): 297–306.

———. 'A Further Note on Romans 1'. *NTS* 13 (1966–7): 181–3.

Hughes, P.E. *Paul's Second Epistle to the Corinthians* (Grand Rapids: Eerdmans, 1962).

Hultgren, A.J. 'Paul's Pre-Christian Persecutions of the Church: Their Purpose, Locale, and Nature'. *JBL* 96 (1976): 105–7.

Hunter, A.M. *The Unity of the New Testament* (London: SCM, 1943).

Hyldahl, N. 'A Reminiscence of the Old Testament at Romans i.23'. *NTS* 2 (1955–6): 285–8.

Jervell, J. 'Paul in the Acts of the Apostles: Tradition, History, Theology.' Pages 297–306 in *Les Actes des Apôtres: Traditions, redaction, theologie* (ed. J. Kremer; Gembloux: J. Duculot; Leuven: Leuven University Press, 1979).

———. *The Unknown Paul: Essays on Luke-Acts and Early Christian History* (Minneapolis: Augsburg, 1984).

Jewett, R. *Dating Paul's Life* (London: SCM, 1979).

Johnson, L.T. *The Acts of the Apostles*, SP (ed. D.J. Harrington; Collegeville, MN: Liturgical Press, 1992).

Keck, L.E. *Paul and His Letters*, Proclamation Commentaries (Philadelphia: Fortress, rev. edn, 1988 [1979]).

Keener, C.S. *Acts: An Exegetical Commentary* (4 vols; Grand Rapids: Baker, 2012–15).

———. 'First-Person Claims in Some Ancient Historians and Acts'. *JGRChJ* 10 (2014): 9–23.

———. *The IVP Bible Background Commentary: New Testament* (Downers Grove, IL: IVP, 1993).

Kim, S. 'Jesus, Sayings of.' Pages 474–92 in *Dictionary of Paul and His Letters* (ed. G.F. Hawthorne, R.P. Martin and D.G. Reid; Downers Grove, IL / Leicester: IVP, 1993).

———. *The Origin of Paul's Gospel* (Grand Rapids: Eerdmans, 2nd edn, 1984 [1981]).

Klausner, J. *From Jesus to Paul* (New York: Menorah, 1943 [1939]).

Knox, J. *Chapters in a Life of Paul* (New York: Abingdon, 1950).

———. *Chapters in a Life of Paul* (rev. and ed. D.R.A. Hare; Macon, GA: Mercer University Press, rev. edn, 1987).

———. 'Chapters in a Life of Paul – a Response to Robert Jewett and Gerd Lüdemann.' Pages 341–64 in *Colloquy of New Testament Studies: A Time for Re-*

appraisal and Fresh Approaches (ed. B.C. Corley; Macon, GA: Mercer University Press, 1983).

———. '"Fourteen Years Later": A Note on the Pauline Chronology'. *JR* 16 (1936): 341–9.

———. 'The Pauline Chronology'. *JBL* 58 (1939): 15–29.

Kraft, H. 'στῦλος.' Page 281 in *Exegetical Dictionary of the New Testament*, vol. 3 (Grand Rapids: Eerdmans, 1993).

Kreitzer, L.J. 'Eschatology.' Pages 253–69 in *Dictionary of Paul and His Letters* (ed. G.F. Hawthorne, R.P. Martin and D.G. Reid; Downers Grove, IL / Leicester: IVP, 1993).

Kümmel, W.G. *Introduction to the New Testament* (trans. H. Clark Lee; Nashville: Abingdon, 1975).

———. *Theology of the New Testament* (trans. J.E. Steely; London: SCM, 1974 [1972]).

Kuntz, J.K. 'Arabia/Arabians.' Page 63 in *The Dictionary of Bible and Religion* (ed. W.H. Gentz; Nashville: Abingdon, 1986).

Ladd, G.E. *A Theology of the New Testament* (Grand Rapids: Eerdmans, 1974).

Lake, K. 'The Apostolic Council of Jerusalem.' Pages 195–212 in *The Beginnings of Christianity*, vol. 5 (ed. F.J. Foakes-Jackson and K. Lake; London: Macmillan, 1933).

Lentz, J.C. *Luke's Portrait of Paul*, SNTSMS 77 (Cambridge: Cambridge University Press, 1993).

Lightfoot, J.B. *Notes on Epistles of St. Paul from Unpublished Commentaries* (London: Macmillan, 1895).

———. *St Paul's Epistles to the Galatians* (London / New York: Macmillan, 1890).

Longenecker, R.N. *Galatians*, WBC 41 (Dallas: Word, 1990).

———. *Paul, Apostle of Liberty* (New York: Harper & Row, 1964).

Lüdemann, G. *Paul, Apostle to the Gentiles: Studies in Chronology* (London: SCM, 1984 [1980]).

Maddox, R. *The Purpose of Luke-Acts* (Edinburgh: T&T Clark, 1985).

Manson, T.W. *Studies in the Gospels and Epistles* (ed. M. Black; Manchester: Manchester University Press, 1962).

Marguerat, D. 'Paul After Paul: A (Hi)story of Reception.' Pages 70–89 in *Paul and the Heritage of Israel: Paul's Claim upon Israel's Legacy in Luke and Acts in the Light of the Pauline Letters* (ed. D.P. Moessner, D. Marguerat, M.C. Parsons and M. Wolter; London / New York: T&T Clark, 2012).

Marshall, I.H. *1 Peter*, IVPNTC (ed. G.R. Osborne, D.S. Briscoe and H. Robinson; Downers Grove, IL / Leicester: IVP, 1991).

———. *The Acts of the Apostles: An Introduction and Commentary*, TNTC (Leicester: IVP; Grand Rapids: Eerdmans, 1980).

———. *Luke: Historian and Theologian* (Exeter: Paternoster, 3rd edn, 1988 [1970]).

———. 'Luke's View of Paul'. *SwJT* 33 (1990): 41–51.

———. 'The Place of Acts 20.28 in Luke's Theology of the Cross.' Pages 154–70 in *Reading Acts Today: Essays in Honour of Loveday C. Alexander*, LNTS

427 (ed. S. Walton, T.E. Phillips, L.K. Pietersen and F.S. Spencer; London / New York: T&T Clark, 2011).

McNeile, A.H. *New Testament Teaching in the Light of St Paul's* (Cambridge: Cambridge University Press, 1923).

———. *St Paul: His Life, Letters, and Christian Doctrine* (Cambridge: Cambridge University Press, 1920).

Metzger, B.M. *A Textual Commentary on the Greek New Testament* (London / New York: UBS, 1975 [1971]).

Moessner, D.P., D. Marguerat, M.C. Parsons and M. Wolter, eds. *Paul and the Heritage of Israel: Paul's Claim upon Israel's Legacy in Luke and Acts in the Light of the Pauline Letters* (London / New York: T&T Clark, 2012).

Moule, C.F.D. 'Christology of Acts.' Pages 159–85 in *Studies in Luke-Acts: Essays Presented in Honor of Paul Schubert* (ed. L.E. Keck and J.L. Martyn; London: SPCK, 1968 [1966]).

Moulton, J.H. *A Grammar of New Testament Greek, I: Prolegomena* (Edinburgh: T&T Clark, repr. 1988 [1906–76]).

Mounce, R.H. *The Essential Nature of New Testament Preaching* (Grand Rapids: Eerdmans, 1960).

———. 'Preaching, Kerygma.' Pages 735–7 in *Dictionary of Paul and His Letters* (ed. G.F. Hawthorne, R.P. Martin and D.G. Reid; Downers Grove, IL / Leicester: IVP, 1993).

Mount, C. *Pauline Christianity: Luke-Acts and the Legacy of Paul*, NovTSup 104 (Leiden: Brill, 2002).

Munck, J. *The Acts of the Apostles*, AB 31 (Garden City, NY: Doubleday, 1967).

———. *Paul and the Salvation of Mankind* (London: SPCK, 1959).

Murphy-O'Connor, J. *Paul: A Critical Life* (Oxford: Oxford University Press, 1996).

———. 'Pauline Missions before the Jerusalem Conference'. *RB* 89 (1982): 71–91.

Neusner, J. *The Rabbinic Traditions about the Pharisees before 70*, vol. 1 (Atlanta: Scholars Press, 1999).

Nock, A.D. *Early Gentile Christianity and Its Hellenistic Background* (New York: Harper & Row, 1964).

O'Neill, J.C. *Paul's Letter to the Romans* (Harmondsworth: Penguin, 1975).

———. *The Recovery of Paul's Letter to the Galatians* (London: SPCK, 1972).

Oepke, A. *Die Missionspredigt des Apostel Paulus: Eine biblisch-theologische und religionsgeschichtliche Untersuchung* (Leipzig: Hinrichs'sche Buchhandlung, 1920).

Orr, W.F., and J.A. Walther. *1 Corinthians: A New Translation, Introduction with a Study of the Life of Paul, Notes and Commentary*, AB (New York: Doubleday, 1976).

Pak, J.Y.-S. *Paul as Missionary: A Comparative Study of Missionary Discourse in Paul's Epistles and Selected Contemporary Jewish Texts*, European University Studies, Series 23: Theology 410 (Frankfurt: Peter Lang, 1991).

Park, E.C. *Either Jew or Gentile: Paul's Unfolding Theology of Inclusivity* (Louisville, KY / London: Westminster John Knox, 2003).

Pervo, R.I. *Dating Acts: Between the Evangelists and the Apologists* (Santa Rosa, CA: Polebridge, 2006).

———. *The Making of Paul: Constructions of the Apostle in Early Christianity* (Minneapolis: Fortress, 2010).

———. *The Mystery of Acts: Unraveling Its Story* (Santa Rosa, CA: Polebridge, 2008).

———. *Profit with Delight: The Literary Genre of the Acts of the Apostles* (Philadelphia: Fortress, 1987).

Phillips, T.E. *Paul, His Letters, and Acts*, Library of Pauline Studies (Peabody, MA: Hendrickson, 2009).

———. 'Paul as a Role Model in Acts: The "We"-Passages in Acts 16 and Beyond.' Pages 49–63 in Acts and Ethics, New Testament Monographs 9 (ed. T.E. Phillips; Sheffield: Sheffield Phoenix Press, 2005).

Porter, S.E. *Paul in Acts* (Peabody, MA: Hendrickson, 2001 [1999]).

———. *Verbal Aspect in the Greek of the New Testament, with Reference to Tense and Mood*, SBG 1 (New York: Lang, 1989).

Rackham, R.B. *The Acts of the Apostles: An Exposition* (London: Methuen, 1906).

Räisänen, H. *Paul and the Law* (Tübingen: Mohr Siebeck, 1983).

Ramsay, W.M. *The Bearing of Recent Research on the Trustworthiness of the New Testament* (London: Hodder & Stoughton, 1915).

———. *The Church in the Roman Empire before A.D. 70* (London: Hodder & Stoughton, 4th edn, 1895).

———. *Historical Commentary on St. Paul's Epistle to the Galatians* (New York: G. P. Putnam's Sons, 1900. Repr., Grand Rapids: Baker, 1979).

———. *Pauline and Other Studies in the Early Christian History* (London: Hodder & Stoughton, 1906).

———. *St Paul the Traveller and the Roman Citizen* (18th ed. London: Hodder & Stoughton, 1935 [1895, 1920]).

Rapske, B.M. *The Book of Acts and Paul in Roman Custody*, vol. 3 of *The Book of Acts in Its First Century Setting* (Carlisle: Paternoster; Grand Rapids: Eerdmans, 1994).

———. 'The Importance of Helpers to the Imprisoned Paul in the Book of Acts'. *TynBul* 42 (1991): 3–30.

———. 'Review of *Luke's Portrait of Paul*, by John Clayton Lentz Jr.'. *EvQ* 66 (1994): 347–53.

Reicke, B. *The Epistles of James, Peter and Jude*, AB 37 (New York: Doubleday, 1964).

Reymond, R.L. *Paul, Missionary Theologian: A Survey of His Missionary Labours and Theology* (Fearn: Christian Focus, 2000).

Richards, E.R. *Paul and First-Century Letter Writing: Secretaries, Composition and Collection* (Downers Grove: InterVarsity, 2004).

———. *The Secretary in the Letters of Paul* (WUNT 2:42; Tübingen, Mohr-Siebeck, 1991).

Ridderbos, H. *Paul: An Outline of His Theology* (London: SPCK, 1977 [1966]).

Bibliography

Rienecker, F., and C. Rogers. *Linguistic Key to the Greek New Testament* (Grand Rapids: Zondervan, 1976, 1980).
Riesner, R. *Paul's Early Period* (Grand Rapids: Eerdmans, 1998).
Robbins, V.K. 'The We-Passages in Acts and Ancient Sea Voyages'. *BRev* 20 (1975): 5–18.
Robertson, A., and A. Plummer. *A Critical and Exegetical Commentary on the First Epistle of St Paul to the Corinthians*, ICC (Edinburgh: T&T Clark).
Robertson, A.T. *A Grammar of the Greek New Testament in the Light of Historical Research* (Nashville: Broadman Press, 1934 [1914, 1915, 1923]).
Robinson, B.W. *The Life of Paul* (Chicago: Chicago University Press, 1918).
Roetzel, C. *Paul: The Man and the Myth* (Minneapolis: Fortress, 1999 [1997]).
Sanders, E.P. *Paul and Palestinian Judaism: A Comparison of Patterns of Religion* (London: SCM, 1977).
——. *Paul the Apostle's Life, Letters and Thought* (Minneapolis: Fortress, 2015).
Schmithals, W. *Paul and James*, SBT 46 (trans. D.M. Barton; London: SCM, 1965).
Schoeps, H.J. *Paul: The Theology of the Apostle in the Light of Jewish Religious History* (trans. H. Knight; London: Lutterworth Press, 1961 [1959]).
Schütz, J.H. *Paul and the Anatomy of Apostolic Authority*, SNTSMS 26 (Cambridge: Cambridge University Press, 1975).
Schweizer, E. 'Concerning the Speeches in Acts.' Pages 208–16 in *Studies in Luke-Acts: Essays Presented in Honor of Paul Schubert* (ed. L.E. Keck and J.L. Martyn; London: SPCK, 1968 [1966]).
Segal, A. *Paul the Convert: The Apostolate and Apostasy of Saul the Pharisee* (New Haven, CT / London: Yale University Press, 1990).
Senior, D., and C. Stuhlmueller. *The Foundations for Mission* (London: SCM, 1983).
Sheeley, S.M. 'Getting into the Act(s): Narrative Presence in the "We" Sections'. *Perspectives in Religious Studies* 26 (1999): 203–20.
Stanton, G.N. *Jesus of Nazareth in New Testament Preaching* (Cambridge: Cambridge University Press, 1974).
Stern, D.H., trans. *The Jewish New Testament: A Translation of the New Testament that Expresses Its Jewishness* (Jerusalem: Jewish New Testament Publications, 1991 [1979, 1989, 1990]).
Steyn, G.J. *Septuagint Quotations in the Context of the Petrine and Pauline Speeches of the Acta Apostolorum* (Kampen: Kok Pharos, 1995).
Tajra, H.W. *The Trial of St. Paul: A Juridical Exegesis of the Second Half of the Acts of the Apostles*, WUNT 2.35 (Tübingen: Mohr Siebeck, 1989).
Taylor, N. *Paul, Antioch and Jerusalem: A Study in Relationship and Authority in Earliest Christianity*, JSNTSup 66 (Sheffield: JSOT Press, 1993).
Thornton, C.-J. *Der Zeuge des Zeugen. Lukas als Historiker der Paulusreisen*, WUNT (Tübingen: Mohr Siebeck, 1991).
Thrall, M.E. *2 Corinthians 8–13*, ICC (London / New York: T&T Clark, 2000).
Trenchard, E.H. 'The Acts of the Apostles.' Pages 1335–86 in *The Pickering*

Bible Commentary for Today (ed. G.C.D. Howley, F.F. Bruce and H.L. Ellison; London / Glasgow: Pickering & Inglis, 1979).

Turner. M. *The Holy Spirit and Spiritual Gifts Then and Now* (Carlisle: Paternoster, 1996)

Tyson, J. *Marcion and Luke-Acts: A Defining Struggle* (Columbia, SC: University of South Carolina, 2006).

Urch, E.J. 'Procedure in the Courts of the Roman Provincial Governors'. *CJ* 25 (1929): 93–101.

Vielhauer, P. *Geschichte der urchristlichen Literatur* (Berlin: de Gruyter, 1975).

———. 'On the "Paulinism" of Acts.' Pages 33–50 in *Studies in Luke-Acts: Essays Presented in Honor of Paul Schubert* (ed. L.E. Keck and J.L. Martyn; trans. W.C. Robinson Jr and V.P. Furnish (London: SPCK, 1968 [1966]). This translation of the original article, 'Zum "Paulinismus" der Apostelgeschichte', *EvT* 10 (1950–51): 1–15, was previously published in *Perkins School of Theology Journal* 17 (Fall, 1963).

Walton, S. 'The Acts – of God? What Is the "Acts of the Apostles" All About?' *EvQ* 80 (2008): 291–306.

———. *Leadership and Lifestyle: The Portrait of Paul in the Miletus Speech and 1 Thessalonians* (Cambridge: Cambridge University Press, 2007).

Watson, F. *Paul, Judaism and Gentiles: A Sociological Approach*, SNTSMS 56 (Cambridge: Cambridge University Press, 1986).

Wedderburn, A.J.M. 'The We-Passages in Acts: On the Horns of a Dilemma'. *ZNW* 93 (2002): 78–98.

Weiss, J. *Earliest Christianity: A History of the Period A.D. 30–150*, vol. 1 (New York: Harper, 1959 [1914, 1937]), originally published as *Das Urchristentum* (1914); then as *The History of Primitive Christianity* (trans. F.C. Grant; New York: Harper & Brothers, 1937).

Weissenrieder, A. *Images of Illness in the Gospel of Luke: Insights of Ancient Medical Texts*, WUNT 2.164 (Tübingen: Mohr Siebeck, 2003).

Wenham, D. 'Acts and the Pauline Corpus, II: The Evidence of Parallels.' Pages 215–58 in *The Book of Acts in Its Ancient Literary Setting*, vol. 1 of *The Book of Acts in Its First Century Setting* (ed. B.W. Winter and A.D. Clarke; Grand Rapids: Eerdmans, 1993).

———. *Paul: Follower of Jesus or Founder of Christianity?* (Grand Rapids: Eerdmans, 1995).

———. 'The Paulinism of Acts Again'. *Themelios* 13 (1988): 53–5.

Wenham, D., and S. Walton. *Exploring the New Testament: A Guide to the Gospels and Acts* (Downers Grove, IL: IVP, 2001).

Wessel, W.W. 'Arabia.' Pages 83–6 in *The Illustrated Bible Dictionary*, Part 1 (ed. J.D. Douglas; Leicester: IVP, 1980).

Wilckens, U. 'Interpreting Luke-Acts in a Period of Existentialist Theology.' Pages 60–83 in *Studies in Luke-Acts: Essays Presented in Honor of Paul Schubert* (ed. L.E. Keck and J.L. Martyn; London: SPCK, 1968 [1966]).

Williams, C.S.C. *The Acts of the Apostles*, BNTC (ed. H. Chadwick; London: A&C Black, 2nd edn, 1964 [1957]).

Wilson, M.R. *Our Father Abraham: Jewish Roots of the Christian Faith* (Grand

Bibliography

Rapids: Eerdmans, 1989).
Wilson, S.G. *The Gentiles and the Gentile Mission in Luke-Acts*, SNTSMS 23 (Cambridge: Cambridge University Press, 1973).
Witherington III, B. *The Acts of the Apostles. A Socio-rhetorical Commentary* (Grand Rapids: Eerdmans, 1997).
——. *The Paul Quest: The Renewed Search for the Jew of Tarsus* (Downers Grove, IL / Leicester: IVP, 1998).
Wood, H.G. 'The Conversion of St. Paul: Its Nature, Antecedents and Consequences'. *NTS* (1954–5): 276–82.
Worley, R.C. *Preaching and Teaching in the Earliest Church* (Philadelphia: Westminster, 1967).
Wright, N.T. 'The Messiah and the People of God: A Study in Pauline Theology with Particular Reference to the Argument of the Epistle to the Romans' (PhD dissertation, University of Oxford, 1980).
——. *What St. Paul Really Said: Was Paul of Tarsus the Real Founder of Christianity?* (Oxford: Lion, 1997).
Wuest, K.S. *Wuest's Word Studies from the Greek New Testament: For the English Reader*, vol. 1 (Grand Rapids: Eerdmans, 1973, repr. 1992 [1950–53]).
Zerwick, M., and M. Grosvenor. *A Grammatical Analysis of the Greek New Testament* (Rome: Biblical Institute Press, rev. edn, 1981 [1966]).

Index of Authors

Achtemeier, P.J.   90n, 95n, 99n, 152
Adams, S.A.   106n, 152
Arndt, W.F.   111n, 152
Arrington, F.L.   109n, 152
Ascough, R.S.   16n, 152

Barnes, A.   108n, 152
Barrett, C.K.   10n, 16n, 18n, 20n, 76n, 77n, 124n
Bauckham, R.J.   98n, 152
Bauer, W.   111n, 152
Baur, F.C.   1, 2, 2n, 3, 3n, 15n, 86, 86n, 90, 90n, 100, 103, 119n, 152
Betz, H.D.   7, 8n, 78n, 141n, 152
Bock, D.L.   70n, 106n, 107n, 152
Bornkamm, G.   23n, 58, 58n, 121n, 152
Bovon, F.   16n, 17n, 152
Bowers, W.P.   80n, 153
Bruce, F.F.   4n, 12n, 16n, 21n, 23n, 24n, 41n, 75n, 76n, 77n, 81, 81n, 82, 83, 83n, 86n, 87n, 97n, 107n, 108n, 110n, 112, 112n, 128n, 140n, 143, 143n, 153, 161
Buckwalter, H.D.   16n, 153
Bultmann, R.   47n, 51n, 58n, 121n, 153

Burchard, C.   122n, 153
Burton, E.D.W.   80n, 153
Bussmann, C.   45n, 46n, 153
Butticaz, S.   39, 39n, 68n, 69n, 143n, 153

Cadbury, H.J.   11n, 15n, 106n, 107, 153
Caird, G.B.   6n, 45n, 154
Campbell, W.S.   10n, 106n, 107, 154
Caragounis, C.C.   ii, 19n, 33n, 154
Carson, D.A.   107n, 154
Carter, C.W.   11n, 154
Chae, D.J.-S.   9n, 10n, 18n, 23n, 9n, 37n, 40n, 49n, 50n, 66n, 67n, 69n, 70n, 86n, 88n, 91n, 94n, 116n, 131n, 134n, 149n, 154
Chase, F.H.   41n, 154
Chilton, B.   4, 4n, 100n, 154
Collins, R.F.   32n, 154
Conzelmann, H.   8n, 38, 16n, 21n, 26n, 28n, 47, 47n, 49, 77n, 84n, 93n, 106n,
Crossan, J.D.   4, 4n, 155

Danker, F.W.   111n, 155
de Wette, W.M.L.   26n, 155
Deissmann, A.   33n, 52n, 80n, 155
Dibelius, M.   3n, 15, 15n, 16, 16n, 17, 18n, 26n, 76n, 106n,

Index of Authors

118n, 121n, 157
Dodd, C.H. 45n, 46n, 47, 47n, 49, 49n, 50n, 51n, 56n, 121n, 155
Drane, J. 20n, 41n, 155
Dunn, J.D.G. 11n, 13n, 14n, 16n, 18n, 46n, 47, 48, 48n, 49, 107, 107n, 124n, 142n, 155

Earle, R. 11n, 155
Edwards, T.C. 51n, 155
Elliott, N. 47n, 155
Ellis, E.E. 16n, 43n, 155
Enslin, M.C. 82, 82n, 155
Eusebius. 11, 11n, 12, 12n, 88n, 109n, 148, 155

Fee, G.D. 32n, 33n, 95n, 155
Fitzmyer, J.A. 107n, 154, 155
Flichy, O. 17n, 155
Foakes-Jackson, F.J. 12n, 13n, 14, 14n, 153, 156, 158

Gager, J. 7n, 78n, 88n, 141, 149, 156
Gärtner, B. 16n, 21n, 156
Gasque, W.W. 2n, 16n, 17, 17n, 39n, 40n, 42n, 43n, 86n, 143n, 156
Gempf, C. 19n, 40n, 156
Gingrich, F.W. 111n,
Goodenough, E.R. 78n
Goodspeed, E.J. 35n, 89, 89n, 90n, 156
Green, M. 98n, 156
Grosvenor, M. 19n, 90n, 163
Guthrie, D. 36n, 92, 92n, 103, 110n, 156

Haenchen, E. 3, 16, 16n, 28n, 41, 43, 72, 72n, 92n, 94, 94n, 103n, 108n, 121n, 122n, 141n, 156
Hahn, F. 91n, 95n, 103n, 156

Hall, D.R. 90n, 156
Hanson, R.P.C. 16n, 21n, 95n, 100n, 103, 103n, 107n, 156
Harnack, A. 2, 2n, 5, 10n, 11, 15n, 26, 143n, 156
Hawthorne, G.F. 153, 157, 158, 159
Hays, R.B. 39, 39n, 70, 70n, 156
Hemer, C.J. 3, 3n, 4n, 5, 5n, 8, 8n, 10n, 12n, 20n, 76n, 90, 90n, 106n, 107, 107n, 143n, 146, 146n, 156
Hengel, M. 2n, 4, 4n, 10n, 13n, 57n, 80n, 81n, 88n, 89, 89n, 95, 95n, 98n, 103, 103n, 105n, 107n, 112n, 122n, 123, 123n, 124, 124n, 125n, 142n, 143n, 151n, 156
Holmberg, B. 4n, 157
Holzner, J. 95n, 98n, 157
Hooker, M. 18n, 157
Hughes, P.E. 91, 91n, 157
Hultgren, A.J. 121, 122n, 157
Hunter, A.M. 47n, 49n, 157
Hyldahl, N. 18n, 157

Jervell, J. 13n, 16n, 45n, 151, 151n, 152, 157
Jewett, R. 4n, 119n, 157
Johnson, L.T. 79n, 82, 82n, 85n, 91n, 157

Keck, L.E. 45n, 52n, 58n, 154, 156, 157, 159, 161, 162
Keener, C.S. ii, 4, 4n, 5n, 9n, 10n, 11n, 12n, 17n, 24n, 43n, 76n, 81n, 103n, 106n, 107n, 111n, 143, 143n, 146n, 147n, 149n, 150, 150n, 151n, 157
Kim, S. 57n, 85n, 121n, 157
Klausner, J. 58n, 121n, 150n, 157
Knox, J. 3, 3n, 4n, 5, 10, 10n, 79, 81n, 119, 119n, 120,

	120n, 122, 126n, 151, 157	Neusner, J.	122n, 159
Kraft, H.	97n, 158	Nock, A.D.	95n, 104n, 159
Kreitzer, L.J.	35n, 158		
Kümmel, W.G.	36n, 106, 106n, 158	O'Neill, J.C.	149n, 159
Kuntz, J.K.	80n, 158	Oepke, A.	46n, 159
		Orr, W.F.	33n, 51n, 159
Ladd, G.E.	6n, 58n, 61n, 158		
Lake, K.	4n, 84n, 91n, 119n, 153, 158	Pak, J.Y.-S.	51n, 54n, 159
		Park, E.C.	95n, 159
Lentz, J.C.	16, 16n, 84n, 106n, 152, 158, 160	Parsons, M.C.	17n, 153, 156, 158, 159
Lightfoot, J.B.	33n, 90n, 158	Pervo, R.I.	1n, 3, 3n, 4n, 22n, 81, 81n, 84n, 90n, 96n, 102, 102n, 112n, 142n, 160
Longenecker, R.N.	12n, 17n, 46n, 80n, 84n, 158		
Lüdemann, G.	8n, 84n, 119n, 157, 158	Phillips, T.E.	1, 1n, 2n, 3n, 17n, 106n, 159, 160
		Plummer, A.	33n, 161
Maddox, R.	21n, 158	Porter, S.E.	1n, 4n, 13, 13n, 6n, 17n, 21n, 33n, 43, 44n, 46n, 104, 104n, 105n, 106n, 141n, 142n, 143n, 150n, 152, 160
Manson, T.W.	83n, 91, 91n, 158		
Marguerat, D.	17n, 29n, 41n, 43, 43n, 94n, 143n, 153, 155, 156, 158, 159		
Marshall, I.H.	1, 1n, 16n, 24n, 28n, 31, 31n, 41n, 76n, 85n, 88n, 89, 89n, 90n, 99n, 107n, 143, 143n, 158	Rackham, R.B.	13, 13n, 160
		Räisänen, H.	8, 8n, 78n, 141n, 149n, 160
		Ramsay, W.M.	2n, 12n, 15n, 86n, 91n, 107n, 109n, 143n, 160
Martin, R.P.	153, 156, 157, 158, 159	Rapske, B.M.	16n, 85n, 111, 111n, 112n, 160
McNeile, A.H.	3n, 18n, 119n, 159		
Metzger, B.M.	32n, 159	Reed, J.	4, 4n, 155
Moessner, D.P.	16, 17n, 153, 155, 156, 158, 159	Reicke, B.	98n, 99, 99n, 160
		Reid, D.G.	153, 156, 157, 158, 159
Moo, D.J.	107n, 154		
Moule, C.F.D.	40n, 77n, 159	Richards, E.R.	81n
Moulton, J.H.	33n, 159	Ridderbos, H.	33n, 160
Mounce, R.H.	45n, 47n, 49n, 57n, 159	Rienecker, F.	97n, 160
		Riesner, R.	4n, 8n, 74n, 80n, 81n, 84n, 103n, 122, 122n, 130n, 142n, 160
Mount, C.	16n, 159		
Munck, J.	4n, 43n, 95n, 103, 103n, 107n, 112, 112n, 143n, 159	Robbins, V.K.	106n, 160
		Robertson, A.	33n, 78, 160
Murphy-O'Connor, J.	80n, 85n, 119n, 120n, 122n, 159	Robertson, A.T.	33, 33n, 161
		Robinson, B.W.	80n, 161
		Robinson, H.	158

Index of Authors

Roetzel, C.	119n, 161		19n, 20, 21, 21n, 22, 22n, 23, 23n, 24, 24n, 25, 25n, 26, 26n, 27n, 28, 28n, 29, 29n, 30, 30n, 31, 31n, 32, 32n, 34, 35, 36, 36n, 38, 38n, 39, 39n, 40, 40n, 41, 42, 42n, 43, 43n, 44, 46n, 59, 144, 162
Rogers, C.	97n, 160		
Sanders, E.P.	16n, 46n, 52n, 58n, 62n, 161		
Schmithals, W.	88n, 161		
Schoeps, H.J.	31n, 161		
Schütz, J.H.	51n, 161		
Schweizer, E.	75n, 161	Walther, J.A.	33n, 51n, 159
Schwemer, A.M.	2n, 4n, 10n, 13n, 80n, 88n, 89n, 95n, 98n, 103n, 105n, 123n, 124n, 125n, 151n, 157	Walton, S.	8n, 9n, 17n, 41n, 46n, 65n, 70n, 76, 76n, 90n, 142n, 143n, 159, 161, 162
Segal, A.	4n, 93n, 161	Watson, F.	8n, 69n, 78n, 141n, 162
Senior, D.	4n, 54n, 161	Wedderburn, A.J.M.	106n, 162
Sheeley, S.M.	106n, 161	Weiss, J.	1n, 11n, 46, 46n, 47n, 48, 48n, 87, 87n, 120n, 162
Stanton, G.N.	46n, 49n, 50n, 57n, 161		
Stern, D.H.	xi, 161	Wenham, D.	20, 20n, 58n, 90n, 142, 162
Steyn, G.J.	61n, 161		
Stuhlmueller, C.	4n, 54n, 161	Wessel, W.W.	80n, 162
		Wilckens, U.	16n, 39n, 162
Tajra, H.W.	110, 110n, 111n, 161	Williams, C.S.C.	83n, 89, 90n, 92n, 105n, 109n, 162
Taylor, N.	8n, 78n, 80n, 141n, 161	Wilson, M.R.	83n, 162
		Wilson, S.G.	84n, 124, 124n, 162
Thornton, C.-J.	4n, 107n, 143n, 161	Witherington III, B.	4n, 10, 10n, 11n, 77n, 78n, 107n, 141n, 143n, 162
Thrall, M.E.	84, 84n, 161		
Trenchard, E.H.	109, 109n, 161		
Turner. M.	ii, 59n, 70n, 154, 161	Wolter, M.	17n, 153, 156, 158, 159
Tyson, J.	16n, 161	Wood, H.G.	121n, 163
		Worley, R.C.	49n, 163
Urch, E.J.	110n, 161	Wright, N.T.	67n, 69n, 77n, 163
		Wuest, K.S.	12, 12n, 13n, 163
Vielhauer, P.	3, 3n, 5, 10, 15, 15n, 16, 16n, 17, 17n, 18, 18n, 19,	Zerwick, M.	19n, 90n, 163

Index of Scriptural References

Genesis
15:4-5   37
15:6   37
18:32   19n

Leviticus
4:20   27n
4:26   27n
4:31   27n
4:35   27n
5:10   27n
5:13   27n
5:16   27n
5:18   27n
6:7   27n
14:19–20 27n
19:22   27n

Numbers
15:25   27n
15:28.   7n

Deuteronomy
29:4   70

1 Kings
4:29   x

Nehemiah
9:30-31   19n

Psalms
2:7   69
4:6   82

16:10   69
27:1   82
32:1-2   27
44:3   82
89:15   82
104:1-2   82

Isaiah
6:9-10   69, 70
9:2   82
29:10   70
55:3   69

Ezekiel
1:27-28   82

Daniel
1:17   x

Jonah
3:10   19n
4:11   19n

Matthew
10:5-6   87n
15:21-28 87n
24:36   34
26:24   51n

Mark
1:15   37
7:24-30   87n

10:45   31

Luke
1:1-4   106, 117
1:3   11, 106
2:11-12   30
23:34   19
24:25-27 51n
24:27   61
24:44-47 61, 70
24:44-48 57n
24:45-47 51n

John
1:4   82
4:22   87n
13:23   12
18:14   28n
19:26   12
20:2   12
21:7   12
21:20   12

Acts
1–12   101
1–15   106
1:1   11, 106, 117
1:8   39, 148
1:22   61n, 96
1:23   21
2:14-39   58n
2:23   31

168

Index of Scriptural References

Acts (continued)		9:17	123	13:5	65n, 68n, 75, 85, 131
2:24	61n	9:20	60, 65n, 67n, 85	13:6-12	72n
2:25	51n	9:21	121n, 122, 123	13:8	75
2:30	61n			13:9-11	72
2:30-31	51n	9:22	31, 60, 62	13:9-12	43n, 71
2:31	61n	9:23-25	125, 134	13:13	99, 109n, 129n
2:36	58n	9:26	92, 125		
2:38	26	9:26-28	42n, 125	13:14	65n, 68n, 72n, 85, 131
3:13-15	30	9:26-30	89		
3:13-26	58n	9:28-29	131	13:16-37	29
3:15	61n	9:29	42n	13:17-41	58n
3:17	18, 19	9:30	122, 125	13:19	28, 31
3:19	19, 26	10-11	78n, 96, 141	13:22	60
3:19-21	98	10:34-35	28n	13:23	30, 71
3:26	61n, 67n, 68	10:36-43	58n	13:23-37	62
4:2	61n	10:39-42	21	13:26	67n, 68n, 131
4:10	61n	10:40	61n		
4:10-12	31, 58n	10:42	58n	13:26-31	57n
4:12	58n	10:43	26	13:26-37	9
5:30	61n	11	90, 92n	13:27	18, 19, 31, 36, 75
5:30-32	58n	11:1-18	90n		
5:31	26	11:19-30	117	13:27-30	69
5:42	61	11:25	122	13:27-35	42n
6:5-6	111	11:25-26	125	13:27-36	73
6:8-8:3	117	11:25-30	135	13:27-37	37
7:54-8:3	121n	11:27-30	89, 92, 126, 135	13:28-29	21
8:3	121			13:28-30	31, 61
8:5-25	14	11:28	105n	13:29	36
8:26-40	14	11:29	92	13:29-30	75
9	90, 124	11:30	82	13:30	61n, 71
9:1	123	12:12	99	13:30-37	61
9:1-2	121n	12:17	101	13:31	61, 68n
9:1-9	71	12:25	82, 99, 126	13:32	68n, 71
9:1-19	42n, 124	12:25-28:31	117	13:32-33	69
9:1-30	117	13	17, 27, 28, 30, 44	13:32-36	36
9:3-16	71			13:32-37	30, 71
9:4	82	13–14	127	13:33	30, 60, 61n
9:7	82	13:1	135n	13:33-35	75
9:10-19	124	13:1-5	127	13:33-37	69
9:11	122	13:1-15:35	135	13:33-47	70
9:13-14	121n	13:2	71, 126	13:34	61n, 71
9:15	42n, 45, 67, 67n, 86, 123	13:2-3	42n	13:34-37	29
9:15-16	134	13:4-5	129n	13:37	26, 29, 61n,

169

Acts (continued)		14:21-22	129	15:38-40	129n
	71	14:21-25	115, 139	15:40	108, 145
13:37-39	30	14:22	131	15:40-16:6	127, 139
13:38	26, 28, 68n,	14:23	130	15:41	129
13:38-39	26, 28, 28n,	14:23-25	37	16:1-3	85, 108, 115,
	39, 75, 75n	14:25	129		135
13:39	28, 75	14:26-27	127	16:3-5	113
13:40-41	19, 42n, 69,	14:27	14, 66, 71,	16:4	83, 108
	134		76, 86, 131	16:4-5	129
13:41	66	15	90, 90n, 91,	16:5	139
13:43	65, 129, 139		92, 94, 100	16:6-10	42n, 66, 71,
13:44-47	65n	15:1	83n, 89		127
13:44-50	66	15:1-2	14, 25, 91,	16:8	66, 86
13:46	66, 67n, 68,		92, 127	16:10	12, 67, 108,
	87	15:1-3	93		109, 145
13:46-47	36, 42n, 67n,	15:1-34	89	16:10-17	105
	68, 69, 134	15:1-35	135	16:11	127
13:46-48	66	15:2	93	16:11-12	129n
13:48-49	69	15:3	66, 76, 86,	16:11-15	66
13:48-50	42n		131	16:12	135
13:49	65	15:3-4	145	16:12-20:2	127
13:50	134	15:3-34	91	16:13	67
13:51	66	15:4	71	16:14	71
14	9	15:5	89	16:15	115
14:1	65, 65n, 68n,	15:7	137	16:16-18	72
	85, 131	15:9	93	16:17	67n, 108,
14:2	66, 69	15:9-11	28n, 93		109, 145
14:3	72	15:11	93	16:18	112
14:4	96	15:12	71, 72, 76,	16:18-20:1	112n
14:5	131, 134		86, 131	16:19-23	84
14:7	67n	15:13	137	16:19-40	131
14:8-10	72, 72n	15:13-19	101	16:19-17:13	108
14:8-18	43n, 71	15:13-21	101	16:20	108
14:14	96	15:22-29	145	16:22-23	85, 132
14:14-19	66	15:25-36	135	16:22-24	134
14:15	18, 20, 64,	15:27	108	16:23-34	43n
	65, 67n	15:30	83, 127	16:23-40	134
14:16	19	15:32	108, 135n	16:25-36	72
14:17	20	15:34-35	127	16:31	75
14:19	42n, 65n, 69,	15:35	67n, 75, 127	16:32	67
	134	15:36	67n, 75, 139	16:37	79
14:19-20	12, 72n	15:36-41	135	16:37-38	84
14:20-28	129n	15:37-38	109n	16:40	107, 115,
14:21	65, 67n, 129	15:37-39	137n		129, 139

Index of Scriptural References

Acts (continued)

17	9, 18, 20, 21, 39		63n	19:8-11	131
		17:31-32	61	19:9	66, 69, 116
17:1	108, 127	17:32	61n	19:9-10	8, 65n
17:1-3	68n, 85	18:1	127	19:10	41, 139
17:1-9	55	18:1-3	113	19:11-12	72
17:2	57n, 65n	18:1-22	108	19:12	72n
17:2-3	51n, 60, 62, 69	18:2	114, 136	19:20	131
		18:3	137	19:21	116, 128
17:3	31, 60, 61n, 67n, 74	18:4	62, 65n, 68n, 85	19:22	135
				19:23-24	132
17:4	66	18:4-5	69, 73	19:23-41	134
17:4-5	66	18:5	31, 60, 115, 135, 139	19:26	132
17:5	69			19:26-27	64
17:5-8	132	18:5-6	73	19:28-34	84
17:5-9	131, 134	18:6	42n, 65n, 66, 67n, 68, 69, 87, 133	19:29	137n
17:5-13	114			20:1	112, 131
17:7	63			20:1-2	129, 129n, 139
17:10	65n, 68n, 69, 85, 114, 127, 132	18:6-17	42n		
		18:8	66	20:1-3	129
		18:9-10	71	20:3	131
		18:11	8, 41, 133	20:4	111n, 112, 116, 137n, 137n, 139
17:12	66, 69	18:12	65n, 133		
17:13	66, 67n, 131, 132	18:12-17	131, 134		
		18:8	114, 133	20:5	109
17:13-15	139	18:16	66	20:5-6	109, 129n
17:13-16	21n,	18:17	114, 133, 136	20:5-15	105n, 112
17:14	108, 115, 129n, 135			20:5-21:18	105, 145
		18:18	65n, 85, 136	20:17	129
17:15	127, 135	18:18-19	113, 136	20:7-12	72n
17:15-16	115, 127	18:18-23	129n	20:13-14	129n
17:16	20, 108, 127	18:19	62, 68n, 73, 85, 136	20:15	109
17:17	65n, 68n, 69, 85			20:16	86, 128
		18:21	127	20:16-38	130
17:18	21, 61, 61n, 67n	18:21-22	108	20:17-35	116
		18:22	127	20:17-38	38, 76, 110
17:22-31	17, 20n, 58n	18:23	115, 128, 139	20:18	50n, 76
17:23	18			20:18-19	138
17:24-25	18	18:24-28	114	20:18-35	9, 139
17:24-31	20	18:26	136	20:18-36	76
17:28-30	18	18:28	31, 57n, 61	20:19	76n, 77n, 131
17:29-30	64	19	128		
17:30	18, 19, 20, 65	19:1	114	20:20	50n
		19:8	65n, 68n, 69, 85	20:20-21	130
17:31	20, 21, 61,			20:20-24	42n

171

Acts (continued)		21:30-36	84	24:23	13, 110, 111
20:21	65	21:37	122	24:25	21
20:22	71	21:39	122	24:27	85
20:22-23	77	21:40	122	24:27-26:32	13
20:24	67, 77, 129, 130, 138	22	124	25:3	134
		22–26	9	25:8	7
20:25	67n	22:1	68n	25:9	85
20:28	31, 31n, 42, 77	22:2	122	25:10	79
		22:2-16	83	25:10-12	85
20:29	77	22:3	122	25:19	42n, 58n, 61, 61n
20:31	50n, 76n, 138	22:3-4	121		
		22:3-5	121n	25:21	85
20:33-34	77n	22:4	134	25:25	85
20:33-35	137	22:6	124	25:27	134
20:34	50n, 137	22:6-11	71	26	124
20:36-38	140	22:6-16	42n	26:4	68n, 122
21	22, 25, 84, 94, 100	22:7	82	26:4-5	121
		22:14	82, 123	26:4-23	83
21–28	117, 129	22:15	67, 123	26:6-7	61
21:1	110	22:16	124	26:6-8	42n, 58n, 61
21:1-17	98	22:17-21	42n, 67n, 71, 80n, 81, 87	26:8	61n
21:1-18	105n, 112			26:9-11	121n
21:1-19	128	22:19	121n	26:12	124
21:4	131	22:21	66, 86	26:16	123
21:8-9	111	22:23-29	84	26:16-17	123
21:9	66	22:25-29	79	26:16-18	67, 67n, 123
21:10-14	129	23:1	68n	26:12-23	42n
21:11-14	131	23:6	58n, 61, 61n, 121	26:14	82, 122
21:17	82, 110			26:16	82
21:18	110, 111, 137	23:11	71	26:17	68n, 86
		23:12	134	26:18	28
21:19	86	23:15	134	26:20	62, 65, 66, 86, 124, 134
21:20	82, 93	23:18	134		
21:21	86	23:27	79	26:22	61
21:21-24	23n	23:34	122	26:22-23	7, 29, 51n, 61, 62, 70
21:22-24	101	24:1	111		
21:23-24	22	24:12	7	26:22f	29
21:24	26	24:14-15	42n, 61, 62, 70	26:23	31, 61, 61n, 67n, 86
21:24-26	85				
21:25	25, 94	24:15	58n, 61	26:32	85
21:26	22, 82, 86	24:17	42n, 82, 98, 129	27:1	111, 112
21:27ff	98			27:1-28:14	129n
21:27-36	131, 134	24:21	42n, 58n, 61, 61n	27:1-28:16	105, 106, 112, 145
21:29	137n				

Index of Scriptural References

27:1-29	105n	1:10-13	139	3:20-21	75n
27:2	111n, 137n	1:11-13	130	3:20-26	75
27:23-24	71	1:11-15	116	3:21	20, 28n
28:1-16	105n	1:15	56, 67, 67n	3:21-22	71
28:3-6	72n	1:16	8, 37, 42, 65,	3:22	28, 67n, 94,
28:7-9	72n		67n, 87, 87n,		149
28:16-17	134		149	3:23	19
28:17	7, 68n, 68n,	1:16-17	68, 75	3:23-24	27
	85	1:18-32	18, 39, 49	3:23-25	27
28:17-29	65n	1:18-2:16	20n	3:24	27, 42n, 77
28:19	68n, 85	1:19-20	18	3:24-25	48n
28:21-28	42n	1:20	18	3:25	18, 19, 77
28:23	42n, 57n, 61,	1:21	18	3:25-26	20
	62, 63, 68n,	1:22-25	64	3:28	28n, 75n
	70	1:32	18	3:31	149
28:23-28	68, 69	2:4	19, 58n	4	149
28:25-27	70	2:4-5	20, 65	4:1	68
28:25-29	66	2:5	58n	4:1-25	68
28:26-27	134	2:6	99n	4:5	37
28:26-28	70	2:6-7	28n	4:6	27
28:28	65n, 66, 67n,	2:9	67n	4:7-8	19
	69, 87	2:10	67n	4:9-12	37
28:31	61, 63, 67n,	2:12-15	42n	4:11	28
	145	2:13	25	4:13	42n
		2:13-15	23	4:13-16	37
Romans		2:14-15	66	4:14	28n
1	18, 39	2:16	21, 49, 58n,	4:16	77
1:1	45, 123		63n	4:24-25	42n 4:25 27,
1:1-4	49, 68	2:17-24	47, 49		48n, 56n, 57
1:2	42n, 71	2:17-27	149	4:25	58n, 62n
1:2-3	57n, 70	2:17-29	66	5–8	56
1:2-4	37, 58n, 60,	2:20	25	5:1	75n
	61, 62	2:22	64	5:2-5	24
1:3	30	2:25	25, 86, 149	5:5	71
1:3-4	21, 29, 48n,	2:25-29	23, 42n	5:6	56n
	56	2:26-29	66	5:8	27, 56n, 58n
1:4	30, 56n, 58,	3	19, 27	5:9	42n, 77
	58n, 62n	3:1	86, 149	5:10	30
1:5	42n, 67n,	3:1-2	25, 67, 87n,	5:15-21	77
	123		149	6:4	21, 21n, 56n,
1:7	38	3:9-10	149		62n
1:9	30, 60	3:9-20	67n	6:5	56n
1:9-10	139n	3:10-18	47, 49	6:7	28
1:9-14	56	3:20	28n	6:9	56n

Romans (continued)		9:25-26	66, 68, 70, 99n	11:25	66
6:10	56n			11:25-26	38, 70
6:18	28	9:25-33	42n	11:26	149
6:22	28	9:27-29	66, 70, 134	11:28-32	134
7:4	56n	9:27-33	65n, 134	11:32	19, 20
7:7	149	9:30-33	66	12:4-8	38
7:12	23, 25, 86, 149	9:33	75n	12:9-16	38
		10:1	67, 86, 87, 123, 148	12:9-21	57
7:13	23, 86			12:11	138
7:14	23, 25, 86, 149	10:4	28, 28n	12:21	58n
		10:8-9	49, 56, 58n	13:1	75n
14:13	102	10:9	21, 21n, 42n, 47, 48n, 56n, 57, 62n, 75n	13:8	25
7:16	23, 25, 86, 149			13:8-14	57
				13:10	25
7:22	25, 86	10:11-13	28, 68	13:11-14	36
8:3	30	10:12	94	13:12-14	99n
8:7	25	10:12-13	67n, 149	14:1	102
8:11	21, 21n, 56n, 62n	10:13	124	14:1-23	57
		10:15	67n	14:1-15:7	38
8:19	36	10:17	47	14:2-6	25n
8:19ff	58n	10:19	66	14:4	102
8:23	36	10:19-21	42n	14:5	25n
8:28-30	37	10:20	66, 68, 70	14:5-6	86
8:29	30	10:21	19, 20, 65n, 66, 70, 134	14:8	138
8:31-34	42n, 57			14:9	42n, 56, 56n, 57
8:32	30	11:1	68, 121, 134, 149		
8:33	71			14:9-12	63n
8:34	48n, 49, 56n, 58n	11:7-8	65n	14:10	21, 102
		11:7-9	66	14:14	83
9–11	134	11:7-10	66, 134	14:20	83
9:1-3	87	11:7-17	134	14:27	63
9:1-4	65	11:8	70	15:8-9	87n
9:1-5	67, 86, 123	11:8-10	71	15:8-12	37
9:3	68, 148	11:11	66, 70	15:9-12	70
9:4	25, 86	11:13	67n	15:15-16	67n, 71, 131
9:4-5	87n, 149	11:13-14	148	15:15-21	42n
9:5	58n	11:14	38, 65, 66, 67, 86, 87, 123	15:18	71
9:6-29	37			15:18-19	76
9:10	68			15:19	43n, 80, 80n
9:10-29	71	11:16	67	15:19-20	130
9:15	68	11:17-20	67	15:20	67n
9:22	19	11:17-24	65n, 87	15:20-21	148
9:23	68	11:20	66	15:23-24	56, 67, 116, 126, 130
9:24	37	11:24	67		

Index of Scriptural References

15:23-25	128	1:27-29	96	6:11	75, 75n
15:24	128n	1:30	27, 42n	6:12-20	38
15:25	116	1:31	71	6:14	21, 21n, 62n
15:25-26	97	2:1	38, 51, 67n	6:18-20	99n
15:25-27	97, 129	2:1-2	52, 73, 74	6:19-20	53
15:25-31	42n	2:2	48n, 51, 54, 61, 74	6:20	42n, 77
15:25-32	126			7	6, 148
15:28	128n	2:3	76n, 138	7:17-19	53, 73
15:30-32	77	2:4	43n, 72	7:17-20	24
15:31	98, 129	2:4-13	59	7:23	42n
15:32	126	3:2	6	8	6, 25n, 148
16:3	136	3:3-4	38	8:1-13	83
16:3-4	136	3:4-5	98	8:4	64
16:3-5	113	3:4-6	114	8:4-13	25
16:4-5	38	3:5-9	71	9:1	71, 82, 123
16:7	68, 136	3:10	71	9:1-2	145
16:11	68	3:10-15	38, 52	9:1-18	96
16:16	38	3:12	99n, 137	9:5	137
16:17	38	3:16	71	9:5-6	96
16:17-19	139	3:16-17	99n	9:6	42n, 77n, 135, 137n
16:21	68, 135, 137n	3:22	114		
		4:3-5	21	9:7	77
16:25	67n	4:5	34, 52, 63, 63n	9:11-12	137, 137n
16:25-26	76			9:14	67n
16:25-27	37	4:6	114	9:15-18	137n
		4:8-13	133	9:16	45, 67, 67n, 130
1 Corinthians		4:10	138		
1:1	71, 114, 136	4:11-13	133	9:17	123
1:2	38, 77	4:12	77n, 137	9:18	67n
1:6	51, 52	4:16-17	53	9:19-20	65
1:7	52, 63	4:17	50n, 53, 135, 139	9:19-22	148
1:7-8	34, 52			9:19-23	22, 23, 25, 59, 67, 73, 77, 87
1:9	30	4:20	63, 63n		
1:11-13	38	5:5	52		
1:12	98, 114, 137	5:9	53	9:20	24, 25, 26
1:14	114, 136	5:9-11	50n	9:20-21	73
1:17	45, 67, 67n, 130	5:9-13	38	9:22	138
		5:10-11	64	9:27	67n
1:21	71	5:11	53	10	148
1:21-25	52	6:5	63	10:7	64
1:23	48n, 54, 67n, 61, 95	6:6	38	10:12	77
		6:9	64	10:14	64
1:23-25	73	6:9-10	3, 63n, 99n	10:14-30	83
1:26-29	99n	6:9-20	53	10:19-20	64

175

1 Corinthians (cont'd)		15:12	19, 34	1:3-10	131
10:25-33	25	15:12-15	52, 62	1:8-10	131, 133
10:32	77	15:12-52	34	1:8-11	133
10:32-33	24, 25	15:12-56	35, 36	1:16	128
11:2	6, 34n, 50n	15:12-57	32, 33, 34, 41	1:18	56n 1:14 52
11:16	77			1:19	51, 58, 60, 67n, 100, 135
11:22	77	15:14	52		
11:23	51	15:15	21, 21n, 51, 52, 62n, 73	1:23	128
11:23-26	50n			2:4	76n, 138
11:34	51n	15:17	52	2:12	66
12–14	6, 148	15:20	52, 73	2:12-13	127
12:2	64	15:20-28	63	2:17	77n, 137
12:12-26	38	15:20ff	58n	4:1	138
12:13	67n	15:22-25	63	4:5	51, 67n
12:25	38	15:23	38	4:6	82
12:28	39	15:24	63n	4:7-12	133
13:1-7	99n	15:28	30	4:8-9	133
15	18, 7, 148	15:35	52	4:8-12	131
15:1	9, 67n	15:49	33n	4:16-5:10	149
15:1-2	51, 130	15:49-52	33	5:1-10	35
15:1-4	31, 68, 73, 95	15:50	63n	5:10	21, 63n, 99n
		15:51	33n	5:14-15	130, 138
15:1-7	49	15:51-52	32	5:14-21	48n
15:1-8	6, 7, 74	15:52	33	5:18-19	19
15:1-11	51n	16	6	5:19	27
15:2	67n	16:1	97, 126	6:1	71
15:3	58n, 95, 149	16:1-4	82, 91, 97	6:1-10	133
15:3-4	29, 37, 58n, 61, 62, 69	16:1-6	128	6:4-5	84, 133
		16:2	97	6:4-10	131, 134
15:3-5	42n	16:4	77	6:16	59, 64
15:3-7	57n	16:5	128	7:5	138
15:3-8	27, 51n, 73	16:8	136	7:9	58n
15:3-11	48n	16:8-9	128, 131, 139	7:9-10	20, 64
15:4	62n			7:10	58n
15:5	137	16:9	66, 77n, 128, 131, 133	7:12	38
15:5-7	101			8-9	97, 148
15:5-8	58, 61	16:10	135, 139	8-10	82
15:7	101, 137	16:12	114	8:1-5	97
15:8	42n, 82, 123	16:13	77, 139	8:1-15	126
15:9	77, 95, 96, 121n	16:19	113, 128, 136	8:2	132, 133
				8:6	91
15:11	49, 94, 95, 102, 145, 149	**2 Corinthians**		8:10	97
				8:14	97
15:11-12	67n, 145	1:1	38, 135	8:21	102

Index of Scriptural References

9:1	97	12:21	20, 58n	1:19	101
9:12	97	13:1-2	139	1:20	74
10-13	77	13:2	6, 9, 50n, 52, 128	1:21	125
10:1	76n			1:22	121
10:13	71	13:4	96	1:23	67, 12167n, 121n, 122
10:13-16	131	13:9	38		
10:13-18	138			1:23-24	123
10:16	67, 67n	**Galatians**		2	90, 92n
11:4	67n, 139	1	90	2:1	92, 122, 127n
11:5	95, 124, 145	1–2	90		
11:7	67n, 76n, 138	1:1	54, 62n, 124, 145	2:1-2	84
				2:1-3	91, 103, 125
11:7-11	77n	1:2	38	2:1-9	135
11:9	137n	1:4	27, 58n	2:1-10	42n, 88n, 89, 90, 90n, 94
11:13	139	1:6	74, 96		
11:13-15	95	1:6-9	67	2:2	53, 67n, 92
11:21	133	1:7	53, 74, 97	2:2-3	125
11:22	67	1:8	67n, 74	2:3	91
11:23-25	84, 85	1:9	67n	2:4	89, 91, 93
11:23-26	133	1:11	6, 53, 67, 74	2:4-5	91, 91n
11:23-27	131, 134	1:11-12	42n, 149	2:4-9	93
11:24	22, 65, 134	1:12	51n, 82, 95, 123, 124, 145	2:4-10	91, 103, 127, 135
11:24-26	77n				
11:25	129	1:12-16	123	2:5	93, 126, 127
11:26	134	1:13	77, 121, 121n, 122	2:6	94, 97, 145
11:28	38, 39, 138, 140			2:6-10	91
		1:13-14	59	2:7-8	67n
11:32	80	1:13-16	54, 83	2:7-9	22, 83, 84, 88, 145
11:29-30	138	1:14	68, 121, 122		
11:32-33	125	1:15	123, 126	2:7-14	137
12:1-4	71	1:15-16	42n, 45, 53, 67n, 71, 123	2:9	97, 101, 127
12:1-5	82			2:10	42n, 90, 94, 97, 102
12:1-10	133	1:16	30, 60, 67, 67n, 74, 123, 124		
12:5	138			2:11	97
12:9-10	96, 138			2:11-13	128
12:9-11	138	1:16-17	125	2:11-14	96, 135
12:10	131	1:17	80, 124	2:11-21	135
12:11	124	1:17-18	80	2:12	78n, 96, 97, 101, 141
12:12	72	1:17-19	92		
12:13-17	77n	1:18	42n, 125	2:13	127
12:14	128	1:18-19	84, 89, 101, 125, 137	2:14	25, 83n
12:14-17	137			2:15-16	75, 149
12:14-18	137n, 139	1:18-20	125	2:16	28n, 74, 75n
12:20	38	1:18-24	121	2:19	28n

177

2:19-20	138	6:12-15	54	2:6-11	30
2:20	27, 30	6:14	54, 74	2:8-9	58
3	149	6:15	24, 25	2:17	140
3:1	48n, 74, 134			2:19-23	135
3:1-4	49	**Ephesians**		2:22	115
3:1-5	7, 53, 59, 72, 74	1:4	37, 99n	3	30
		1:7	26, 27, 27n, 42, 77	3:4-6	23
3:2	149			3:4-11	59, 83
3:5	72	1:15-19	139n	3:5-6	1, 21n
3:7-8	68	1:20	62n	3:6	68
3:8	68	2:2	63n	3:7-14	138
3:10	28n, 102	2:8-9	75n	3:9	28n, 75n
3:11	28n, 74, 75n, 149	2:10	99n	3:13-14	138
		3:1	134	3:17-18	115
3:13	42n, 58n, 149	3:3	116	3:17-19	54
		3:5-12	76	3:18	76n, 138
3:13-14	27	3:6	68	3:20	30, 36
3:15-25	68	3:7-12	37	4:2	38
3:16	37	3:14-21	139n	4:5	36
3:23	149	4:1	134	4:9	115
3:23-25	149	4:2	76n, 138	4:10	115
3:28	67n, 94	4:21-22	116	4:32	27
4:4	30, 37	5:2	58n		
4:6	30, 49	5:5	63, 63n	**Colossians**	
4:8	18, 64	6:19-20	130	1:3-14	139
4:10-11	86	6:20	134	1:4	130
4:12-15	65	6:21	116, 137n, 139	1:5-7	57
4:13	53, 67n			1:6-9	56
4:13-14	12			1:7	56
4:14	139	**Philippians**		1:7-9	130
4:19	138	1:1	135	1:9	140n
4:25	80	1:3-4	139n	1:9-14	139n
4:28	37	1:3-6	71	1:10	99n
5:2-3	149	1:7	134	1:12-13	63n
5:2-4	28n	1:8	139	1:13	30
5:6	24, 25	1:9-11	139n	1:13-14	27
5:11	67n, 121	1:14	134	1:14	26, 42n
5:13	99n	1:15-18	25n	1:15-23	56
5:19-21	53, 54, 64, 99n	1:17	134	1:20	42n
		1:17-18	67n	1:21-23	57
5:20-21	54	1:21-24	35	1:23	45, 56, 67n
5:21	50n, 63n	1:27	115	1:25-27	37, 76
5:22-23	102	1:29-30	132	1:28	67n
6:10	62	2:3	76n	2:1	138, 139

Index of Scriptural References

2:5	139	2:8	74	5:1-2	7, 9, 35, 50n, 55
2:12	21, 21n, 56n, 62n	2:8-9	50n	5:1-3	34
2:13-14	27	2:9	67n, 74, 77n, 114, 137n	5:2	55
2:20	56n	2:11	138	5:6	77
3:1	56n	2:12	63n, 137	5:6-11	36
3:1-17	57, 62	2:14	56, 114, 132	5:9-10	74
3:11	67n, 94	2:14-16	42n, 77n, 134	5:10	55
3:12	76n	2:15	55	5:20	27
3:12-14	99n	2:15-17	132	5:23	55, 63
3:13	27	2:17	114		
4:3-4	130	2:18	139	**2 Thessalonians**	
4:14	105	2:19	63	1:1	100, 134, 135
4:3	66	3:1	21n, 127	1:4	56
4:7	116, 137n, 139	3:1-2	127	1:5	63n, 132
4:10	136, 137n	3:1-6	114, 139	1:7	55
4:10-14	105n	3:2	71, 134	1:7-10	63
4:10-15	12	3:4	9, 56, 59, 132	1:8-10	63n
4:11	63n, 99	3:6-7	134	1:11-12	139n
4:14	23, 12	3:10	38, 139	2:1ff	55
4:17	138	3:11-13	139n	2:1-2	36
		3:13	63	2:1-5	7, 35
1 Thessalonians		4	148	2:1-12	35, 36
1:1	38, 100, 134, 135	4:1-2	50n, 55	2:3	35
1:2	139n	4:2-3	99n	2:5	21, 35, 48, 50n, 55
1:4-6	50n, 59	4:5	64	2:6	35, 137n
1:5	43n, 72	4:6	6, 9, 50n, 55	2:8	137n
1:6	55, 66, 74, 132	4:7-8	99n	2:13	37
1:9	54, 64	4:9	99n	2:14-16	42n
1:9-10	20, 49, 54n, 58n, 59, 65, 98	4:9-10	55	2:15	9, 50n, 55
		4:10	139	3:3-5	139n
1:10	30, 34, 48, 48n, 54, 55	4:11	9, 50n, 55	3:4	50n
		4:12	6	3:6	9, 50n, 55
2:1-2	132	4:13	5	3:6-10	55
2:2	54, 64, 74, 114, 127, 132	4:13-18	6, 7,	3:7-8	137
		4:13-5:11	32, 33, 34, 36, 41, 149	3:7-10	6, 77n
2:4	45	4:14	55, 58n, 62n	3:8	137n
2:5-12	55	4:15	32, 33, 33n	3:10	9, 50n, 55
2:6-9	76n	4:15-16	63		
2:7	138	4:16	55	**1 Timothy**	
		4:17	33	1:12	45, 123
				1:12-14	83

179

1:13	19, 121n	**Titus**		2:15	99n	
1:18	50n	1:3	45	2:24	58n	
2:4	19	1:10	139	3:8	99n	
2:7	67n	2:14	27, 58n, 99n, 102	3:11	99n	
4:14	50n			4:3-4	99n	
6:15	63	3:8	99n, 102	4:8-10	99n	
6:16	82	3:12	137n, 139	5:12	100	
6:18	62	3:14	102	5:13	99, 100	

2 Timothy

		Philemon		**2 Peter**	
1:3	139n	4	139n	1:1	88
1:6	50n	19	134	1:12-13	50n
1:8	134	23-24	105	3:1	50n
1:13	50n	24	12, 99, 136, 137n	3:2	50n
1:16	134			3:11-12	99n
2:2	50n			3:11-14	36
2:3	134	**Hebrews**		3:14-16	98
2:8	50n	9:12	27	3:15	98
2:9	134	9:15	27	3:15-16	36n
3:10-14	50n	10:10-12	27	3:16	98
3:11	133				
3:13	139	**James**		**1 John**	
3:17	102	2:1	102	1:5	82
4:1	21, 63n	3:17-18	102	2:7	50n
4:5	138	4:11-12	102	2:10	99n
4:6-7	138			2:21	50n
4:7	138	**1 Peter**		2:24	50n
4:8	21	1:1	88	3:11	50n
4:10-11	105, 112	1:12	50n	5:5	47
4:11	12, 13, 99, 136, 137n	1:14-16	99n		
		1:17	99n	**2 John**	
4:12	137n, 139	1:22	99n	5–6	50n
4:16	111n	1:25	50n		
4:18	63n	2:9-10	99n	**Jude**	
4:19	36	2:10	88	5	50n
4:30	137n	2:11-12	99n		
		2:12	99n		

Index of Subjects

Abraham 37, 41, 68, 149
Achaia 126, 127, 128, 133
Acts of the Apostles
   a record of the gospel message 8, 9, 21, 29
   as a Primary source 1, 12, 54, 180
   as secondary authority 45, 119n
   as unhistorical ix, 1, 3, 9, 41, 93n, 142
   authorship of Acts 10, 10n, 11, 12, 107n
   coloured by Luke's agenda 4, 120
   credibility of Acts 3, 8, 50, 72, 80, 90, 105, 107, 113, 119, 150
   critical scholarship on 1, 2n, 8, 12, 16, 16n, 17, 105n
   historicity of Acts 2, 3, 5
   history of earliest Christianity 3, 15, 143, 148
   Luke's account of Paul 3, 4, 5, 10, 41, 77, 78, 87, 102, 103, 119, 120, 123, 127, 128, 140, 141, 142, 143, 144, 147, 151
   purpose of Acts 3, 9, 76n, 93n, 120, 146, 147
   reliability of Acts 2, 3, 4, 5, 10, 13, 16, 39, 44, 46, 46n, 59, 60, 83, 89, 102, 120, 140, 143, 144, 146
   sceptical scholarship on Acts 5, 78, 141, 142
   source for Pauline studies 1, 4
   sources of Acts 112
   speeches in Acts 15, 39, 41, 43, 46n, 61
Agabus 126
Agrippa 13, 61, 62, 111, 112, 124
Ananias 123, 123n, 124, 133
Anti-Marcionite prologue 11, 12, 109n
Antioch (Syrian) (*see also* Pisidian Antioch)
   8, 12, 13, 13n, 14, 71, 75, 88, 90, 92, 93, 97, 99, 101, 108, 109, 109n, 112, 113, 125, 126, 127, 128, 135, 136, 146
Antioch incident 25, 81, 86, 89, 96, 98, 100, 127, 128
Apollos 61, 113, 114
Apostles
   Jerusalem apostles 22, 32, 42, 46, 47, 49, 58, 82, 84, 90, 92, 92n, 93, 93n, 94, 95, 97, 98, 100, 101, 103, 106, 108, 110, 120, 124, 125, 125n, 126, 135, 137, 145, 149
   Paul the apostle 2, 3, 4, 12, 13, 14, 25, 44, 52, 55, 57, 67, 71, 72, 75, 78, 81, 84n, 87, 96, 105, 112
Apostolic decree (*see also* Jerusalem Council decree)
   22, 79, 83, 83n, 84, 94, 100,

101, 102, 108
Arabia   16, 96, 97, 98, 124, 149, 188, 193
Areopagus   18, 19, 20, 64
Aristarchus   105, 109, 109n, 112, 137
Artemis   64
Athens   18, 19, 19n, 20, 61, 64, 65, 108, 113, 115, 127

Baptism   123, 123n, 124
Barnabas   13, 14, 71, 89, 90n, 91, 92, 93, 96, 99, 100, 125, 126, 127, 129, 135, 137, 139
Berea   8, 66, 108, 113, 114, 115, 127, 130n, 132, 134

Caesarea   7, 13, 14, 85, 108, 110, 111, 111n, 112, 125, 127, 129, 132, 147
Catholicism   3, 15
Christian origin   3
Christianity   1, 31n, 86n, 93n, 95, 96, 99, 120, 148, 151
Christians   19, 24, 27, 42, 64, 76, 86, 123, 126
Christology   3, 15, 21, 29, 30, 46n, 58n, 144
Christophany   83, 123, 123n, 124, 150
Chronology   3, 79
Church-planting   x, 4, 45, 46, 48, 96, 144
Cilicia (*see also* Tarsus)   121, 122, 125, 127
Circumcision   22, 23, 24, 24n, 25, 26, 73, 83, 85, 86, 87, 88n, 89, 91, 92, 92n, 93, 94, 95n, 96, 100, 149
Collection (*see also* Relief fund)   6, 79, 81, 82, 91, 92, 92n, 94, 97, 98, 100, 101, 102, 126, 129, 148
Colossae   116, 130, 140n
Colossians   56, 57, 116, 148

Comparison/compare   2n, 9n, 10, 10n, 15n, 16, 17, 20, 21, 23, 24, 30, 40, 41, 43, 44, 46, 46n, 59, 60, 64, 66, 70, 72, 73, 76, 77, 79, 81, 87, 107, 120, 124, 131, 134, 137, 140, 142, 142n, 143, 144, 145, 146, 147, 148, 149, 150
Compatibility   5, 59, 72, 77n, 78, 92n, 103, 117, 137, 141, 142, 143, 145, 146, 147, 148
Consensus   1, 6n, 18, 41, 90, 117
Corinth   6, 7, 8, 33, 34, 41, 52, 60, 62, 63, 71, 72, 73, 74, 75, 77, 88, 91, 95, 97, 98, 98n, 100, 108, 113, 114, 115, 117, 126, 127, 128, 128n, 129, 130, 133, 133n, 134, 135, 136, 137, 138, 139, 144
Corinthians   7, 21, 27, 33, 34, 34n, 37, 41, 51, 51n, 52, 53, 60, 61, 63, 64, 69, 72, 73, 78n, 94, 95, 96, 97, 98, 113, 114, 116, 125, 128, 131, 132, 133, 133n, 135, 136, 137, 138
Crispus   113, 114, 136
Cross   20, 21, 30, 31, 52, 53, 54, 57, 59, 74, 76

Damascus   13, 42, 60, 62, 80, 82, 83, 106, 123, 123n, 124, 125, 134, 147
David   27, 29, 30, 47n, 56, 60
Derbe   75, 127
Diaspora   22, 23n, 122
Didache   49, 49n
Discrepancy   5, 79, 85n, 90, 92, 102, 103, 145, 146, 150

Epaphras   56, 57, 105
Ephesian elders   9, 40, 63, 76, 106, 130, 131, 137, 139, 144, 146
Ephisians   27n, 116, 138
Ephesus   6, 8, 31, 41, 63, 64, 65, 72,

Index of Subjects

102n, 106, 108, 109, 113, 114, 116, 117, 126, 127, 128, 130, 131, 132, 134, 136, 139

Equality
of Jew and Gentile 40, 49, 67, 87, 88n, 149

Eschatology 3, 15, 17n, 31, 32, 36, 36n, 39, 39n, 40, 144, 149

Evangelism (*see also* Mission)
8, 9, 25, 25n, 40, 43, 59, 60, 63, 67, 75, 77, 117, 128n, 129, 130, 144

Evangelist 9. 60, 117, 129, 130, 140, 148

Eyewitness 11, 13, 58, 105, 106, 107, 112, 117

Farewell speech 106, 110, 130, 139, 146, 148

Felix 62, 84, 110, 111, 112n

Festus 61, 110, 111

Forgiveness of sins 26, 27, 27n, 28, 31, 42, 75

Fulfilment 29, 31, 37, 42, 51, 52, 59, 61, 62, 68, 69, 70, 73

Galatia 7, 12, 12n, 25, 29, 53, 54, 64, 65, 72, 74, 75, 75n, 77, 78n, 86, 88, 89, 91, 95, 96, 97, 100, 105, 109, 113, 126, 127, 128, 129, 130, 139, 144, 149

Galatians 6, 7, 8, 12, 18, 24n, 25, 27, 29, 40, 41, 53, 54, 57, 64, 72, 80, 86, 86n, 88, 89, 90, 94, 95, 97, 102, 103, 121, 122, 124, 126, 127, 127n, 140, 145, 149

Gamaliel 122, 122n

Gentiles
apostle to the Gentiles 67, 68, 127, 144
mission to the Gentiles 32, 36, 37, 70, 79, 80, 80n, 86, 93, 95, 97, 117, 135, 140

God
call of God 62, 66, 67, 71, 85,
forbearance of God 19
kindness of God 19, 20, 65
Lord of heaven and earth 18
the Creator 18
the Judge 21
word of God 8. 68, 75, 87, 12, 133
wrath of God 65

God-fearers 85, 87n

Godly life 52, 54, 55, 57, 60, 99, 115

Gospel
gospel message 6, 8, 40, 42, 65, 70
Paul's gospel 22, 47, 48, 49, 58, 65, 70, 74, 118n, 132

Gospel of Luke 11, 13, 106, 107, 109n, 112, 117, 118, 118n

Gospel of Mark 118

Gospel of Matthew 118

Grace (*see also* God: God's grace)
20, 27, 38, 59, 67, 77, 81, 93, 94

Great commission 148

Greeks 8, 25, 62, 65, 130, 131

Hardship 35, 36, 39, 114, 129, 131, 133, 133n, 138n, 148

Hard work 76, 77n, 133, 137

Historians 4, 15n, 16n, 42, 146

Holy Spirit 14, 42, 53, 58, 70, 71, 72, 148

Hypothesis 18, 40, 102

Iconium...8, 75, 133, 134

Idolatry 18, 19, 20, 54, 64

Idols 6, 20, 25n, 54, 58n, 59, 64, 65, 83, 144, 148

Ignorance 18, 19, 20, 23, 64

Israel 38, 66, 67, 68, 71, 80, 120, 134, 149

James 22, 25, 82, 92, 96, 97, 101, 102, 110, 121, 125, 137, 145, 146

Jerusalem
apostles in Jerusalem 22, 32, 46,

49, 82, 84, 92, 92n, 94, 95, 100, 103, 106, 120, 124, 135, 145, 149
church in Jerusalem 14, 23n, 30, 91, 100, 101, 121, 135n, 145, 146
city of Jerusalem 8, 13, 14, 22, 40, 42, 45, 61, 69, 71, 77, 79 80, 80n, 81, 82, 89, 90, 90n, 91, 92, 92n 93, 94, 95, 7, 98, 99, 101, 102, 103, 104, 110, 110 111, 111n, 112, 113, 116, 120, 121n, 122, 124, 125, 125n, 126, 127, 128, 129, 130, 131, 134, 135, 138, 140, 145, 148
temple in Jerusalem 7, 81, 85, 110

Jerusalem Council 14, 22, 48, 72, 83, 88, 89, 90, 90n, 91, 92, 93, 96, 97, 101, 126, 127

Jerusalem Council decree (*see also* Apostolic decree) 22, 79, 83n, 84, 100, 101, 102, 108

Jesus Christ (*see also* Messiah, Son of God)
19, 21, 24, 27, 31, 37, 38, 40, 52, 53, 54, 57, 59, 60, 61, 62, 63, 69, 71, 74, 75, 76, 87, 93, 105, 113, 123, 124, 149
ascension of Christ 14, 63
Judge 20, 47, 47n, 61, 63
Saviour 30, 42, 47n, 60, 71
second coming of Christ 34, 63

Jews
ethnic Jews 26, 27, 28n, 38, 63, 66, 68, 71, 73, 95, 98, 114, 123, 148
in Diaspora 23n, 28n, 73, 132, 134, 136
Paul first goes to Jews 27, 42, 68, 70, 79, 86n, 87, 102
Paul preaches to 24, 31, 40, 42, 47, 59, 60, 62, 66, 67, 69 75, 77, 87n, 88, 88n
Paul preaches to Jews and Gentiles 37, 38, 40, 52, 62, 65, 68, 77, 87, 94, 103, 123, 126, 130, 131
refuse to believe in Jesus 37, 42, 65, 66, 68, 70, 131, 132, 133, 134, 134n
unbelief of Jews 42, 66, 68, 70, 134, 134n

John Mark (*see also* Mark) 99, 100, 105, 109n 135, 136, 137

Judaism 22, 54, 83, 120, 121

Judaizers 7, 9, 25, 29, 40, 83, 86, 88, 92, 93, 94, 95, 96, 97, 100, 100n, 145, 149

Judea 93, 121, 121n, 122

Justification by faith 7, 22, 26, 27, 28, 29, 40, 52, 68, 74, 75, 86, 149

Kerygma 46, 47, 47n, 48, 48n, 49, 51, 51n, 58

Kingdom of God 27, 53, 54, 63, 69, 131, 144

Law
Mosaic Law 22, 23n, 26, 28, 62, 69, 71, 75, 86, 89, 100
law not to be imposed on Gentiles 24, 29, 83, 89, 93
Paul's attitude to the law 22, 23, 24, 25, 26, 73, 87, 88n, 102, 149, 149n
role in salvation 25, 26, 28, 29, 40, 102
salvation apart from the law 29, 40, 71, 74
value of the law 86

Lord (*see also* Jesus Christ, Son of God)
21n, 30, 31, 32, 34, 35, 36n, 42, 47, 47n, 51, 52, 54, 55, 56, 57, 58, 59, 63, 65, 66, 67, 71, 72, 73, 74, 79, 82, 93, 94, 98, 101, 123, 124, 129, 130, 131, 133,

Index of Subjects

137, 138, 139
Lucan scholarship (*see also* Scholars) 106
Luke
  a companion of Paul...1, 2, 2n, 11, 12, 13, 14, 81, 82, 105n, 107, 111, 117
  a credible historian 59, 74, 80, 90, 107, 113, 119, 134, 142, 145, 147, 150
  as a creative author 4, 4n, 8, 80, 102, 106, 108, 109, 110, 117, 118, 146, 150
  as a historian 42
  as a Thucydidean reporter 39
  the author of Acts 2, 2n, 5, 8, 10, 11, 12, 13, 14n, 15, 107, 112, 118, 150
  the doctor 11, 12, 105, 105n, 107, 108
Luke's credibility 59, 74n, 76, 80, 90, 107, 113, 119, 134, 142, 145, 147, 150
Luke's portrait of Paul 3, 4, 5, 8, 10, 14, 15, 16, 17, 21, 39, 40, 41, 46, 46n, 60, 63, 70, 78, 79, 89, 90, 103, 105, 107, 113, 119, 120, 129, 140, 141, 142, 142n, 143, 145, 147, 150, 151n
Lydia 71, 115, 139
Lystra 19, 64, 65, 75, 127, 133, 134

Macedonia
  people of 67, 107, 127, 132
  region of 71, 97, 107, 109, 113, 115, 126, 127, 128, 129, 132, 133, 135, 139
Mark (*see also* John Mark) 99, 100, 109n
Marriage 6, 148
Messiah (*see also* Jesus Christ, Son of God)
  Jesus the Messiah 37, 38, 40, 47, 56, 59, 60, 62, 68, 87, 87n

  messiahship 22, 26, 62
Methodology 5, 9, 9n, 17, 23, 26, 39, 40, 41n, 42n, 44, 46, 47, 49, 119, 120, 144, 147, 148, 149
Miletus 76n, 77n, 109, 110, 113, 116, 129, 139
Miracles (*see also* Signs and wonders) 13, 39n, 42, 53, 71, 72, 76, 131
Mission (*see also* Evangelism)
  1, 14, 32, 36, 37, 39, 42, 47, 60, 65, 66, 70, 79, 80, 80n, 85, 86, 87, 88n, 93, 95, 95n, 97, 99, 100, 117, 135, 140
Missionary journeys (*see also* Paul's missionary work)
  11, 12, 13, 14, 25, 40, 63, 71, 72, 75, 81, 89, 98, 99, 100, 101, 106, 108, 109, 112, 113, 117, 120, 126, 127, 128, 129, 131, 135, 136, 139, 140, 146, 147
Missionary message 5, 9, 27, 43, 44, 46, 47, 48, 49, 53, 54, 59, 144
Missionary preaching (*see also* Paul's missionary preaching)
  5, 9, 9n, 17, 19, 29, 29n, 32, 35, 40n, 44, 45, 45n, 46, 46n, 47, 48, 49, 50, 51n, 54, 54n, 55, 56, 57, 59, 60, 62, 72, 77, 81, 86, 87, 117, 144, 148
Moses (*see also* Law of Moses)
  26, 28, 61, 62, 69, 75, 86, 93, 100
Muratorian Canon 11

Nabatean kingdom 80
Natural theology (*see also* Theology)
  15, 17, 17, 18, 21, 21n, 144
Nazirite vow 22, 23, 23n
New Testament (*see also* Old Testament)
  1, 15n, 17n, 29n, 47n, 49n, 50, 68, 95, 122, 143

Old Testament (*see also* New Testa-

ment)
    10, 42, 57, 58, 59, 60, 61, 62,
    68, 69, 70, 73, 80, 88n, 122, 134

Parousia 31, 32, 33, 34, 35, 35n, 36,
    38, 39, 39n, 41, 48, 52, 55, 58,
    60, 63, 98
Pastor (*see also* Paul: a pastor)
    8, 9, 41, 60, 140
Pastorals 5, 5n, 50n
Paul
    a church planter 9, 42, 129, 130,
      140
    a Hellenistic Jew 18, 122
    a letter writer 79, 81, 83, 98
    a missionary apostle 8, 9, 42, 126,
      133, 140, 147
    a pastor 8, 9, 41, 60, 140
    a Roman citizen 79, 84, 84n, 85,
      112
    a theologian 8, 9, 41, 60
    an evangelist 9, 130
    apostolic self-awareness of 116
    co-workers of 81, 98, 99, 100, 108,
      108n, 109, 109n, 111, 114, 115,
      120, 134, 136, 137, 140, 145,
      146, 147n
    Luke's hero 4
    pre-Christian life of 13, 106, 121
    relationship with Jerusalem 79, 84,
      92, 93, 96, 100, 101, 102, 103,
      104, 140, 145
    the historical Paul 2, 4, 10, 15, 17,
      19, 102, 103, 143, 151
    the Jewishness of 67, 79, 85, 88, 89,
      102, 103, 145
    the Lucan Paul 5, 7, 9, 15, 19, 20,
      21, 22, 28, 30, 31, 37, 40, 42,
      44, 59, 60, 61, 62, 63, 65, 66,
      67, 68, 69, 70, 71, 72, 73, 74,
      75, 76, 77, 82, 84, 85, 86, 87,
      93, 97, 111n, 117, 121, 122,
      122n, 124, 130, 131, 133, 134,
      138, 139, 144

the real Paul 15, 19, 20, 22, 31, 40,
      42, 43n, 44, 59, 60, 62, 63, 66,
      69, 70, 71, 72, 73, 75, 76, 77,
      79, 81, 82, 85, 86, 95, 103, 117,
      124, 131, 134, 138, 140, 143,
      144, 145
Paul of Acts 1, 2n, 3, 15, 20, 22, 30,
    69, 70, 79, 84, 104, 117, 129,
    130, 138, 140, 143n
Paul of the letters (*see also* Paul's
    letters, Pauline corpus)
    1, 2n, 3, 20, 22, 28, 30, 41, 69,
    79, 89, 104, 117, 130, 138,
    142, 143n
Paul's apostolic ministry 13, 67, 96,
    146
Paul's letters (*see also* Paul of the
    letters, Pauline corpus)
    9n, 10n, 24, 31, 41, 43, 46, 58n,
    59, 63, 64, 72, 73, 76, 77n, 78,
    78n, 79, 81, 82, 98, 102, 103,
    103n, 113, 120, 126, 130, 134,
    136, 137, 139, 141, 143, 144,
    147, 148, 150, 151, 151n
    autobiographical remarks 10,
      119, 121
    credibility of Paul's accounts 10,
      78
    follow-up letters 6, 41, 43, 50, 60,
      76, 144, 148
    rhetorical element of 78, 78n, 101,
      140, 141, 144, 151n
Paul's life and ministry 3, 5, 8, 10,
    11, 13, 58n, 78n, 96, 119, 120,
    131, 140, 146, 147, 151, 151n
Paul's missionary preaching (*see also*
    Missionary preaching)
    5, 9, 9n, 17, 19, 29, 29n, 32, 35,
    40n, 44, 45, 45n, 46, 46n, 47,
    48, 49, 50, 51n, 54n, 55, 56, 57,
    58, 59, 60, 62, 72, 73, 77, 81,
    86, 87, 117, 144, 148
Paul's missionary work (*see also*
    Missionary journeys)

Index of Subjects

29, 50, 52n, 63, 65, 67, 71, 72, 73, 74, 76, 78, 81, 84, 86, 89, 96, 115, 121, 126, 127, 130, 131, 134, 135, 135n, 138, 141, 145, 148, 149

Paul's theology (*see also* Theology) 17, 23, 39, 40, 41, 43, 143, 144

Pauline corpus (*see also* Paul's letters) 5n, 41, 99

Paulinism 3, 15

Pentecost 128, 131

Persecution...13, 36, 55, 56, 59, 76, 76n, 114, 120, 121n, 122n, 129, 131, 132, 133, 134, 138n

Peter 1, 19, 25, 26, 50n, 58, 60, 78n, 81, 88, 91, 92, 93, 94, 95, 96, 97, 98, 98n, 99, 99n, 100, 100n, 101, 103, 104, 121, 125, 135, 137, 141, 146, 148

Pharisees 121, 140

Philip 14

Philippi 66, 109, 112n, 115, 117, 127, 130, 132, 134, 146

Phrygia 127, 128, 139

Pilate 21, 31, 69

Pisidian Antioch (*see also* Antioch) 8, 19, 28n, 29, 60, 61, 62, 73, 75, 91, 133, 134

Priscilla and Aquila 113, 136, 137

Prison 14, 72, 100, 101, 108, 111, 112, 115, 121, 133, 134

Prophets 37, 39n, 60, 61, 62, 69, 70, 71, 75, 100, 135n

Redemption 27, 27n, 28, 31, 80

Redemptive history 32, 36, 37, 38, 39, 40

Relief fund (*see also* Collection) 42, 82, 91, 92, 97, 99, 126

Reminder formula... 9, 46, 50, 50n, 57, 60, 144

Repentance 19, 19n, 58, 58n, 59, 63, 65, 130, 144

Resurrection
resurrection of Jesus 7, 14, 19, 20, 21, 26, 29, 31, 32, 34, 37, 40, 42, 47, 48, 48n, 51, 52, 53, 54, 55, 56, 57, 58, 58n, 59, 60, 61, 62, 62n, 69, 73, 74, 76, 80, 86, 96, 149
resurrection of believers... 6, 7, 32, 34, 35, 52, 62, 63, 148

Righteousness 20, 27, 37, 71

Rome 8, 10, 13, 25, 40, 45, 61, 62, 64, 68, 69, 71, 81, 85, 88, 88n, 98, 100, 111, 111n, 112, 113, 114, 116, 117, 126, 128, 128n, 129, 130, 134, 136, 147, 148

Sabbath 25n, 62, 69

Salvation (*see also* Soteriology) 17n, 22, 23, 24, 25, 26, 28, 29, 30, 37, 38, 42, 46n, 52, 54, 58n, 59, 65, 66, 69, 70, 74, 76, 86, 87, 88, 89, 93, 94, 95, 100, 102, 149

Samaria 14, 101

Sanhedrin 14, 110

Scholars 1, 3, 4, 5n, 12, 16, 17, 17n, 18, 39n, 41, 45, 46, 46n, 48, 59, 65, 79, 81, 91, 92n, 103, 105, 107n, 108, 109, 117, 121, 123, 142, 143, 145

Scholarship 1, 2, 3, 5, 8, 16, 78, 103, 106, 141, 112n

Scriptures 29, 31, 37, 42, 47n, 51, 57, 60, 61, 62, 63, 66, 68, 69, 70, 71, 73, 74, 75, 87, 122, 134n

Signs and wonders 72, 76

Silas 60, 72, 81, 100, 107, 108, 109, 114, 115, 127, 132, 134, 135, 135n

Sin 20, 53, 54, 64

Son of God (*see also* Jesus Christ, Messiah) 30, 31, 37, 42, 47, 47n, 49, 51,

53, 55, 56, 58, 60, 61, 63, 73, 74, 100, 122
Sopater 109, 137
Sosipater 137
Sosthenes 113, 114, 136
Soteriology (*see also* Salvation) 23n, 26, 46n
Spain 139, 151, 154
Suffering
  of believers 53, 114, 132
  of Christ 31, 61, 62, 69, 73
  of Paul 111, 114, 115, 120, 132, 133, 134, 140, 147
Synagogues 8, 22, 60, 61, 62, 68, 74, 85, 86, 87n, 102, 114, 131, 136, 145
Syria 109n, 113, 121, 125, 127, 129, 136

Tarsus(*see also* Cilicia) 13, 122, 122n, 125
Theology (*see also* Paul's theology) 1, 3, 4, 5, 6, 10, 15, 16, 16n, 17, 17n, 18, 21, 21n, 23, 24, 28, 39, 40, 41, 43, 46, 46n, 58, 58n, 70, 81, 103, 135, 143, 144, 146, 150, 151

Theophilus 11, 118
Thessalonica 8, 35, 55, 60, 62, 66, 72, 74, 74n, 75, 77, 105, 113, 114, 115, 117, 126, 127, 130, 132, 134, 135, 144
Timothy 22, 23, 24, 26, 50n, 53, 60, 81, 85, 86, 99, 100, 108, 109, 111, 114, 115, 127, 128, 134, 135, 139
Titus 11, 80, 91, 91n, 92, 92n, 105, 109n, 125, 136
Troas 65, 66, 108, 108n, 109, 127, 129
Tübingen School 1, 12, 81, 98n, 103, 143
Tychicus 109, 116, 137
Tyrannus hall 116, 131

Uncircumcision 24, 25, 73, 95n, 127

We-passages 5, 11, 105, 105n, 106, 106n, 107, 108, 109, 110, 112, 113, 116, 117, 146

Zealots 94, 122, 125

www.ingramcontent.com/pod-product-compliance
Lightning Source LLC
Chambersburg PA
CBHW050636300426
44112CB00012B/1820